THE GREAT SYRIAN REVOLT AND
THE RISE OF ARAB NATIONALISM

Modern Middle East Series, NUMBER 22

Sponsored by the
Center for Middle Eastern Studies (CMES)

The University of Texas at Austin

THE GREAT SYRIAN REVOLT

and the Rise of Arab Nationalism

MICHAEL PROVENCE

UNIVERSITY OF TEXAS PRESS · AUSTIN

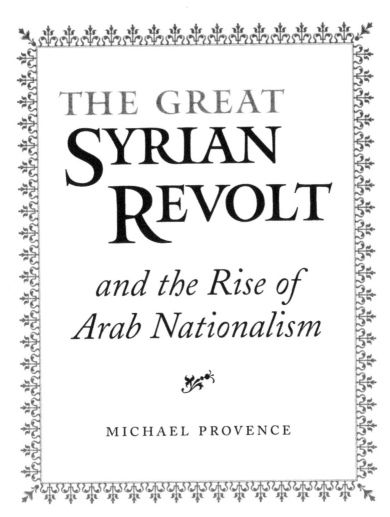

Printed in the United States of America

First edition, 2005

Requests for permission to reproduce material from this work should be sent to

Permissions, University of Texas Press, P.O. Box 7819, Austin, TX 78713-7819.

♾ The paper used in this book meets the minimum requirements of ANSI/NISO Z39.48-1992 (R1997) (Permanence of Paper).

Library of Congress Cataloging-in-Publication Data

Provence, Michael, 1966–
The great Syrian revolt and the rise of Arab nationalism / Michael Provence.—1st ed.
p. cm. — *(Modern Middle East series, no. 22)*

Includes bibliographical references and index.

ISBN 0-292-70635-9 (hardcover : alk. paper)
ISBN 0-292-70680-4 (pbk. : alk. paper)

Summary: *"A history of the largest and longest-lasting people's revolt in the Arab East, which attempted to liberate Syria from French Mandate rule in 1925"*—Provided by publisher.

1. Syria—History—Insurrection, 1925–1927. 2. Mandates—Syria. 3. French—Syria. I. Title. II. Modern Middle East series (Austin, Tex.) ; no. 22.
DS98.P76 2005
956.9104'1—dc22

2004025106

To the memory of

Bill O'Brien

1961–2000

CONTENTS

MAPS AND ILLUSTRATIONS

ACKNOWLEDGMENTS

It is a pleasure to record my thanks to the people who contributed to this book. The indelible traces of wonderful teachers and friends are imprinted on each page, and the existence of this project is unimaginable to me without their help. Rashid Khalidi, Cornell Fleischer, and Beshara Doumani generously guided the dissertation from which it grew. They have long supported my endeavors.

Many people have read, commented on, and encouraged my efforts over the years. I would like to acknowledge a debt of gratitude to Dennis Cordell, Philip Khoury, David Yaghoubian, Abdallah Hanna, Thomas Philipp, Ronald Inden, James Hopkins, Frank Peter, Nadine Méouchy, Peter Sluglett, Hasan Kayalı, Eugene Rogan, James Gelvin, Abdul-Rahim Abu Husayn, Ziad Abu Shaqra, Hasan Amin al-Biʿayni, Fandi Abu Fahkr, Khairia Kasmieh, Ira Lapidus, Cristoph Schumman, John Meloy, Robert Blecher, Stefan Weber, Astrid Meier, Adil Samara, Sana al-Wazir, Cristoph Melchert, Soo Yong Kim, Joseph Logan, Talal Rizk, Jens Hanssen, Anne Broadbridge, Bruce Craig, Rusty Rook, Ussama Makdisi, Kamal Salibi, Roger Owen, Farouk Mustafa, Edward Thomas, Hesham el-Rewini, Andrea Boardman, Joseph Esherick, Engin Akarlı, Muhammad Tarabayh, Gavin Brockett, Ken Garden, David Peters, Maurice Pomerantz, Stefan Winter, and Hayrettin Yücesoy. It has been my great good fortune to benefit from their help and friendship. They are blameless if I did not always listen or understand good advice generously offered.

I have been the grateful recipient of much institutional support. I thank the History Department at the University of California at San Diego, the Clements Department of History at Southern Methodist University, the Center for Middle Eastern Studies at the University of Texas, the Center for Middle Eastern Studies and the History Department at the University of Chicago, the Mellon Foundation, the Fulbright-Hays Commission of the United States Department of Education, the Fulbright Commission's Institute of International Education, and the University of California, Berkeley. In Damascus, I benefited from the invaluable archival collections of the

Historical Documents Center (Markaz al-Wathâ'iq al-Târîkhiyya) under the direction of Mme. D'ad al-Ḥakîm. The Institut Française d'Etudes Arabes de Damas, under the direction of Professor Dominique Malet, Dr. Nadine Méouchy, and Dr. Michel Nieto, was my institutional home for more than two years. The German Archaeological Institutes in Damascus and Beirut graciously welcomed me and provided much help. In Beirut, Jafet Library and the History Department at the American University in Beirut (AUB) were tremendously hospitable. In France, the Ministère des Affaires Etrangères, Archives Diplomatiques, in Nantes was a wonderful place to work and provided me every courtesy. Pierre Fournié helped with photos, and Jerome Cookson created the maps. At the University of Texas, Annes McCann-Baker, Wendy Moore, Carolyn Cates Wylie, and Kathy Lewis guided the book, and its anxious author, with sympathy, skill, and patience.

Finally, this work would never have been possible without the love and support of my family. My parents, grandparents, and parents-in-law have encouraged and supported me in ways too great to recount. Lor Wood has been a source of inspiration. She shared it all.

ABBREVIATIONS

AUB	American University of Beirut
FO	British Foreign Office
IFEAD	Institut Française d'Etudes Arabes de Damas
IJMES	*International Journal of Middle Eastern Studies*
MAE	Ministère des Affaires Etrangères
MWT	Markaz al-Wathâ'iq al-Târîkhiyya
SHAT	Service Historique de l'Armée Terre

TRANSLITERATION

Arabic words have been transliterated into Latin script according to the system employed by *IJMES*. The diacritic ^ has been used to indicate long vowels. Ottoman Turkish words have been rendered into Latin script according to the rules of modern Turkish. Names and words reasonably familiar to the English-speaking reader have been rendered in their familiar form (for example, Druze rather than *durûz*).

CHAPTER 1

Introduction

The Jebel Druse is a country of great feudal chiefs, whose efforts are directed to preserving the powers by which they live. What we call progress means in their eyes the loss of their privileges and later on perhaps the partition of their lands. With regard to the inhabitants, who are ignorant or unmindful of any better fate, they are deeply rooted in their serfdom and are as conservative as their masters. They have no aspirations for a system of greater social justice nor *[sic]* for a better communal life.

—*Testimony to the League of Nations Permanent Mandates Commission investigating the Syrian Revolt, Geneva, 1926*[1]

Syrians, remember your forefathers, your history, your heroes, your martyrs, and your national honor. Remember that the hand of God is with us and that the will of the people is the will of God. Remember that civilized nations that are united cannot be destroyed.

The imperialists have stolen what is yours. They have laid hands on the very sources of your wealth and raised barriers and divided your indivisible homeland. They have separated the nation into religious sects and states. They have strangled freedom of religion, thought, conscience, speech, and action. We are no longer even allowed to move about freely in our own country.

To arms! Let us realize our national aspirations and sacred hopes.

To arms! Confirm the supremacy of the people and the freedom of the nation.

To arms! Let us free our country from bondage.

—*Excerpt from a rebel manifesto signed by Sulṭân al-Aṭrash and issued on 23 August 1925*[2]

In late July 1922 a small group of men waited in the shade of a tree alongside a lonely road in rural southern Syria. Syria was a new country in 1922. The victorious European powers had carved it out of the defeated Ottoman Empire in the wake of the First World War in 1918. Less than two years

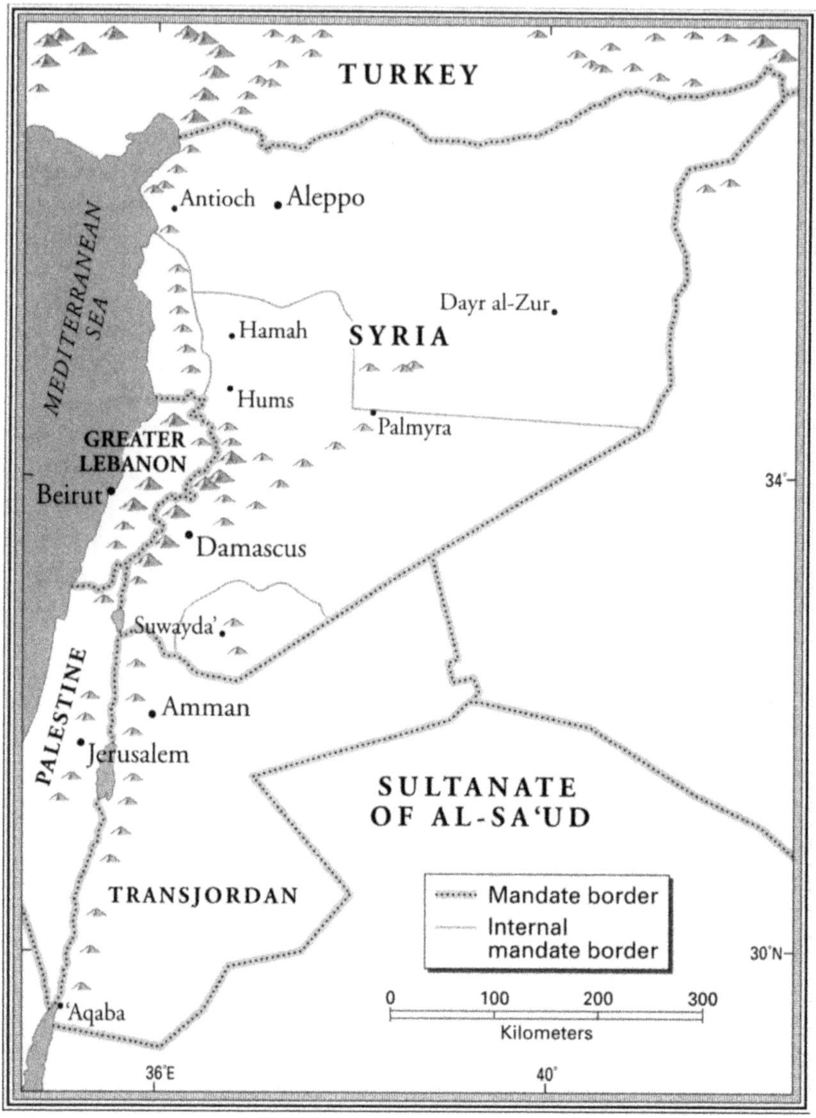

FIGURE 1. Greater Syria under mandate rule

later, in 1920, France occupied the country against the wishes of most of its inhabitants, including the men under the tree by the road that day.

They sat above a gravel track which followed the curve of a gentle hill. The long hillside above the road was covered with old olive trees and jagged black basalt boulders. The hillside below the road descended to a plain spreading as far as the eye could see in the midsummer haze. It was carpeted by recently harvested wheat fields, now reduced to a golden stubble, dotted with grazing sheep. The men were armed with rifles and sabers and sat on horseback, waiting patiently, smoking and talking in low tones.

Soon a dust cloud on the horizon signaled the approach of vehicles. The conversation stopped; and one among them, a short young man with a huge mustache that spanned his face, began to issue curt directions. The man giving orders was thirty-one-year-old Sulṭân al-Aṭrash. He had piercing blue eyes and the short, powerful stature of a wrestler. He had gathered the men together to stop a convoy and free a prisoner that the convoy was expected to be transporting to Damascus, the capital, some 100 kilometers north.

The first of three vehicles rounded the corner and came into full view. The men waited anxiously for Sulṭân al-Aṭrash's signal to attack. The cars were armored wagons, each with a machine gun protruding from a small turret. As the cars presented themselves, the horsemen charged down the hill, splitting off to engage each vehicle and completely surprising the drivers. Sulṭân al-Aṭrash was said to have leapt from his horse onto one of the cars, lifting the hatch and killing the three French soldiers inside with his saber. The other cars responded with a panicked hail of gunfire; but the horsemen were too quick, and the other cars were immobilized too. Four soldiers were killed, including the convoy's commander, and five soldiers were captured. The armored wagons held only soldiers, and the prisoner that they had sought to free was nowhere to be found.

Unknown to the would-be rescuers, French authorities had taken the prisoner, Adham Khanjar, to Damascus by airplane that morning. The French had accused Khanjar of taking part in an assassination attempt against a French general in 1921, and he had escaped to the British League of Nations mandate of Transjordan. In July 1922 he and a band of guerrillas had tried to cross the border to sabotage the electrical generating station in Damascus. The band had been dispersed at the border. With the French authorities in pursuit, Adham Khanjar sought refuge at the house of Sulṭân al-Aṭrash, a Druze shaykh and well-known enemy of the French mandatory government.

Sulṭân al-Aṭrash was not in his village, and French officers captured and arrested Adham Khanjar. When Sulṭân al-Aṭrash learned that Khanjar had sought refuge at his house and was in French captivity, he went to the provincial capital at Suwaydâʾ to protest the breach of customary law before the French authorities. According to customary law and Arab codes of honor, a guest who sought protection had to be welcomed and protected by his host.

The prestige and honor of rural leaders was linked to their ability and willingness to uphold such customs of hospitality.

Sulṭân al-Aṭrash was already locally famous as a charismatic firebrand in the southern region of Ḥawrân and Jabal Ḥawrân. Jabal Ḥawrân was the mountain homeland of the Druze, a minority sect that had often been at odds with the Ottoman state. In 1910 the Ottoman government hanged Sulṭân al-Aṭrash's father for insurrection, while his son served in the Balkans as an Ottoman army conscript. Toward the end of the First World War he joined the British-supported Arab Revolt against the Ottoman Empire. After 1920 he focused his opposition to French rule. While Sulṭân al-Aṭrash was a rural shaykh from a rebellious minority sect, he had also become a Syrian nationalist. He had been exposed to new nationalist ideas while in the army and during the war, when he sheltered fugitive Syrian nationalists on the run from the Ottoman authorities in Damascus. After the war, Sulṭân al-Aṭrash maintained his contacts with Syrian nationalists, including men like Adham Khanjar, a Shî'a from the west, who was suspected of ties to Amîr 'Abdallâh, Hashemite prince of Transjordan. They sought a unified Greater Syria, including the French and British mandates of Syria, Lebanon, Palestine, and Transjordan, independent and undivided by borders.

While Adham Khanjar was imprisoned, Sulṭân al-Aṭrash sent a series of telegrams to the native and French authorities protesting the breach of customary law. To the native governor, his cousin Salîm al-Aṭrash, he argued that the breach was an insult to the honor of the Druze and to Syria. To the French authorities he argued that the breach was in violation of previous agreements between the mandate government and the Druze. His relatives rejected his appeal, and the French argued that his protests were excuses for lawlessness and refused to release the prisoner.[3] Sulṭân al-Aṭrash failed to rouse Jabal Ḥawrân, but he managed to gather his brothers and a few friends to launch an attack to free Khanjar. French forces responded to the destruction of the convoy by issuing warrants for the rebels, bombing their villages, and destroying their houses.

In 1922 French authorities considered Sulṭân al-Aṭrash a minor provincial outlaw in a country full of outlaws and rebels against the mandatory occupation. Many Druze of Jabal Ḥawrân considered him a hero; but the Druze had experienced many rebellions against the Ottoman government, and his call to revolt was not widely popular. Sulṭân al-Aṭrash hoped to spark a wider revolt that would provide the Druze with the greater autonomy that they had managed to wrest from the Ottoman state. Perhaps he hoped to lead the Druze and Syrians generally in a national uprising to expel France from the Middle East.

The uprising failed. Sulṭân al-Aṭrash and a few others fled over the border to Transjordan and launched periodic guerrilla raids against French forces. The mandate government executed Adham Khanjar, but less than a year later the government pardoned Sulṭân al-Aṭrash and his comrades. French officials hoped that they would lay down their arms and return to lead quiet lives in their villages, isolated from the wider currents of nationalist politics. It was not to be.[4]

GREATER SYRIA AND OTTOMAN RULE

Greater Syria, comprising the modern states of Syria, Jordan, Israel/Palestine, and Lebanon, became part of the Ottoman Empire in 1516. For the next four centuries the degree of control exerted by the central state in Istanbul waxed and waned. The agricultural lands, pasture, and trade routes of the region thrived when the state was strong. Agriculture contracted when the state was weak, and the zones of nomadic pasture increased. As trade and its revenue were lost to the state, powerful local families or outside powers filled the void left by state contraction. The principal cities—Damascus, Aleppo, Ḥamâh, and Jerusalem—remained important and commanded their agricultural hinterlands and trade routes. Damascus and Jerusalem were also important pilgrimage stations and destinations, which added to their economies and their significance to the central government. In the late nineteenth century, after decades of administrative reform, the state haltingly renewed control and divided the region into the three Ottoman provinces *(wilâyat)* of Syria, Aleppo, and Beirut and the special administrative district *(sanjaq)* of Jerusalem and the separate governate *(mutaṣarrifiyya)* of Mount Lebanon. Coastal cities like Beirut, Haifa, and Tripoli became more important as the Ottoman Arab provinces were incorporated into world trade networks for the export of grain, oranges, and silks and the import of European manufactured goods.

The land was fertile, the cities rich and cultured. From Palestine in the south to the Taurus Mountains in the north, the eastern Mediterranean met the land along a well-watered coastal plain. In the south the plain was wide and ascended gradually to a plateau; higher mountains separated the zone of increasingly marginal agricultural land from the steppe and finally the Syrian desert. Farther north, in the present-day states of Lebanon and Syria, the edge of the plateau became a coastal mountain range, ascending from a narrow plain to sometimes snow-capped peaks in a few kilometers. Beyond the coastal or Mount Lebanon range lay the Biqâ'a (Bekaa) valley; while less well watered than the coastal zone, the valley was always fertile. Beyond it rose a second mountain range, the Anti-Lebanon, separating the fertile zone from the steppe and desert to the east.

Damascus nestled on the far slope of the eastern mountains, at the end of a small river that watered the city and made it an oasis on the edge of the desert. Vast and densely cultivated gardens surrounded Damascus at the foot of the mountain and produced much of the city's food. To the south of the city, and to the east of the Anti-Lebanon range, lay the plain of Ḥawrân, an area of rich volcanic steppe land that had produced vast wheat harvests in Roman times and had often reverted to nomadic pastureland in times of weak government control. To the east rose a remote volcanic spur called variously Jabal Ḥawrân, Jabal al-'Arab, or Jabal Druze, the final outpost of settled agriculture between Syria and the Euphrates in Iraq.

The human geography of Greater Syria was similarly rich. Arabic was the common language of the whole region, spoken by Jews, Muslims, and Christians of the various sects. Although some of the minorities retained separate liturgical languages, and a few villages of mixed Muslim and Christian habitation preserved spoken Aramaic, Arabic vastly prevailed in daily life. Literary Ottoman Turkish was the language of government, while literary Arabic was used for commercial records, religion, intellectual pursuits, and law.

The coastal regions were typically the home of Sunnî Muslims, both merchants in the cities and peasants in the villages. The mountain areas were often home to the minority sects that sought refuge or isolation from the majority. Among them were the Maronite Christians, who maintained an indigenous rite in union with Rome, in the region of Mount Lebanon; the Druze, who derived their esoteric religion from certain elements of Ismâ'îlî Shî'îsm, also in Mount Lebanon and in a few other isolated areas; and the 'Alawî, who practiced an esoteric faith also derived from Shî'îsm, west of Ḥamâh and in the mountains in what became northern Syria and southern Turkey. Ismâ'îlî Shî'a lived in a few mountain villages west of Ḥamah; and Imamî or Twelver Shî'a lived in the gardens of Damascus and in what came to be southern Lebanon near Jabal al-'Âmil. Orthodox and Greek Catholic Christians lived in agricultural villages and in the cities, while Jews mostly lived in the cities. The nomads, who were divided by vocation and tribe between permanent nomads and semisedentary nomads, were mostly Sunnî, though there were also Orthodox Christian nomads in the plain of Ḥawrân.

The hand of the state was necessarily light on the Arab provinces. The imperial center rarely had the resources or the will to impose direct rule on its distant possessions and ruled instead through local elites. The Ottoman provincial ruling classes were, like the ruling classes of the state center, primarily Sunnî. The top political families of Damascus usually got their start in government service (either civil or, more likely, military) and later became tax brokers, government officials, and eventually big landlords. These families provided generations of sons for high positions in local government and religious/legal leadership. They served as mediators between the central state and local society. Albert Hourani famously sketched the outlines of their world in his article "Ottoman Reform and the Politics of Notables" in 1968.

The prominent position of the leading families depended both on access to state authority and on independent power rooted in the local society. The political behavior of such families was characterized by caution and ambiguity. They sought to maintain balance between both poles of their power and avoided appearing to be either enemies or mere instruments of state authority.[5] Hourani's description of Ottoman provincial society emphasized three social groups, the State, the Notables, and, by implication, the *ra'îya* or state subjects. The notable class mediated between the vast majority considered *ra'îya* and the tiny minority that represented the state, in the form of a rotating elite of provincial governors and garrison commanders that Istanbul frequently reassigned.

Hourani described a negotiated and contested power relationship. Philip Khoury later demonstrated that the overarching role of the imperial power was eventually transferred to the civil and military functionaries of the French mandate after 1920. Under both Ottoman and French rule, the political notables struck a bargain in which they enjoyed variable and qualified access to political power and tremendous economic power in return for minimizing the political aspirations of the great mass of the subject population.[6]

Local power was based on control of land and agricultural surpluses. Claims to represent a "natural leadership" were based on the ability to dispense patronage among the dependent subordinate classes, whether peasants or inhabitants of a given urban quarter dominated by a notable family. Families from Damascus and Ḥamâh owned entire villages in the surrounding regions. Single extended families controlled scores or even hundreds of villages comprising thousands of individuals. The share of agricultural produce retained by peasants often barely met the level of subsistence. Leading families usually lived in Damascus in grand houses that included multiple courtyards and scores of rooms on two or three levels. Dozens of family members might inhabit a single house, but leading families often owned several houses. The houses dominated the urban quarters in which they were situated, and the families supported all kinds of activities in the quarter from youth clubs to Ṣûfî orders to trade and craft guilds. The leading families also owned large areas of urban real estate, which they leased for commercial and residential purposes. Most merchants and traders in a given quarter might turn to the principal local notable as landlord, employer, protector, contract guarantor, moneylender, and dispute arbiter, among other things.[7]

Seismic changes in late Ottoman provincial society had made such patronage networks less comprehensive than they had once been. Integration into world markets had made new mercantile families more prominent. In the Maydân neighborhood of southern Damascus in particular, grain merchants and exporters worked outside the system of patronage and protection, dealing directly with grain cultivators when they could and emphasizing commercial relations rather than government connections. Large areas of agricultural land were brought under the plow and were not subject to the old arrangements. Peasants migrated to areas where they could approach the status of independent proprietors rather than chattel. New educational institutions fostered the emergence of new classes.

The tremendous wave of social change finally crested and broke between 1918 and 1949, but the story of the old notables remained dominant. Scholars, and the members of the notable families themselves, continued to interpret history as the story of the scions of a dozen Damascus families. Arab nationalism was understood as the ideology of a tiny elite; and until the 1990s scholars focused obsessively on the writings of scarcely a score of extraordinarily privileged men. Few scholars explained how an elite ideology of intellectuals and wealthy landowners had suddenly burst forth in 1920 to fill the streets of Damascus with ordinary people protesting for national rights and an end to European occupation. The nationalist independence movement of the interwar period was broadly understood to be the political preserve of the same dozen families, and the elite emphasis of written history was undisturbed.[8]

The great mass of the subject population remained silent and presumably supine. So while historians readily explained the bargains that the powerful made with the still more powerful, no one seemed to be able to explain the bargains made between the comparatively weak and numerous and the comparatively powerful and few. How, in other words, did the notable class deliver the tacit consent or at least grudging acquiescence of those it sought to dominate in concert with the imperial power? How did ordinary people feel about their peripheral role in politics? When uprisings emerged, who led and who followed? What did Syrian nationalism mean in 1925?

OTTOMAN REFORM

The Ottoman reform movement emerged in the first half of the nineteenth century. Reformers worked to strengthen the military, extend central government control, and improve revenue collection. By the end of the century the cumulative results of reform had reached most Ottoman subjects. The hand of the state extended to social and geographical terrains that it had never before touched. The private ownership of state agricultural land became codified and legalized in 1858. State education was expanded first in military academies in the imperial capital, then in medical schools and civil service academies, and eventually in scores of provincial secondary and preparatory schools organized along similar lines as the central academies. Military and bureaucratic reform and the idea of Ottoman patriotism went together as the state's reformers helped to create an imperial elite of modern, educated Ottomans, with decreasing legal distinctions by religion or sect. Efforts at universal conscription and elite state education served these goals.

Legal reform of landholding was particularly important in the provincial regions. Legally speaking, most agricultural land had been the property of the state, while heritable cultivation rights lay with the peasants who worked it. The land law of 1858 was intended to insure tax revenues of agricultural lands and regulate an existing market in land. Lands that had been effectively, if not legally, under the control of peasants, however, often became the private property of urban notables. Peasants feared the extension of government control in taxation and military conscription and rarely registered their lands, while urban notables with greater resources and legal know-how manipulated the registration process to consolidate their holdings. Provincial elites had been tax collectors and brokers of agricultural lands, and the new laws made it possible for them to become landlords, drawing them and the lands they controlled more firmly into the embrace of the state but also bestowing new rights in return.[9] Land reform measures were intended to bring peasants under state control. The law's intentions were mostly subverted by provincial elites. In the areas of Greater Syria long under intensive cultivation, urban absentee landlords became more powerful, while cultivators became weaker and probably poorer. Although the state sought to increase revenue, and provincial elites sought to increase their control of land, sometimes powerful forces pulled in other directions.

International trade increased tremendously in the nineteenth century. Cotton from India and Egypt fed the textile mills of Lancashire, and manufactured cloth and other goods were exported to the Ottoman Empire via its thriving Mediterranean ports. Wheat, cotton, silk, and other agricultural products became the major exports from Greater Syria. Sometimes the Ottoman state helped to facilitate the new trade, but more often it was the work of Ottoman subjects adjusting to and profiting from new realities. Enterprising peasants and merchants opened up new areas of the Arab Ottoman realms to settled agriculture and often staunchly resisted state attempts to levy taxes on their labor. Vast areas of rain-fed farmland were wrested from nomads and government neglect and brought under the plow.

The independent-minded people of these frontier regions felt that they had earned the right of relative independence from the state and deeply resented late nineteenth century efforts to conscript their sons and tax their agriculture. In Ḥawrân south of Damascus, in the Jazîra east of Aleppo in the middle Euphrates river valley, and elsewhere, such independent farmers regularly fought the bedouin and the state and developed a frontier warrior ethos that opposed the assertion of state or urban notable authority over their regions.[10] Inhabitants of such regions resisted government registration of their land because they feared the extension of state authority; but, unlike peasants in longer-settled regions to the west, they also resisted efforts by urban notables to register land on their behalf. They sought to preserve their independence both from the state and from provincial elites and would-be landlords. Independent peasant proprietors forged commercial bonds with new mercantile classes in the cities, especially grain merchants.

The Ottoman state responded to centrifugal forces in the late nineteenth century with both threats and enticements. Rural rebellions were suppressed with military force, and urban schools were built to educate and indoctrinate subjects in the benefits of the Ottoman system. Urban elites were the first to experience modern education. They sent their sons and daughters to be educated in schools set up by French, British, and American missionaries. The Ottoman government responded by opening state preparatory schools in the imperial capital like the famous Galatasaray Lycée in Istanbul and eventually provincial preparatory or Iʿdâdiyya schools like Maktab ʿAnbar in Damascus. More numerous secondary or Rushidiyya schools were opened in provincial cities all over the empire. State secondary and preparatory schools were intended to provide training and retain the loyalty of elites. It was only later educational efforts, particularly provincial military schools and other academies in the capital, that were intended to foster new provincial elites and to draw the sons of the frontier regions into the state system.[11]

Decades of military repression preceded the policy of drawing rural inhabitants into the state's embrace through education and public works. By the final decade of the nineteenth century, however, Ottoman policy had turned more or less in the direction of enticement rather than punishment. The government built wagon roads and railways, opened telegraph offices, established mail service, opened local schools, and established special scholarships for young men from rural areas. The new institutions were widely mistrusted, since rural inhabitants correctly saw that telegraphs conveyed intelligence, roads brought government agents and police, and school rosters recorded names of children later to be taxed and perhaps conscripted for distant (and possibly fatal) military service. Still, education and the government jobs it often brought were increasingly attractive. By the first decade of the twentieth century there were secondary schools in Damascus for military service, civil service, and female students. Within a few years demand soared, and it was ever more difficult to secure a place in the government schools.

The final Ottoman decades were full of trauma and hope. In 1908 a revolution replaced the aging autocrat Abdülhamid II with a constitutional government. Elections were held, and all Ottoman provinces sent representatives to the reopened Parliament. Reform had touched everyone, but with reform came new internal pressures to match the crushing pressures from outside. Nationalist and separatist movements had emerged among the minority populations in the empire. Italy invaded and annexed Ottoman Libya. Balkan Christians fought devastating wars to achieve national independence. Armenian, Greek, and Arab populations in Anatolia and Greater Syria were alienated by the increasing ethnic Turkish orientation of state elites. The new constitutional government, besieged from all sides, became more dictatorial and less representative. The idea of a nation made up of all imperial Ottoman subjects was strained to the breaking point.

In 1914 a Serbian nationalist assassinated the heir to the throne of the Hapsburg Empire. The assassination, in the former Ottoman provincial capital of Sarajevo, led to the First World War and the destruction of the Ottoman Empire. The people of Ottoman Greater Syria suffered tremendously between 1914 and 1918. The government conscripted hundreds of thousands of men, and hundreds of thousands died in the famine that accompanied the war. A revolt against the Ottoman army and in support of the British emerged in Ḥijâz province of western Arabia. Arab rebels entered Damascus at the end of the war with British troops. The Amîr Fayṣal, leader of the revolt and son of Sharîf al-Ḥusayn, the former Ottoman religious governor of Mecca in Ḥijâz, believed that Britain had promised the rebels an Arab kingdom stretching from Iran to the Mediterranean. Britain and France, however, had produced a series of secret and mutually contradictory agreements over the postwar disposition of the Ottoman realms. Their secret agreements with one another would take precedent over agreements with non-European wartime allies.

The agreements led to the partition of the Arab Ottoman lands and most present-day borders. Borders and ruling arrangements were negotiated and casually drawn in London and Paris. Amîr Fayṣal was crowned king of the new state of Syria in March 1920. The British had supported Fayṣal and his new kingdom; but in the face of French claims to Syria, Britain withdrew its support, Fayṣal fled to become British-supported king of the British mandate for Iraq, and France occupied Syria in July 1920. France's League of Nations mandate over Syria lasted twenty-six years, until 1946. Armed opposition to European occupation emerged immediately in Syria, Iraq, Palestine, and elsewhere. Men from what had been the unruly fringes of empire led resistance movements everywhere. Sulṭân al-Aṭrash was one of them.

THE GREAT SYRIAN REVOLT

In the summer of 1925, five years after France occupied Syria, the largest, longest, and most destructive of the Arab Middle Eastern revolts began. It brought together veterans of the Great War and earlier postwar rebellions and served as a template for later revolts, such as the revolt in Palestine in 1936. Contrary to the expectations of the mandatory power, the uprising began in an apparently remote and supposedly backward rural region. It spread to Damascus and came to include most regions and social strata of mandate Syria, rural and urban. For more than two years a ragtag collection of farmers, urban tradesmen and workers, and former junior officers of the Ottoman and Arab armies managed to challenge, and often defeat, the colonial army of one of the most powerful countries in the world.

After five years of French military rule, the memories of war and famine and the defeat of the Ottoman Empire remained acute and bitter. Likewise, memories lingered of the British-supported Arab kingdom led by Amîr Fayṣal between the end of World War I and the imposition of the mandate under France. Syrians had watched with awe as irregular Turkish military units expelled would-be European occupiers by force of arms and the Turkish state emerged from the ashes, under the leadership of former Ottoman army officer Mustafa Kemal (Atatürk).[12]

Like the Turkish war of independence, the Great Syrian revolt began away from the urban centers. But while the circumstances of occupation in Istanbul and the surrender of the last Ottoman sultan to the French and British dictated resistance from distant central Anatolia, the rural origins of resistance in Syria were less clear. By 1925 the occupation and pacification of Syria was presumed complete. Mandate authorities considered the cities of Damascus, Aleppo, and Ḥamâh the likely hotbeds of anticolonial nationalist resistance and systematically denied the elite nationalist politicians of those cities any role in ruling mandate Syria. The French had intentionally separated sectarian groups from one another and separated the rural regions from the cities by the creation of internal borders and autonomous "statelets." They sought to limit intersectarian coalitions and to isolate the countryside from the urban contagion of nationalist agitation. Few imagined that nationalist resistance would emerge in the countryside and spread to the cities—yet this is precisely what happened.

The Great Revolt was a mass movement, and its tactics of armed revolt were far more radical than much of the elite leadership of Damascus was prepared to embrace. Its leaders were not members of the great landowning notable families who sought to become national leaders in an incremental process of negotiation with the French. The revolt was one of the signal events in the emergence of mass politics in the Arab world. It was a decisive breakdown of the elite-dominated system of the "politics of notables" (theorized by Albert Hourani and discussed above).

The axis of the revolt was the grain trade. Migrants from the minority Druze sect had settled and pacified the southern countryside in large numbers during the mid- and late nineteenth century. With the help of an emerging merchant class, mostly from the Maydân quarter of Damascus, they expanded the wide cultivation and export of Ḥawrânî grain. These relationships and tensions helped foster the Great Revolt. Preexisting trade networks were precisely the conduits through which rebellion and nationalist agitation flowed. Grain production was based on contractual agreements between each village leader and a Damascene merchant. Just as the village leaders were not great landlords or estate holders, the merchants were rarely from the great landowning families of Damascus, who usually had vast holdings in other parts of Syria.[13]

The Ottoman state had played little role in pacifying the southern countryside but continually sought to exploit the agricultural surplus. The tension between the state and the rural inhabitants led to numerous revolts throughout the nineteenth century. Often Damascene merchants were aligned with the rebellious rural regions, while the great notables were aligned with the Ottoman state, since both the state and its highest local officials sought to profit from the agricultural surplus of the region. The 1925 revolt began in the southern grain-producing region of Jabal Ḥawrân and quickly spread to the Maydân quarter of Damascus. Many of the revolt's leaders emerged from the Ḥawrân or from the Maydân and had some connection to the grain trade. They were more militant in tactics and aims than the nationalist elite of Damascene notables, some of whom were eventually compelled to join the uprising in order to escape imprisonment and to preserve their political credibility. Several mandate and postindependence-era political leaders emphasized their role in the revolt. For example, future president Shukrî al-Quwwatlî escaped arrest and spent the revolt in Amman and Cairo, Jamîl Mardam Bey spent the revolt in Haifa, and Fakhrî al-Bârûdî was in jail after August 1925, to mention three of the most prominent. In later years, involvement in the revolt became a signifier of nationalist commitment, and these politicians and many others claimed a central role.[14]

French mandate authorities failed to comprehend the significance of the relationships and the connections among regions, classes, and sectarian groups in Syria. They sought to divide and govern mandate Syria along a series of supposedly timeless sectarian and geographical divisions. Jabal Ḥawrân was one such division. The French identified all of Syrian rural society as feudal and exploitative, with resulting deep, but ill-defined, class cleavages.[15] The notion of feudal domination in the Druze region fails to account for the rise of rebel solidarity between supposed lords and serfs and likewise fails to explain the revolt's urban appeal once it spread beyond their region. How and why did people whom the French viewed as exploited and exploiter join together to resist their self-appointed liberators? Economic relations that the French, and many subsequent scholars, believed separated rural people from one another and from urban populations actually brought them together. Ottoman secondary education forged links between people of diverse class, regional, and sectarian origins. When these groups joined together and began to articulate a nationalist vision, whose vision was it?

CONTRASTING NARRATIVES

The Great Revolt was a seminal, albeit contested, event in the Syrian national narrative, and secondary works in Arabic are numerous. The revolt was represented as a heroic episode in the colonial history of Syria. Broad coalitions of Syrians from the inland southern heartland of Bilâd al-Shâm—the lands of Damascus—joined together to resist colonial oppression. Just as the 1960s were a heyday for nationalist politics in Syria, they were also a heyday for studies of the revolt. The correspondence between the revolt and an era of postindependence nationalist ferment was not coincidental.

Advocates of different Syrian national narratives incorporated the revolt into their visions of Syrian history as the postcolonial state took shape.[16] They emphasized the nationalist, nonsectarian aspects of the revolt and tended to be less interested in the local aspects, as represented by the Druze and the beginnings of the uprising. Most secondary works were written by people who had some close, usually family, connection to the revolt. They brought a more or less critical gaze to an episode that showed how diverse regions and sectarian groups had united for a common goal in the formation of the Syrian Arab nation—a nation that all recognized was decidedly not homogenous. The revolt could serve as an example, a touchstone for unity, but also (in its sectarian, separatist, and regionalist aspects) as an example of how far the nation had progressed by the 1960s.

Books in this vein have disappeared since the early 1970s. The disappearance is a symptom of the political climate in modern Syria. The generation that fought the revolt is gone, and the memoirs that they left are often unavailable. Most such books are out of print and hard to find. Recent generations have sometimes been disappointed in their nationalist and anti-imperialist convictions by the state of political culture and discourse in modern Syria. There is some interest among younger Syrians in information about their modern history, but it is only satisfied by the innocuous productions of historical soap operas for television.[17] The Syrian nationalist narrative has been codified, and there is little space in it for heroic narratives that compete with the dominant narrative of the late President Ḥâfiẓ al-Asad and the Baʿth Party. The Syrian revolt brought together the Ḥawrân Druze and the Damascene merchant community. Arguably, the potential challenge to the government from one, or both, of these groups since independence has resulted in a certain official reluctance to highlight their heroic collaboration in 1925.

Mandate officials claimed that the revolt was the response of retrograde Druze feudal lords who felt their power threatened by mandatory reforms. They argued relentlessly that the revolt was sectarian and not nationalist. The contemporary record indicates otherwise. Different sectarian groups, regions, and classes joined under the unifying banner, however variable, of Syrian patriotism and nationalism. Further, many among the rebels willingly took orders from leaders of different religions and geographical regions from their own. And while this is clear in the contemporary documents and memoirs, it is also clear in secondary works dealing with the revolt until the early 1970s.[18]

During the 1970s, however, something changed. The revolt became re-colonized; and as Damascus and Syria's ruling apparatus changed with the influence of ʿAlawî military officers and bureaucrats, Syria's colonial history changed too. Syria's military and then its government became the preserve of members of another formerly isolated rural sectarian minority, which had played no major role in the Great Revolt. The national narrative that privileged Damascus and the Druze was displaced by a narrative that included many revolts (in each region, all characterized by an immature political consciousness), eventually united for a final heroic march to true national consciousness and independence under the leadership of the Baʿth Party. The Great Revolt became one in a long line of revolts that included uprisings in the region of Aleppo under the leadership of Ibrâhîm Hanânû and uprisings in the ʿAlawî region east of the coastal city of Latakia under Ṣâliḥ al-ʿAlî. The Great Revolt remains an episode that does not fit neatly into the post-1970 national narrative; therefore, it is usually simply ignored.

Nationalism is not the only motif of works dealing with the revolt. In the last fifteen years books have been published that stress the sectarian aspects of the uprising. The studies of Ḥasan al-Biʿaynî, a Lebanese Druze scholar, are foremost among these.[19] While there is a hegemonic national narrative in Syria that forbids the public discussion of sectarian differences, in Lebanon the national narrative has been highly contested along sectarian lines. Indeed, the factions in the Lebanese civil war were often split by sect, and the war's central issue was arguably a contested vision of national identity.[20] It is no accident that the generation shaped by the war has authored sectarian histories. This is not to say that Biʿaynî seeks to privilege the Druze narrative above the Arab or Syro-Lebanese narrative. Rather, he seeks to stress the important contribution of the Druze to the independence struggle against the French. His works attempt to show that the Druze minority has made a valuable contribution to the history of the Syrian-Arab nation. In making his argument, however, Biʿaynî sometimes makes the larger Syrian-Arab nation disappear. He seems to argue that the Druze *are* the Syrian-Arab nation. In foregrounding the heroic actions of the Druze, Biʿaynî obscures the connections that gave the revolt of 1925 its nationalist dimensions.

Another notable sectarian history is that of Kais Firro.[21] Firro is an Israeli-Druze scholar. The Druze community in Israel is the main non-Jewish group not considered Arab by the government. Identity thus remains a contentious issue, particularly for Druze intellectuals like Firro. The Israeli state has largely succeeded in its Druze policy, while the French mandate failed. The French attempted to separate the Druze from the larger mandate Arab population, and the Great Revolt is proof that they failed. The Israeli state, by a more nuanced policy of enticements and a tacit, multitiered model of Israeli citizenship, succeeded in greater measure in separating the Druze from the larger Palestinian Arab population. Still, the question of identity is not settled, as Firro makes clear. Like Biʿaynî, he considers the Druze part of the Arab nation. His detailed narrative history of the Druze is an impressive scholarly work. It chronicles the Druze in what became Syria, Lebanon, and Palestine, from earliest times until the 1950s.

The emphasis on religious divisions and sectarian essentialism has a long history in much western scholarship on the Middle East. The earliest memoirs of the revolt, written as apologies by French officers who had been involved, stressed the impenetrable and ageless mix of sectarian fanaticism and backward feudalism that they claimed was the defining characteristic of the rebels. These men saw their careers as colonial functionaries in dire jeopardy and desperately sought to justify the colonial role and their actions to a skeptical French public. In so doing, they utilized a whole palette of racist, orientalist, and essentialist stereotypes. They sought to destroy and discredit any rationally understandable explanation for the uprising and to portray themselves as the blameless couriers of civilization to uncomprehending and ungrateful savages.[22] Sectarian conflict was a theoretical necessity for French colonialism in Syria, since the entire colonial mission was based on the idea of protecting one sectarian community, the Maronite Christians, from the predations of others. Without sectarian conflict, colonial justification evaporates.

The difference between the viewpoint of mandate officials and former mandate citizens reveals an interesting contrast. With few exceptions, Syrian writers on the Great Revolt have been self-conscious and forthright about the assumptions and political commitments that their work aims to advance. The European chroniclers of France's mandate spoke from a position of authority that required no justification or examination. They neither mentioned nor examined their assumptions and political commitments but usually veiled them behind a screen of self-described "objectivity." It should not be a surprise that the works of those who sought to advance a privileged argument for European supremacy over the rest of the world have worn less well over the decades than the works of those who spoke forthrightly for resistance against that same supremacy. It is deeply unfortunate, however, that the lesson has not been learned. Americans and Europeans still publish books and articles about postcolonial countries that advance the shopworn theories of their colonial forebears. Many still insist on their objectivity and fitness to define, and indeed to rule, the rest of the world.

Two texts in English stand above all others for the history of Syria during the mandate and beyond: the encyclopedic works of Philip Khoury and Hanna Batatu.[23] Both of these books achieve a level of comprehensive narrative detail that will probably never be matched. They utilized a wide range of normative sources, including extensive interviews with elderly Syrians who played key roles in modern history. Many of these people have since died. Despite their richness of detail, both works are concerned ultimately with urban elite politics. Khoury makes a path-breaking contribution to understanding the machinations of traditional urban elites in interwar nationalist politics. Batatu, by contrast, seeks to explain how members of a rural sectarian community became the new postindependence urban elite and ruling class. Khoury devotes four chapters to the Great Revolt. He treats the mandate period from 1920 to 1945, and the revolt specifically, from the perspective of changes in the "politics of notables." Ultimately, Khoury accepts and reproduces the claims of hegemonic representation made by the mandate and postindependence nationalist elite, who viewed themselves as the uncontested representatives of the nation.[24]

Batatu rightly seeks the roots of today's Syrian regime in the countryside. For Khoury, the rural-urban connection is fairly undefined, though he clearly acknowledges its importance, while Batatu subjects the relationship between urban and rural regions to broad thematic generalizations that cannot be sustained from region to region. He writes in detail about the origins and conditions of the various peasant communities in Syria, in explaining the rise of the Asad regime. He has little to say, however, about their historical relations with one another or with the cities. Batatu's analysis of the rise of Ḥâfiẓ al-Asad from a humble mountain village is unlikely to be matched. But when he generalizes about the condition of all Syrian mountain regions and the people who lived there, he is on shakier ground. For while the ʿAlawî sect (from which Asad came) and the Druze sect (from which many of the Great Revolt's fighters came) share apparently esoteric religious beliefs, mountainous native regions, and a tradition of rebellion, they share few other elements. There were vast differences in ownership of land, in social and economic relations, and particularly in commercial and social integration with the surrounding regions. The ʿAlawî mountains were historically far more isolated than the southern regions, and their development and social conditions reflect this difference.

The emergence of nationalism in Greater Syria has also received much scholarly attention. This is part of the aim of Khoury's book on the mandate and is central to his earlier book.[25] Others have also devoted much attention to the rise of nationalism; while they have made unprecedented contributions, none has dealt with nationalism in the city and the countryside.[26] Many other scholars have devoted the major part of their research to the rise of

Arab nationalism, and yet they have all concentrated on urban nationalism—usually among a narrow elite of notables and intellectuals—and ignored the countryside.[27] The gap is difficult to understand, since during the mandate the population of Syria's three biggest towns (Damascus, Aleppo, and Ḥumṣ) was never more than 20 percent of the total population.[28] Additionally, there is no doubt that the countryside was always of supreme importance for urban dwellers, as a source of wealth for the notability and as the provider of food for the entire urban population. Until quite recently, agriculture and pastoralism were the bases of most of the country's wealth, whether in grain, woolen and cotton textiles, or olive oil and its products. Finally, as Hanna Batatu and others have noted, the entire government power structure of today's Syria is composed of people of rural origin. The late Syrian president Ḥâfiẓ al-Asad made frequent reference to his peasant background.[29] The dearth of studies on the rural regions is thus all the more inexplicable since, unlike most other examples of anticolonial nationalist struggles, the countryside ultimately prevailed over the urban leadership to dominate the postindependence government.

The existing histories reflect the deep misgivings and biases of urban dwellers regarding the countryside. Scholars, whatever their origin, are usually members of an urban elite and naturally focus their attention on people that they can identify with and relate to. The lack of rural studies also reflects the usual dearth and difficulty of access to sources for rural history and the comparative wealth and ease of access to sources for urban areas. Given the importance of the southern countryside in the economy of Damascus and the central position of the Great Revolt in modern Syrian history, neither of these problems applies. The local sources, the memoir accounts, and particularly the French archives are extraordinarily rich for the Great Revolt and southern Syria.

No study has traced the relationships between rural and urban regions and their influence on nationalist politics from the Ottoman period into the mandate. This book examines these relationships. It makes connections between events and social conditions that have not been made in print before. The political economy of grain production and the resultant social and commercial interactions made possible broad resistance to the colonial state and the rise of nationalism in the countryside. The spread of state-subsidized military education in the late Ottoman period likewise fostered popular nationalism and resistance. The uprising is thus illustrative of several previously neglected historical processes, including rural-urban integration, the rise of new merchant and professional military classes, and—related to both of these and perhaps most importantly—the emergence of popular Syrian-Arab nationalist identities.

THEORIZING INSURGENT AND NATIONAL CONSCIOUSNESS

Over twenty years ago Benedict Anderson published a widely influential book titled *Imagined Communities.* Anderson argued that intellectuals and various historical forces had created an illusion of simultaneous common experience from which people could imagine themselves part of a vast national community. Anderson was marginally more charitable toward the aspirations of recently imagined national communities than other theorists of nationalism had been. For example, in a book of almost equally wide influence, Eric Hobsbawm argued by implication that the nation-state, which in his conception was the only basis for national identity, was not only an imagined community but actually an *imaginary* community, destined in the future to disappear as a focal point of human consciousness. Hobsbawm, one of the twentieth century's greatest historians, thereby not only casually dismissed the national aspirations and consciousness of Palestinians, Kurds, and numerous stateless others but dismissed as essentially meaningless, or at least tragically pointless, the sacrifices of millions of dead in formerly colonized countries all over the world. Both Hobsbawm and especially Anderson conceived nationalism as a vaguely central European phenomenon imported to the colonial world in modular packages, to be selected or rejected but rarely reshaped in any substantial way. I would argue that each was gravely, though perhaps only inferentially, influenced by the still looming specter of the European wars of the twentieth century.[30]

Partha Chatterjee points out the central problem with all this: "If nationalisms in the rest of the world have to choose their imagined community from certain 'modular' forms already made available to them by Europe and the Americas, what do they have left to imagine?"[31] The question is appropriate: although Europeans and Americans certainly took nationalism seriously while they fought bloody wars over it, these theorists of nationalism seem to say, today thinking people the world over ought to abandon the concept of national identity altogether. This stance is notably uncharitable to many outside Western Europe and North America who find their national communities—imagined or not, but certainly not imaginary—quite literally under siege from all sides.

Chatterjee and earlier theorists of anticolonial nationalism, like Frantz Fanon, provide insights with which to consider anticolonial and nationalist resistance. Both Chatterjee and Fanon examine in detail the various communities and classes that make up the colonial nation-state. Chatterjee writes of the need for a pluralist "fragmentary" view of the nation from the perspective of India of the 1990s. Fanon, by contrast, writes from the perspective of the Algerian war of independence, which he joined after the French government sent him to serve in a hospital in Algeria.[32] Both are useful in making sense of nationalism and resistance in Syria.

The Syrian revolt was a catalyst for the formation of popular notions of Syrian-Arab identity. People who perhaps had not thought much about being part of a larger national community willfully entered a desperate struggle against a clearly, but negatively, defined enemy. When rebels and insurgents conceived notions of their "imagined community," the conception was theirs; they did not borrow it from someone else, or take it from a book, or adopt one of the modular theories of national identity current today. They imagined it themselves, in negative relation to the colonial occupier. In this process of imagining, they incorporated elements that made sense to, and coexisted with, their existing ideas of self. Because new notions of identity were historically and culturally subjective, they differed from place to place, along with different local histories. Such notions of identity resist easy categorization and generalization.[33]

A hypothetical example of how identity can shift, form, and re-form may be useful. While a peasant insurgent from a given village might identify herself as an inhabitant of village X, member of family Y, Muslim, Syrian, Arab, woman, another insurgent might identify himself as a resident of city quarter A, member of family B, Druze, Syrian, Arab, man. These different facets of identity coexist, mingle, and overlap, depending on context and situation. There is no easily discernible natural hierarchy among one's facets of identity. And yet, when people who have only one or more facet in common face an enemy that is clearly an "Other" (such as a colonial military power), a new facet can emerge, or a preexisting facet may be pushed to the foreground, as a basis for collective action. When these two hypothetical insurgents join together to resist a colonial oppressor, for example, they do not hold identical conceptions of their national identity. The way one conceives or imagines the community obviously differs from person to person. But it is the common *notion* of membership that is important, not the common understanding of what membership means. At moments of intense collective crisis, this notion of common membership can expand dramatically, almost overnight, and erase or subordinate differences between members of a single national community. The Syrian revolt of 1925 was such a moment of crisis.[34]

Notions of popular identity and consciousness are notoriously difficult to quantify and analyze. Intellectuals leave letters, newspaper editorials, and memoirs. They often articulate their ideas and ideologies with attractive consistency and theoretical neatness. Subaltern historical actors leave few of these traces and must be known by the symbolic content of their actions and the efforts of their enemies to suppress both their resistance and their collective consciousness. Their actions are often characterized by seeming ambiguity and historical opacity. Seen through the lens of intellectual history, subaltern consciousness offers little consistency or theoretical neatness. Histories of resistance to mandate rule have long been dominated by detailed accounts of urban notables and their intellectual production. I argue here that the near-total emphasis on notables and elite nationalists in this period has obscured the very significant contributions of Syria's non-elite populations to resistance against the mandate. It follows, then, that this book cannot and will not utilize the methods of conventional elite history. Subaltern history and popular consciousness can only be represented by a detailed emphasis on the *actions* of subalterns. Those who tacitly insist that the existence of subaltern national consciousness must conform to elite models will be apt to deny the existence of such consciousness altogether. Orderly categories and tidy theories exist principally in the minds and representations of intellectuals, whether elite nationalists or their chroniclers. I resist the urge to impose order where little was evident and to tidy the ragged edges of a truly vital and uncompromised example of subaltern resistance. Following Partha Chatterjee and others, this book emphasizes and identifies the strengths of the ambiguous, the fragmentary, and the theoretically untidy.

The insurgents clearly agreed on a few things. The leading rebels did not acknowledge the partition of Greater Syria into separate European-ruled colonial states. They freely crossed borders and maintained ties in different areas under European mandate. Many later fled to Transjordan and fought in British-ruled Palestine. The majority of the documents that they left were tactical rather than ideological or strategic. Those few documents that touched upon ideology, however, consistently criticized the partition of Ottoman Greater Syria and demonstrated that the independence and reunification of those lands was the revolt's ultimate goal. There was broad agreement that Greater Syria constituted a single geographical entity. Furthermore, most of the insurgents, both leaders and anonymous fighters, came from rural areas and popular urban quarters. Their dress, their actions, and their language testify to the existence of a common rural Arab culture, centering on ideals of bravery, honor, and common historical memory.

SOURCES

The French Diplomatic Archives in Nantes contain the full documentary record of the French mandate in Syria and Lebanon.[35] During the period of the revolt, the mandate Service des Renseignements (Intelligence Service) compiled daily intelligence bulletins. The bulletins often ran to twenty or thirty pages and covered all events known to the colonial authority in the mandated territory. They included spy reports and the minutes of meetings held by political parties and rebel groups. Within the reports were copies, and often originals, of thousands of intercepted rebel letters and documents. There were reports on the Syrian and foreign press, accounts of battles, and daily reports on each region, including road conditions, rumors, and military operations. Additionally, the archives contain secret special reports on negotiations, submissions to the mandate power, and prisoners, including full court case transcripts, lists of condemned rebels, and transcripts of interviews with captured rebels, as well as private letters between mandate officials and hundreds of pages of intercepted secret British documents that are not in the British Public Records Office. This book draws on 5,000 pages of reports covering the years 1924–1927, few of which have ever been utilized for a history of the revolt.

The mandate archives provide an intimate day-to-day portrait of the French mandate in Syria. But they contain more than a daily record of the repressive apparatus of colonial rule; they also offer the most comprehensive record available of resistance to colonial rule. They are a chronicle of both domination and resistance. In his classic study of rural insurgency in India, Ranajit Guha argues that the collective consciousness of an insurgency is inscribed in negative outlines in the consciousness (and the archives) of its enemies.[36] He contends that insurgency leaves an imprint, a mirror image in negative, on the bureaucratic records of those who seek to dominate it. Just as a glass window smashed by a fist leaves traces on the hand that shattered it, so too must those that the mandatory power sought to control and dominate leave traces of their consciousness on its bureaucratic records.

Not all records documented state repression. The Ottoman state ruled Greater Syria for 400 years, until 1918. Ottoman subjects understood the legal foundations of the state. The sultan was theoretically obligated to insure justice and remain accessible to his subjects. Residents of the most humble village would not hesitate to petition the highest offices of the state to complain about taxes or corrupt officials. Local communities recorded their dealings with their neighbors by written contracts. The sale of agricultural produce was based on annual contracts, which were sometimes written. Marriage contracts were almost always written. Land sales yielded contracts. Payment of taxes left a receipt. I have utilized hundreds of such documents to trace the contours and relations of rural life for the period beginning in 1860.[37]

Many of the participants in the revolt were members of what Hanna Batatu called the lesser rural notability. Sulṭân al-Aṭrash was a member of such a family. These people were literate and more than a few left memoirs, which are valuable and historically unprecedented. They were the *mukhtâr*s or shaykhs of their villages, or perhaps the sons of such men. They might be the largest landholder in a village of small holders. Some were landlords over leased or sharecropped agricultural land. Some had received Ottoman state education, perhaps locally or in the Damascus military preparatory school or even in Istanbul. The early twentieth century was the first time such people wrote down their experiences in the Middle East.[38] Memoirs cover battles against the French and sometimes political battles between the insurgent leaders. These sources describe in detail events that were apparently unknown to French intelligence. While French sources provide powerful evidence of rebel unity and cooperation, insurgent sources indicate the tensions and the costs of maintaining unity. Memoirs furnish a contrast between what the insurgents said about themselves and about each other and what their enemies said about them.

The final major source is the press. Despite censorship and frequent closures, Damascus, like many other cities, was served by a more lively press in 1925 than today. The largest-circulation Damascus daily, *al-Muqtabas,* had an unabashedly nationalist viewpoint; the mandate authority shut it down and jailed its editor, Najîb al-Rayyis, between mid-August and November 1925 and then again in December 1925. There were usually several other newspapers in print in Damascus, though the mandate High Commission completely subsidized a few of them. Sometimes it closed those papers too! The press, both within and outside Syria, is thus an important source. The Paris and London papers are also valuable and contain fiery debates on the uprising and European mandatory occupation. The revolt figured prominently in the Palestinian and Egyptian press too.[39] While the British censored the press in their colonies less vigorously than did the French, the French encouraged anti-British editorials in the Syrian and Lebanese press just as the British encouraged anti-French editorials in the Egyptian, Transjordanian, and Palestinian press.

The Great Syrian Revolt was not an overtly successful example of anticolonial resistance. The revolt did not succeed in ridding Syria of the mandate or even in changing the ruling structure of society; the mandate lasted another twenty years, and those at the highest reaches of Damascene and national politics were unassailable until after independence. The revolt proved to the mandate power that it needed Syria's elites, and, to a certain extent, Syria's elites needed the mandate power. Many who took part in the uprising were killed or exiled from Syria until the late 1930s. The failure of the revolt removed them from political contention. The mandate power and leading Damascus politicians could ignore the exiled insurgents and their uncompromising nationalist visions for more than a decade. Despite its ultimate failure, however, the revolt had the lasting effect of permanently drawing disparate regions together under the idea of a Syrian-Arab nation. In spite of the determined efforts of the mandate power to divide Syrian society permanently, the revolt helped allow Syrians to imagine themselves as a unified nation.

The Great Revolt is significant for more than the emergence of popular nationalism. Many of the historical trends, conflicts, and fissures that have characterized postcolonial Arab politics first emerged during the uprising. Former military officers of mostly modest background challenged older, more prominent, and more conservative notables and their claims to lead the nation. New nationalist classes communicated in the language of their origins and led an expansion and a radicalization of politics, which was initially short-lived but which eventually became the dominant political discourse. Years later radical nationalists of the Ba'th and other Syrian parties took the militants of the Great Revolt as their examples, rather than the notable politicians of the postrevolt era to whom they were opposed. Resistance against occupation remains a potent theme in the Middle East.

The uprising is also important because it signifies the first skirmish of a struggle for leadership in Syria between old urban notables and new rural elites. In Turkey, in Syria, in Egypt, and in Iraq provincial and rural notables ultimately replaced the old Ottoman urban notability in the halls of national power. In every instance this transformation occurred when new classes overturned old classes, usually through the upward mobility provided to them in the army. The revolt of 1925 figures as a formative event in modern Arab history of great and generally unrecognized significance. It defined the contours of future political and class contestation.

The significance of the uprising was clear to its participants at the time. The French almost immediately pardoned its most wealthy and prominent leaders. The mandate government realized the importance of fostering a class of accommodationist notables. All could be forgiven for those with a material and social stake in a system of accommodation with the mandate power.

Nationalist members of this class, dominated by absentee landlords of Damascus and the other cities, also understood the stakes. They determinedly and resolutely facilitated the mandate authority's desire to deny radical revolt veterans any role in Syrian politics. The rebels realized that they had been fully marginalized by exile and by the efforts of their former allies too. Most were exiled from Syria for a decade. Some, killed in revolts in Palestine or Iraq, never returned.

The revolt remains significant for one final and tragic reason. The destruction visited on Syria's cities, towns, and villages was unprecedented. The mandate government, sworn to advance the interests and development of the mandatory population, used collective punishment of entire towns—including wholesale executions, house demolitions, utilization of tanks and armored vehicles in urban neighborhoods, population transfers from region to region, and round-the-clock aerial and artillery bombardment of civilian populations—to pacify the territory under mandate. While these ghastly methods have continued to characterize conflict in the Middle East and elsewhere, it was the distinction of the mandatory government of France to have used them first.

CHAPTER 2

The Ḥawrân Frontier

On 19 July 1925 Druze farmers shot down a French surveillance airplane circling above their mountain home, Jabal Ḥawrân, some 100 kilometers south of Damascus.[1] These were the first shots of a revolt that would last two years, beginning and ending in Jabal Ḥawrân. On the same day Druze rebels attacked French troops in the Jabal. The next day Sulṭân al-Aṭrash led fighters in the occupation of Ṣalkhad, the second town of the Jabal, south of Suwaydâ', the provincial capital.[2] A local uprising, in response to local conditions, had begun. But while local conditions had sown the seeds of revolt in Jabal Ḥawrân, the revolt would not remain local; it would soon involve all of mandate Syria and most of Greater Lebanon.

The Great Syrian Revolt had deep roots in southern Syria. The origins of the uprising, its spread, and the nationalist language that characterized it are thoroughly interwoven in the histories of the people and regions that took part. Just as the social and economic relations between those who supported the uprising predate the French mandate in Syria, the mistrust, suspicion, and animosities that kept some communities apart from the revolt have a history too. The summer of 1925 was the nadir of several years of increasingly dire crisis. Inflation squeezed people's income and savings as the Syrian pound, pegged to the French franc, dropped with the French currency. Merchants, and even the mandate government, demanded Ottoman gold pounds for goods and tax payments. Drought had gripped southern Syria for three or four years. Harvests had declined for several years running, while the tax burden on cultivators had risen. Heavy-handed direct military rule nurtured rising nationalist and anti-imperialist feeling among the mandate populations. A mass uprising against French rule was never preordained, but the perceived illegality and illegitimacy of French colonial rule, coupled with brutality and administrative incompetence, was certain to irritate many of Syria's inhabitants.

When mass armed resistance emerged, French authorities explained it away and justified their own behavior by ascribing resistance to the power struggles between a small group of retrograde "feudal" chiefs who objected to

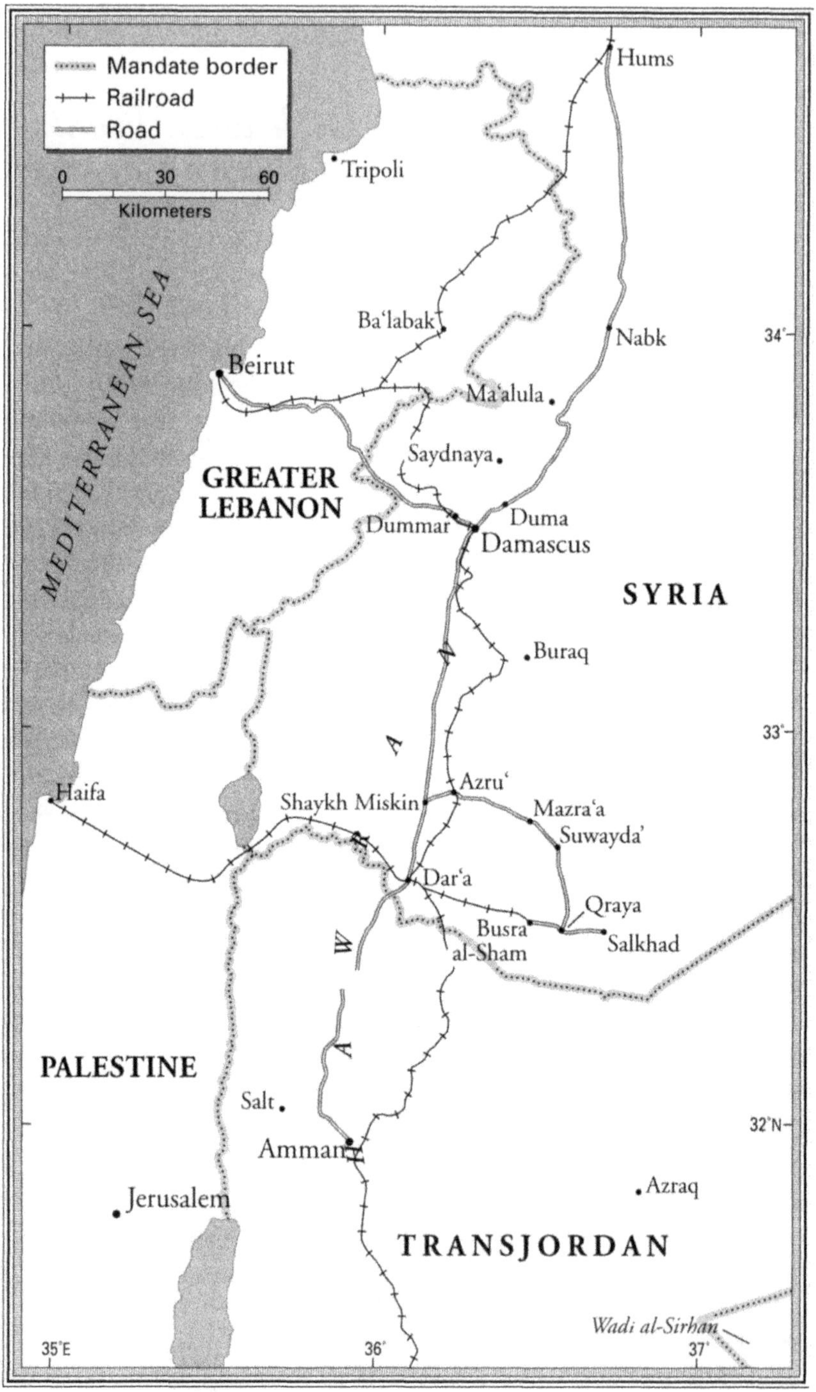

FIGURE 2. Map of Ḥawrân and Damascus

the enlightened reforms that mandate rule brought. When resistance spread to the rest of southern Syria, the mandate power characterized all who resisted as "Druze feudalists," "bandits," or "extremists." Mandate authorities explained that those who resisted opposed progress and sought to defend feudalism. Some were said to be driven by anti-Christian fanaticism, despite the inconvenient fact that Christians participated in the uprising too. Authorities claimed that many simply sought an excuse for plunder. None of the mandate's functionaries and chroniclers could bring themselves to admit the existence of a broad anti-imperialist and nationalist movement against French rule. The uprising was always the "Druze Revolt," invariably accompanied by a reference to the "warlike feudal mountaineers." Few scholars today would use words like "bandit" or "extremist" to describe insurgents against colonial rule, though "terrorist" is perhaps one equivalent. But Druze feudalism has somehow survived, uncritiqued, unexamined, and accepted by all, including many Druze historians themselves.[3]

The economic and social relationships that facilitated the revolt have a history, just as the notion of Druze feudal society has a history. Neither has ever been examined. Ḥawrân Druze feudalism sprang fully formed from the minds of French military officers. It was a montage of popular conceptions of European feudalism mixed with the imperfect understandings of the far more rigidly hierarchical society of Mount Lebanon. The economic and social relations of southern Syria changed over decades, developed by interactions between the inhabitants of the region and sometimes by their relations with the state. This chapter examines these interactions. I wish to show, first, that—due to the efforts of Druze shaykhs and Damascene merchants—southern Syria was well integrated into the economic and social life of Damascus. Second, I seek to argue that the expanding economy and new educational institutions of the Ottoman state served to foster a new social class, which could mount a nationalist, but not elite, challenge to the postwar colonial power more comprehensively than the Ottoman state had ever been challenged. Finally, I wish to demonstrate that Druze feudalism is a mirage, a convincing and durable fake, invented to justify and render coherent a colonial project of military domination.

SETTLING THE FRONTIER

Jabal Ḥawrân rises from the eastern plain of Ḥawrân southeast of Damascus. The plain is vast and fertile and stretches 150 kilometers south from Damascus into what is today Jordan. In most years of good rain, it is covered by a sea of wheat from early spring to midsummer. It is bordered on the west by the southern end of the Anti-Lebanon mountain range, the Jawlân (Golan), and the often snowy peaks of Jabal al-Shaykh (Mount Hermon). It is bordered on the east by the Syrian desert, the gentle slopes of Jabal Ḥawrân, and the volcanic badlands of the Laja'a.

The mountain is hard black basalt with dark and rich topsoil of decomposed basalt. Since Roman times basalt had been the building material of choice, and many of the houses and entire villages that the Druze migrants resettled were already many hundreds of years old. They moved into old villages and built new villages on stony spurs of the mountain—their houses, walls, and animal pens all made from the same black stone. The streets were narrow, the walls high, and the houses close together. Before the large Druze migrations of the 1860s, Ḥawrân peasants and local bedouin lived in some of the mountain villages, often only seasonally. As the Druze migrants increased, they forced aside the villagers and bedouin and cleared more fields of the innumerable basalt rocks and boulders strewn all over the mountain. The basalt made fine material for building new houses as their community expanded and for building even better village fortifications than the heights of the mountain naturally provided.

Jabal Ḥawrân was a safe place for the Druze. Competition for arable land had driven many from Mount Lebanon. Others had come from Palestine or northern Syria. As a small minority, practicing a secretive religion, they perched insecurely on the fringe of the wider Islamic society. Some among the Sunnî Muslim majority saw the Druze as heretics, and the doctrinaire Sunnî Ottoman state had periodically persecuted them. For security and freedom from persecution, they gravitated to remote rural regions far from the centers of state power. While their communities were larger in other parts of the Arab East, Druze peasants had inhabited parts of Jabal Ḥawrân since the seventeenth century.

But it was only after the large migrations of the mid-nineteenth century that the Druze came to dominate. The largest Druze community in Greater Syria was 150 kilometers west of Jabal Ḥawrân in the high coastal mountain range of Mount Lebanon. In 1860 the Druze of Mount Lebanon fought a civil war with their mountain neighbors, the Maronite Christians. Foreign powers, particularly the French and British, were deeply involved in the conflict. Although the Druze defeated the Maronites in Mount Lebanon, the Ottoman state, seeking to avoid further conflict and the threat of even more European interference, authorized a French/Ottoman force to invade Mount Lebanon and protect the Maronites from the Druze. The Maronites had long been unofficial French clients; and they served throughout the nineteenth and twentieth centuries as a "vital interest," justifying French involvement in the affairs of the Ottoman state and Greater Syria. The French intervention in 1860 panicked the Druze inhabitants of Mount Lebanon, and in the period of a month several thousand fled for Jabal Ḥawrân. The migration continued after the end of the war, throughout the 1860s.[4]

When the Druze arrived in Jabal Ḥawrân, they found an environment vastly different from what they had known in Mount Lebanon. Climate and topography were the first immediate differences. Mount Lebanon was truly mountainous, and rainfall was abundant. Tiny plots precipitously terraced on the mountains could sustain a family, due to fine soil and plenty of rain. Land was scarce and population density was high, but the land produced high yields. Jabal Ḥawrân, by contrast, was steppe, nearly desert in some years; and though land was abundant and fertile, rainfall was always scarce. The most generously watered areas of the Jabal never received more than 350 mm in a year, and most areas received much less. Surface water was nearly nonexistent, and the rainfall the mountain did receive ended up under the basalt layer and flowed downhill underground to sustain Lake Tiberias and the aquifer under the oasis of Damascus.

Social life was different too. Mount Lebanon was dominated by noble families, both Druze and Maronite, and the peasants who worked the land for the noble families had much more in common with other peasants than with their landlords. Socially and culturally, the two sectarian communities in Mount Lebanon were very close. Their social practices were similar, and each community was characterized by a rigid and impermeable social hierarchy between peasants and their landlords. Dress, food, social customs, and farming methods were all similar between the Maronites and the Druze. As a migrant population in a frontier region populated by nomads and seminomadic peasants, the Druze in Jabal Ḥawrân found themselves in a much different social and cultural environment than Mount Lebanon. Rather than living side by side with the Maronites, the Druze community there lived side by side with the bedouin and the Jabal Ḥawrân villagers, who were mostly of Christian and settled bedouin origin. Outside forces and influences were much less important; and the European powers, and even the Ottoman state, interfered comparatively little in life in Ḥawrân.

The Druze in Jabal Ḥawrân dressed like bedouin, ate the same food, and followed similar social customs of clan honor and hospitality. In the course of the nineteenth century, as the number of migrants increased, the Druze and the small local bedouin tribes fought one another bitterly for domina-

FIGURE 3. Ḥawrân village street scene. Courtesy Middle East Documentation Center, University of Chicago Library.

tion of the mountain. In the 1860s and 1870s, as the Druze became stronger and more numerous, they decisively defeated the local bedouin and forged new relationships, based on defensive alliances and commercial agreements. As Druze peasants settled more villages and put more and more land under the plow, local bedouin lost pastureland. But the bedouin gained allies against other tribes; and when the grain harvest was finished in the crucial midsummer months, they grazed their flocks on the stubble left on the fields. As the production of grain rose with the increase of Druze migrants, the bedouin prospered too by providing camel transport to Damascus and Haifa for the grain trade.

In Jabal Ḥawrân during the nineteenth century it was labor and not land that was in short supply. Villagers arrived from Lebanon or elsewhere and went to a village where they had relatives or friends. If a new migrant had money or draft animals, or sons who could add to the defensive capabilities of the village, he would buy (or often be given) a house and shares in the communal *(mushâʿ)* land of the village.[5] All those who owned land or shares were *fallâḥîn.* If a migrant did not have money or animals, or other socially desirable attributes, he would contract to cultivate land belonging to someone else. The common arrangement was called *al-râbiʿ*, "a fourth," which denoted the share the laborer received. The contractor was called *al-murâbiʿ*, and landless laborers in general were called *falatiyya.* The land he worked under contract might belong to the shaykh of the village, or to a wealthier peasant who had too much land for his family alone to work, or to an old person who was unable to do the hard work of cultivation. The landlord provided everything necessary for farming: seed, tools, and animals. If the laborer had a house in the village, he would stay there; if not, the landlord provided modest room and board. Life for the new migrants was difficult, and the work of farming usually began with the back-breaking labor of clearing large stones before plowing.

Still, there was much to recommend life in Jabal Ḥawrân. The social hierarchy was much less rigid than in Mount Lebanon, and the goal of most peasant farmers and recent migrants was to purchase communal land in the village and become a small proprietor. It bears mention that landless peasants were always a minority among villagers, and sharecropping arrangements probably only emerged in the second half of the nineteenth century.[6] Statistics from the mandate era show that most were successful in this goal of acquiring land, since ownership was more widespread in Jabal Ḥawrân and the plain of Ḥawrân than in any other part of mandate Syria.[7] Plot size was also smaller than in any other part of the territory under mandate. In any case, there was nothing apart from the renewable *al-râbiʿ* contract, and whatever social ties that may have existed, to keep a peasant from moving on to a new village if land or opportunities were better.

There were no absentee landlords in Jabal Ḥawrân. Shaykhs lived in their villages and worked their own fields. The shaykh of each village was usually merely the first to settle a village and reach an agreement with, or perhaps subjugate, its previous inhabitants. Sons and dependent young men of fighting age were important in claiming a village. The ability to attract young migrants to a village was part of a village shaykh's fitness to lead the village and represent it to the outside. Strength of arms was the actual foundation of local authority in the frontier society, and villages that were secure and well defended from raids by bedouin and others attracted more migrants. The stronger the shaykh of a village, the more favorable the terms he was able to negotiate with local bedouin, with other villages, with outside merchants, and with the state. A copious literature has ascribed the fabled ferocity of the Druze in Lebanon, Palestine, and Jabal Ḥawrân to their sectarian solidarity. In Jabal Ḥawrân, however, the fact of relative social equality far better explains their ability to unite in the face of outside threats to a way of life evidently worth fighting for.

RURAL AUTONOMY AND COMMERCIAL INTEGRATION

During the 1860s the situation in Jabal Ḥawrân changed radically. After eking out a marginal existence on the frontier between the settled and nomadic regions, the Druze came to be the masters of the mountain and later the masters of the Ḥawrân. Several elements facilitated this change. First was population expansion, already discussed above. Second was the growth of local and world markets for agricultural products. Last was the emergence of a new, self-confident, and aggressive chiefly family, anxious to carve out a more important local role.

The Ḥawrân had produced grain for much of Greater Syria and Arabia since Roman times. The production of cereals and settled agriculture had been stagnant in Ḥawrân for at least two hundred years in the mid-nineteenth century.[8] The Ottoman state did not possess the resources or the will to ensure rural security in Ḥawrânî agricultural villages. Peasants became seminomadic, moving to the cities or to more secure areas like central Syria around Ḥumṣ and Ḥamâh. In these regions entire districts, comprising scores of villages, were owned by the Damascene and Ḥamâwî landed notability. In central Syria peasants found greater security but were forced to withstand rapacious absentee landlords and the efficient exactions of the state, which the urban landlords themselves often represented.

The 1860s, in contrast with previous centuries, were a time of booming migration and booming agricultural export markets in Ḥawrân. As the Druze migrants settled and pacified first Jabal Ḥawrân and then the plain, they began to take advantage of this market. The migrants knew the importance of exports from their experience in the silk business in Mount Lebanon. Mulberry trees, silk worms, and silk cocoon production were impossible to sustain in the relatively arid climate of Jabal Ḥawrân, but the migrants were adaptable and learned from their neighbors how to grow the hardy and drought-resistant native Ḥawrânî wheat. Damascus, Beirut, and Haifa were ready outlets for their grain, and the more enterprising shaykhs opened commercial relations on behalf of their villages with merchants from those cities, particularly Damascus.[9]

Wheat exports from Jabal Ḥawrân and the Ḥawrân plain expanded tremendously in the second half of the century. But more than market and demographic forces drove the expansion. In mid-century a new chiefly family, the Aṭrash (plural Ṭurshân), emerged into prominence in Jabal Ḥawrân. The first famous leader of the Aṭrash family, Ismâʿîl al-Aṭrash, completely changed the balance of power throughout the Ḥawrân. Ismâʿîl managed first to bring the local bedouin under his control and actually reverse the payment of tribute or protection money *(khâwa)*, which the Druze had previously paid to the tribes.[10] Under Ismâʿîl the bedouin began to pay tribute money to the Druze for pasture and water. He then attacked and subjugated the formerly dominant Druze clans, wresting supremacy of the mountain from them. He also attempted, with intermittent success, to extend his control over the Muslim and Christian villages of the plain, forcing them to pay protection money and acting as contract agent for their state taxes and for their grain crop with outside merchants.

The leading Druze shaykhs felt that they had earned the right to dominate the mountain and the plain. The Ottoman governors of Damascus and the great landed notables of that city usually disagreed. While the state coveted greater revenues, and the Damascene notability coveted the rich and suddenly prosperous agricultural land of Ḥawrân, Druze martial strength meant that there was usually little they could do to challenge local autonomy and Druze domination. Negotiating from a position of strength, the Aṭrash shaykhs formed commercial bonds with newly prominent Damascene commercial families and avoided business relations with the leading notable families. Damascene notable families derived wealth and prominence from positions in the Ottoman bureaucracy and the ownership of vast tracts of agricultural land, both of which made them potentially dangerous to Druze domination of Ḥawrân. The merchants that the Druze shaykhs chose to deal with were always from the Maydân quarter, the neighborhood outside Damascus' walls, which stretched along the road south to Ḥawrân and the Arabian Peninsula beyond. While these men were often prosperous merchants, they were not part of the Ottoman service or landholding elite. The merchants loaned money to both shaykhs and peasants and contracted to buy the summer wheat crop and other crops consumed locally and exported in smaller quantities, such as chickpeas, grapes, and olives.

These commercial agreements yielded long-term relationships, which facilitated the integration of the Ḥawrân Druze into Damascene cultural and political life. The other rural sectarian minorities of Greater Syria—the ʿAlawîs, the Ismâʿîlîs, and the Shîʿîs of southern Mount Lebanon—did not begin this process of integration with the urban centers until the 1940s. Even more important, the Druze shaykhs dealt with Damascus on their own terms. While Damascene merchants went to villages in Ḥawrân and Ghûṭa, usurious loan contracts in hand, and extracted newly issued Ottoman title deeds from peasants as collateral, the grain merchant families who dealt with the Druze negotiated only with the village shaykhs, who expected to receive fair treatment and who bargained from a position of relative equality with the merchants.[11] Druze villagers held their shaykhs responsible for good interest rates and good crop prices. Maydânî grain merchant families and Druze families thus formed relationships that lasted decades or even generations.

Among the merchants of the Maydân active in this trade were the Muslim Mahâynî, Sukkar, and Bîṭâr families and the Christian ʿAflaq and Shûwayrî families. These merchants built summerhouses in Druze villages and supplied lodging and connections for their customers in Damascus. The sons of Druze shaykhs sometimes lived with the families of their fathers' business partners in Damascus while they attended school.[12]

Life was different for Christian and Muslim Ḥawrânî villages. They did not enjoy such equal relations with the Druze shaykhs who dominated their villages. While Druze protection and domination might be nominally preferable to the mercies of the bedouin, the rapaciousness of the Ottoman state, or the unrestrained usury of Damascene moneylenders, Druze protection came at a heavy price; villagers often welcomed Ottoman troops or even bedouin, if they came to teach the Druze a lesson.[13] After a year or two, though, with heavy government taxes and sometimes conscription demands—coupled with the perpetual inability of the government to deliver security in return for its exactions—the villages would invite the Druze to return or at least acquiesce to a return. This pattern continued into the 1930s.

With the ascendance of the Aṭrash clan and the gradual exploitation of most good land, life became more difficult for Ḥawrân Druze peasants. As Ismâʿîl al-Aṭrash and his descendants were hard on their neighbors, they were also hard on the peasants who lived in the villages they controlled. The Aṭrash shaykhs began to exert authority over all the land adjoining their villages and to insist on the right to allot the shares of communal land as they wished. Ḥawrân Druze society had long dictated that villagers be ready to defend the village behind the shaykh's leadership, but the Aṭrash shaykhs began to evict villagers from their homes and land and replace them with younger, hungrier migrants, who might contribute more readily to the village's complement of young male fighters. As the Aṭrash shaykhs exerted more authority over village life, their authority extended to the control of land. Not only did they insist on the right to supervise the periodic reallotment of communal lands, but they insisted on more shares for themselves personally. By the 1880s most Aṭrash shaykhs received a quarter of village communal land and sometimes conscripted peasants from their villages to work it. Though the land was communal, they periodically utilized their power to dispossess peasants from land that the cultivators actually owned. Such an act triggered an uprising in the final decade of the century.

In 1889 a group of secondary chiefs and peasants formed a coalition to challenge the rule of the Aṭrash chiefs. The community was divided, and the Aṭrash family itself split into opposing camps. The conflict had simmered for several years; and when it finally came into the open, the Ottoman state exploited the opportunity to impose some form of government rule on Jabal Ḥawrân. The power of the great chiefs declined. Peasants earned secure title to their land, or at least their shares, and the chiefs gave up half their shares, to bring the amount of land they controlled in most villages to no more than an eighth. Involuntary evictions stopped.

The cleavages between the Ḥawrân Druze endured. Some would argue that they continue to this day, both between the shaykhs and between members of the Aṭrash family. While a number of Aṭrash shaykhs, especially those from the provincial capital of Suwaydâʾ, accepted Ottoman rule and took positions in the Ottomanized local government, some, particularly those of the southern villages, distant from Suwaydâʾ, continued to decry the lack of unity among the community. The Ottoman state forced the Ḥawrân Druze to accept outside governors *(qâʾimmaqâm)*, among whom were Damascenes, such as Maḥmûd al-Ghazzî, and other outsiders, such as Yûsuf Ḍiyâʾ al-Khâlidî from Jerusalem.[14] The fact of Ottoman rule of law was bad enough; but all the shaykhs resisted outside governors, and several advocated themselves or members of their families for the post.

The final years of the nineteenth century were difficult in Jabal Ḥawrân. State power over the area was vastly increased, the leadership of the Ḥawrân Druze community was split into pro- and anti-Ottoman camps, their control of villages and wheat sales on the plain was more contested than it had been, and grain prices were in sharp and lengthy decline due to worldwide depression. Between 1890 and the First World War, there were two major uprisings against the Ottoman state in Jabal Ḥawrân. In 1896 the Ḥawrân Druze faced an array of Ottoman soldiers, Circassian refugee settlers (armed by the state), hostile bedouin, and Ḥawrânî villagers. Shiblî al-Aṭrash, premier shaykh of the Jabal, had succeeded in his efforts to gain appointment as *qâʾimmaqâm*, and the Ottoman government had relented in its policy of appointing outside governors; but now Shiblî, as an Ottoman employee, could not take his place as the leader of the insurgency.[15] The forces united against them defeated the Ḥawrân Druze, though not without heavy losses for all concerned. The Ottomans, satisfied that they had pacified the Jabal, extended general amnesty and again left the Druze alone.

In 1910, however, two years after the Unionist Revolution in Istanbul, Ottoman soldiers were back. This time they came in response to fighting between Druze and bedouin. With thirty battalions of Ottoman troops, Samî Bâshâ al-Fârûqî met insignificant resistance. While the Ḥawrân Druze leaders were aggressive in defense of what they saw as their rights, they were not suicidal. In the wake of the invasion, Samî al-Fârûqî disarmed the Ḥawrân Druze, and some of the Jabal's young men were taken as conscripts into the Ottoman army. Among them was a twenty-year-old named Sulṭân al-Aṭrash. He spent six months serving in the Balkans, where, among other things, he learned to read and write. Whatever goodwill the experience may have fostered was destroyed when the young man returned to find that his father, Dhûqân al-Aṭrash (shaykh of the southern Jabal village of al-Q̲rayâ), had been publicly hanged by the Ottoman authorities in Damascus, along with five other recalcitrant Druze shaykhs.[16] The executions were not soon forgotten in Jabal Ḥawrân, and they would be cited again and again as proof of Ottoman savagery and, anachronistically, as proof of Druze sacrifices for the Syrian Arab nation.

Ḥawrân Druze villages were not utopian peasant communes. But neither were they bastions of lordly feudal privilege and grinding rural serfdom. The notion of feudal rule and feudal social organization has long characterized accounts of social life in Jabal Ḥawrân. The social system of Jabal Ḥawrân, based as it was on rule by consent and the relatively free movement of labor, had virtually nothing in common with imagined European feudalism, except in the minds of the French officers and civil servants who so desperately sought to justify colonial domination. Their mission dictated the transformation of rural society based on their own imagined history.[17] That French officers viewed Syrian rural society through the prism of the civilizing mission and their own imagined history is unsurprising. What is surprising, however, is that their conceptions, deeply flawed though they were, have survived.

ASSIMILATING THE COUNTRYSIDE: EDUCATION AND THE ARMY

Sulṭân al-Aṭrash was not the only young man of Jabal Ḥawrân to venture outside the mountain homeland for education and military service. Along with others from the unruly fringes of the Ottoman realms, a number of young men from Jabal Ḥawrân experienced the new institutions of Ottoman education in Damascus and even in Istanbul. As the Ottoman state under Sultan Abdülhamid II vigorously repressed expressions of autonomy in the provinces, it also tried to draw the provinces into the unifying culture of the center.[18] An Ottoman local official expressed the two policies vividly in a speech to defiant villagers. "With people like you only two things are possible. One, schools, in which to educate you to see the necessity of law and order . . . the other is the stick. Now, schools take fifteen years to produce a man such as I want; the stick is a matter of five minutes . . ."[19] The stick had been notably ineffective in Jabal Ḥawrân, and by the last decades of the nineteenth century the state had resolved to try other methods of discipline and control.

Assimilation was easier in the urban centers like Damascus, where Ottoman rule had clear benefits, at least for some. Identification with Ottoman culture and power had enduring appeal in the late nineteenth century in the big cities of the Arab East. Damascene elites had innumerable depictions of Istanbul and the Bosporus with Ottoman banners flying, painted on the walls of their houses. They followed the styles of the imperial center with obsessive care.[20] But the state employed imaginative means to draw rural subjects into the government orbit too. Both in the cities and in the countryside the primary means of fostering the assimilation of Ottoman culture and identity were education, the promise of jobs and prestige, and good government. Maktab ʿAnbar, officially known as the Damascus Civil Preparatory School, was the city's most prestigious school and occupied a grand late nineteenth century house built by a Damascene Jewish merchant and confiscated by the government after his bankruptcy. The school has been the topic of many memoirs and scholarly studies. It has long been considered a nursery for Syria's interwar nationalist elite. Philip Khoury has shown that a large percentage of the leaders of the National Bloc, which ruled in concert with the French between 1928 and independence, were graduates of Maktab ʿAnbar.[21]

Maktab ʿAnbar was an elite school. It was expensive and was intended to provide education for boys who were sons of the local Ottomanized elite. ʿAnbar students went on to study in Istanbul at the Imperial Civil Service School, Mekteb-i Mülkiye, at the Ottoman law or medical schools, or at foreign universities. The scholarship on Maktab ʿAnbar has obscured from view the fact that, at least in the provinces, Ottoman education comprised two tiers: one to sustain state elites and one to foster new, admittedly lower-level, inductees into the Ottoman system. While ʿAnbar was an elite, tuition-based, civil preparatory school in Damascus, readying students for high government civil employment, there was also a fully subsidized military secondary school, known locally as the Maktab al-Iʿdâdiyya al-ʿAskariyya, at a relatively distant location outside the city walls in the neighborhood of Barâmka, near the military barracks and parade ground. The Damascus Ottoman military secondary school is virtually unknown to scholars today, but a hundred years ago it was well known throughout Greater Syria. A staggeringly large proportion of the leaders of the Great Syrian Revolt received their schooling there.[22]

Young men of modest rural background rarely attended Maktab ʿAnbar. When they left their villages for the city, it was the military school they entered. They went on to further study at the Ottoman Imperial Military College, the Mekteb-i Harbiye, not the Civil Service School, the Mekteb-i Mülkiye, or foreign universities. The civil educational institutions remained the preserve of the wealthy elite. In the early 1960s Patrick Seale documented the Damascus ruling classes' distaste for the army. He noted that the ascendance of rural military officers in Syria's postcolonial government of the late 1940s had resulted from elite distaste and rural recruiting. The pattern, however, was established much earlier, by the deliberate Ottoman policy of drawing rural people into the state system. When members of the Damascus landed elite sent their sons for higher education, the young men came back as lawyers, engineers, and scholars. When rural shaykhs, village leaders, and middling urban merchants sent their sons for higher education, they came back as graduates of the only schools their families could afford: state-subsidized military academies.[23]

A two-tiered educational system was not the only assimilative reform of late Ottoman rule. Sultan Abdülhamid's government had other, even more innovative, mechanisms for drawing the sons of rural leaders into the Ottoman system. In 1892 the sultan himself conceived and inaugurated the Tribal School in Istanbul. Mekteb-i Aşiret was a multiyear boarding school intended to indoctrinate sons of leading rural shaykhs into Ottoman service.[24] Like military education, it too was completely subsidized. The Tribal School was designed to acculturate and assimilate those who would be the leaders and shaykhs of the previously ungovernable fringe regions of the empire. While Maktab ʿAnbar was designed to instill loyalty in the provincial urban elite, the Tribal School was intended to serve the same purpose among the tribal leaders. The difference was that the indoctrination of provincial urban elites, for whom Ottoman rule brought clear benefits, took place in the provinces, while the much harder job of indoctrinating would-be rural leaders could only take place in the capital. The state intended the Tribal School for boys who would have local influence.

Several of the boys who attended the Tribal School were sons of Druze or bedouin shaykhs from the Ḥawrân. Students came from all over the empire, including Libya, Yemen, Ḥijâz, Iraq, and the Kurdish regions, and at least two of the first eighty-six students came from the Aṭrash clan.[25] From the Tribal School, most young men went on to the Imperial Military School, where they met other Arab students from similar rural and provincial backgrounds. At least some of the boys maintained friendships long after they had left the school to begin their military service. As a matter of policy, they were usually posted near their places of origin. Saʿîd al-ʿÂṣ, who was from a modest background in Ḥamâh and a graduate of both the military school in Damascus and the Harbiye in Istanbul, noted that Ramaḍân Shallâsh, the son of a bedouin shaykh from Dayr al-Zûr, and ʿAlî al-Aṭrash, from the Suwaydâʾ branch of the Aṭrash family, met and became friends at the Tribal School. Their friendship again emerged in 1925, as Ramaḍân Shallâsh came to the countryside of Damascus to join ʿAlî al-Aṭrash and another former comrade from the Ottoman army, Fawzî al-Qâwuqjî, in the fight against the French.[26]

Muḥammad ʿIzz al-Dîn al-Ḥalabî was another young man who benefited from a state military education. He was born in 1889 in the Jabal Ḥawrân town of Shahbâ, where his relatives were locally important Druze shaykhs. For reasons that are unclear, he attended a few years of secondary school in Ankara in central Anatolia, which was then a small town. After a return to Jabal Ḥawrân, he secured a place in the Harbiye in Istanbul, from which he graduated at an unusually young age in 1905. He served in the Ottoman Fifth Army, headquartered in Damascus, after 1905. In 1909 he received command of a reserve cavalry squadron in Dûmâ, just northwest of Damascus, on the Ḥumṣ road. In 1912 he resigned his commission in protest over the Ottoman defense ministry's pacification campaign led by Samî Bâshâ al-Fârûqî in Jabal Ḥawrân and the executions that followed. Muḥammad ʿIzz al-Dîn spent the war years as *qâʾimmaqâm* of the district of al-Zabadânî, in the mountains west of Damascus. After the war, he became an employee of Amîr Fayṣal's government and fought the French invasion of inland Syria at the battle of Maysalûn. When France occupied mandate Syria, he returned to Jabal Ḥawrân, where he became a delegate to the representative council in Suwaydâʾ. He commanded insurgents in the countryside from 1925 until 1927, with often devastating effectiveness. The mandate power exiled him, along with most other military leaders (usually labeled "Sharîfian bandits"), until 1937.[27]

The uprising of 1925 owed much of its national character to the bonds between such former officers. It is impossible to know what experiences they shared in Istanbul and on the battlefields of the Great War, because, as paragons of an emerging Syrian Arab nationalism, they rarely wrote about their Ottoman experiences. Whether the Ottoman project of education and assimilation had served to bind these young men to the Ottoman state or to nascent ideas of Arab nationalism or to both, at different times, there is no question that the experience served to bind them to one another and, in time, to ideas of an independent Syrian state that could be.

The few memoirs they left make it clear that by 1925, when nearly all were in their middle to late thirties, many of them had known one another since they were teenagers. They had met at military school in Damascus, in the Tribal School or at the Harbiye in Istanbul, or in battles in Libya, the Balkans,

Anatolia, Gallipoli, the Arabian desert, and Maysalûn. They were soldiers rather than theorists, and their chronicles and their actions display frustration with and trenchant criticism of the civilian nationalist elite of Damascus. They identified themselves as nationalists and patriots, but their nationalism was practical and unsystematic; they focused on expelling the French from Syria and sometimes mixed in popular Islamic religion, anti-Christian agitation, and even class warfare against urban landlords and notables. It is very likely that people such as these, of modest background and representing an emerging social class fostered by military education, were able to communicate with and organize the resistance of ordinary urban and rural Syrians far better than the self-appointed nationalist elite of intellectuals and western-educated politicians.

THE ARAB REVOLT AND THE ḤAWRÂN DRUZE

Despite the "Sharîfian" epithet used by mandate intelligence officers, not all Arab Ottoman officers joined Amîr Fayṣal in the British-sponsored Arab Revolt. Muḥammad ʿIzz al-Dîn al-Ḥalabî did not, and neither did Fawzî al-Qâwuqjî. Still, many others did join Fayṣal, often after capture by Arab or British forces. In the late summer of 1918, as the Sharîfian army entered Ḥawrân, they were joined by Sulṭân al-Aṭrash and a number of Druze horsemen from Jabal Ḥawrân for the final advance on Damascus. Before the Druze forces joined Fayṣal, however, they signed agreements with his representatives, guaranteeing a high degree of regional autonomy in the state that would emerge from the Ottoman withdrawal.[28]

Direct military involvement was one thing, but some of the Ḥawrân Druze had played a less direct but nonetheless important role in the war since 1916. They had supplied the British-bankrolled Arab army with bread since at least 1917. It was also the Druze, of the southern and traditionally anti-Ottoman part of the Jabal, who sheltered anti-Ottoman Damascene militants in the safety of their mountain. The wartime Ottoman governor of Wilâyat Sûriyya (the Ottoman province of Greater Syria), Aḥmad Jamâl Bâshâ, enacted harsh punitive measures to combat what he perceived as subversive and treasonous activity by Arab nationalists and partisans of Sharîf al-Ḥusayn and his Arab army. He hanged a number of suspected nationalists, and those who could escape went to Cairo or Europe. Along the way many went to Jabal Ḥawrân, where they stayed in villages in the southern Jabal as guests of Druze leaders, among them, Sulṭân al-Aṭrash and ʿAbd al-Ghaffâr al-Aṭrash.[29] While he certainly flew his own standard, Sulṭân al-Aṭrash claimed he was the first to raise the Arab flag over the Jabal.

The first link between Amîr Fayṣal and the Ḥawrân Druze was Nasîb al-Bakrî. Amîr Fayṣal had stayed in the Bakrî family house in the village of al-Qâbûn early in 1916, before the beginning of the Arab Revolt.[30] Nasîb and his brother Fawzî al-Bakrî's ties with Fayṣal dated from before the war and originated with their fathers, ʿAṭâ Allâh al-Bakrî and al-Ḥusayn, the Sharîf of Mecca. Sharîf al-Ḥusayn cemented the connection by appointing Fawzî al-Bakrî his personal bodyguard. During Fayṣal's stay in 1916, Nasîb al-Bakrî organized a meeting of Druze shaykhs, including Sulṭân and Ḥusayn al-Aṭrash, and some Damascene nationalist members of the secret society al-Fatat, to try to gain support for a revolt against Ottoman rule.[31] It was natural that Bakrî would call upon the Ḥawrân Druze for such a project, since their antipathy and periodic armed resistance against the Ottoman state were known everywhere. Sulṭân and Ḥusayn al-Aṭrash met Fayṣal and were impressed with him but declined to lend more than their conditional support to the revolt.

Besides their connection with Sharîf Ḥusayn and Fayṣal, the Bakrîs had long-standing ties with the Ḥawrân and Damascene Druze. Nasîb was born in 1888, and Fawzî was born in 1886. Both were graduates of Maktab ʿAnbar in Damascus. The Bakrîs had houses and commercial connections in their Damascus neighborhood of al-Shâghûr and in the Ghûṭa village of al-Qâbûn. The village was just outside Damascus near the Druze village of Jaramânâ. The Bakrîs were not large landowners by Damascene notable standards, but they did have holdings in and around Jaramânâ and knew various Druze shaykhs well.[32] Amîr Fayṣal made Nasîb his personal secretary, and he also made him his envoy to the Ḥawrân Druze.

The most important contribution of the Ḥawrân Druze to the Arab Revolt was grain. As the war progressed, a crushing famine gripped most of Greater Syria. In Syrian usage, famine and conscription are still collapsed in the Turkish word for land mobilization, *seferberlik,* which evokes all aspects of the horrible suffering of the war years. Linda Schilcher has shown that while grain merchant speculators bore some of the blame for the famine, the most devastating element was effective British blockade of all Arab Mediterranean ports.[33] At the time, it was realized—though apparently not by the Ottoman high command—that grain shortages in Arabia and starvation among the tribes were the principal reason bedouin joined the revolt. While the British kept any grain from entering the country, the Ottoman command, with insufficient food for the army, cut supplies to the coast due to the suspicion (probably well founded) that unscrupulous grain speculators would either hoard grain in Beirut or export it for still higher prices. Meanwhile, with insufficient funds to buy grain on the open market, the Ottoman command was forced to resort to a policy of price fixing for grain producers. When the command was unable to impose a stable grain price, the policy changed to one of more or less forced confiscation, with token payment, of grain stores from both producers and merchants. Only the Ḥawrân Druze had enough independence from the central government to resist confiscation.

British war policy led indirectly to the deaths by starvation of hundreds of thousands in the cities of Greater Syria and in the Ottoman army. The Ottoman high command in Istanbul bore responsibility too and had evidently decided by early 1918 that Greater Syria was lost and that resupply was futile. Enver Pasha, the Ottoman minister of war, constantly sought to divert men and supplies to the Caucasus and even to Azerbaijan. At one point, in midsummer 1918, Enver Pasha offered Ottoman officers on the Arab front double pay and promotion if they accepted reposting to the east Caucasus, where there was no fighting in prospect. Three hundred thousand Ottoman soldiers deserted—most simply to go home, but many deserted to the British and Arab forces. While Ottoman subjects and soldiers starved, the British (well supplied with food and gold to buy grain from the Ḥawrân Druze) dropped beautifully colored and illustrated leaflets on the retreating Ottoman troops, depicting the lavish meals they would enjoy as prisoners and British-Arab soldiers.[34] After the armistice, the British and French flooded the cities of Greater Syria with embargoed and hoarded grain, reaping the goodwill of a grateful populace, who blamed the famine on the defeated Ottomans rather than on their victorious liberators.

Sulṭân al-Aṭrash claimed that the Jabal sheltered and fed 50,000 refugees from the Ottoman army and the famine. He mentioned this by way of deflecting the periodic charge of war profiteering by the Druze, their refusal to sell Ḥawrânî grain to Ottoman-held Damascus at fixed government prices, and their preference for more profitable sales to the British-bankrolled Sharîfian army, a trade that the British encouraged with every means available.[35] While they sheltered and fed thousands of refugees daily, the grain trade continued, in cooperation with Maydânî merchants and local bedouin. Lines of transport, though, moved south toward the British line rather than north toward Damascus or toward Haifa.[36] Sulṭân al-Aṭrash had powerful personal reasons for dislike of the Ottoman state that transcended commercial interests, but not all joined him in abandoning the Ottomans.

The issue of loyalty to the Ottoman state provoked fiery controversy among the Ḥawrân Druze leadership. In an extraordinary exchange of letters between Sulṭân al-Aṭrash and his Ottoman loyalist cousin and titular head of the community, Salîm al-Aṭrash, from August 1918, Salîm accused Sulṭân of stupidly joining what he called the "snuff-box army of Sharîf al-Ḥusayn" and threatened him with expulsion from the community if he continued his financially motivated treachery against the Ottoman state. Sulṭân replied two days later (with great pro-British enthusiasm) that he was not greedy for money, since it was not he who dined at the Damascus Palace Hotel, presumably with Jamâl Bâshâ, "or any other Turk, the murderers of our fathers." He accused Salîm of seeking to place the Druze "under the boot of the most savage state on earth."[37] In 1918 Sulṭân al-Aṭrash was twenty-seven years old, the son of a man hanged by the Ottomans, already a community leader, and a committed partisan of the Hashemites and particularly the British.

Amîr Fayṣal kept his pledge to the Ḥawrân Druze and stayed out of their affairs for the duration of his short rule, though he hardly had the power to interfere during the turbulent twenty-two months.[38] Others did not keep their pledges: when France insisted on enforcing the division of Greater Syria agreed upon with the British and validated by the League of Nations, the British dismissed their pledges to support Fayṣal's kingdom and stood aside as their European wartime allies brought an end to the government of their Arab wartime allies. French intelligence agents had already been circulating in Jabal Ḥawrân to help smooth the way for French rule. When the agents arrived, they found the Ḥawrân Druze divided about their mandate along much the same lines as they had been divided about the Ottomans. Salîm al-Aṭrash supported the mandate as he had supported Ottoman rule, while his cousin Sulṭân al-Aṭrash led the opposition.

Like the Druze, Damascenes were divided in their attitudes toward Fayṣal's Arab government and the prospect of foreign rule. Opposition to Fayṣal and his nationalist and military followers followed generational and class lines. Younger and more humble segments of society tended to support the new government, while older and more established notables looked to the European powers to reestablish order and allow them to assume their customary social roles. The core of Fayṣal's supporters consisted of former Ottoman military officers from modest families. Many were from Iraq and joined the Arab Revolt in 1915 and 1916, but Ottoman officers who had not joined the revolt also flocked to Fayṣal's side after his arrival in Damascus. These officers were more likely to hail from Greater Syria than from Iraq. Apparently there were few hard feelings between them; and former Ottoman army comrades who became wartime enemies easily again became postwar comrades. Fawzî al-Qâwuqjî, Muḥammad ʿIzz al-Dîn al-Ḥalabî, Saʿîd al-ʿÂṣ, and others were among the group who joined Fayṣal after the end of the war. Fayṣal, without a local base of support in Damascus and subject to the opposition of most of the landowning notable families, trusted the officer upstarts and rewarded them with jobs and influence. The landowning elite of Damascus and other Syrian cities mistrusted him and his lower-middle-class military officer supporters.[39] When the French invaded Syria in the summer of 1920, it was Fayṣal's military loyalists who led the doomed popular defense at Maysalûn. Members of the notable families stayed at home and waited for the French to arrive.

A few young men from the upper reaches of Damascene society had lent their support to Fayṣal during his 1916 visit. Many of these were prewar Arab nationalists and had been under threat by the wartime Ottoman government. They included Dr. ʿAbd al-Raḥman al-Shahbandar, who fled into exile with the Druze; members of the Bakrî family, who served as Fayṣal's envoy to the Druze; and members of the Ḥaydar family, who were Shîʿa from Baʿlabak. Not coincidentally, these few also played prominent roles in the Syrian revolt of 1925. Some of these, notably Rustum Ḥaydar, accompanied Fayṣal to Iraq after the French occupation of Syria in 1920. Those who stayed, including Rustum Ḥaydar's relative Saʿîd Ḥaydar and Dr. Shahbandar, became reluctant political strategists for their more militant comrades in 1925. Fayṣal and his radical nationalist and military supporters posed a real challenge to the ruling order of Damascus in 1918 and later. They thus provoked opposition both among the Syrian notable elite and among members of the new French government. Those left behind when Fayṣal fled into exile transferred their opposition to the French mandate authority and to the elite families that helped it function.

The roots of opposition to French rule reached deeply into southern Syria's social and economic history. Changing relations of commerce served to tie perennially rebellious Jabal Ḥawrân to Damascus much more firmly than ever before. Rural shaykhs and Damascene merchants developed new commercial channels, which by the 1920s were already decades old. Commercial contacts led to social contacts, mutual understanding, and a feeling of connectedness. Middling grain merchants in Maydân first became sympathetic to the struggles of the Ḥawrân Druze against the state; and as commercial partners they understood and empathized with the difficulties of their principal suppliers. When Damascenes like Nasîb al-Bakrî kindled wartime revolt against the Ottoman state, it was natural that they should call on Druze shaykhs to join them. Commerce in grain was the origin of these connections, which had not existed twenty or thirty years before. Damascene merchants—many of whom (whether from ideological conviction, capitalist self-interest, or a mixture of both) had become Arab nationalists, Arab renegades from the Ottoman army, fugitive nationalist politicians from Damascus, and grain buyers for the Sharîfian forces—all converged on Jabal Ḥawrân during the war, and all brought new political ideas.

Meanwhile the sons of middling merchants and rural shaykhs from all over Greater Syria had met one another in new state educational institutions. They had served and fought side by side in the Ottoman military and often in the Arab army. Many had joined in the battle of Maysalûn to defend Syria from France. Boys from modest rural and urban backgrounds, they had first experienced military education around the turn of the century. After the war, they returned to their communities (in Jabal Ḥawrân, among their bedouin tribes, in villages, and in urban quarters) as grown men in their thirties, worldly wise and full of new ideas. They were the first generation of nationalists who were not intellectuals or politicians. They could communicate in the language of their origins, and they brought unique experiences of the outside world that gave them credibility as leaders.

These connections have been mostly ignored for seventy-five years. French officers described the origins of the uprising as a mobilization of Druze "feudal lords" against the enlightened polices of mandate rule. Druze "serfs" were so backward that they failed to identify their own best interests when they declined to support their European liberators against their chiefs. Nationalist "extremists" from Damascus came and through fast talk and guile (as the chiefs had tricked the peasants) tricked the chiefs to continue the fight against the mandate. "Bandits" everywhere came and took advantage of disorder for pillage and plunder. Running through the story was the separateness of numerous small segments, sharing little or nothing with other small segments. In the French conception, there was no cohesion and nothing shared between the social strata of Syria. Mandate policy was predicated on, and formulated to emphasize, the divisions of Syrian society. A nationalist movement, united against mandate rule, was an unspeakable prospect for the self-appointed rulers of the mandate over Syria.

CHAPTER 3

Mobilizing the Mountain

Resistance movements emerged in various parts of the Syrian countryside on the eve of the French occupation. Though nationalist feelings and ideas were on the rise all over the country, local articulation differed from place to place. One of those places was Jabal Ḥawrân. Syrian Arab nationalism, as it evolved in Jabal Ḥawrân, was inspired in part by newly prominent nationalists and army veterans in Fayṣal's government and by remembered struggles against the Ottomans and impending struggles against France. Still, the proximity of Damascus and the long-standing contact with the city and its political ferment did not mean that new forms of identity were centrally directed from a smoke-filled room of the Damascene nationalist elite. Local people worked out for themselves what it meant to be part of a larger community. Eventually the countryside came to lead the city in nationalist resistance. The emerging nationalists of Jabal Ḥawrân felt deeply that they were part of a larger Syrian nation, but they articulated their ideas in view of local conditions and local experience. While most agreed that there was one Syrian nation, united against the French occupation, there were many Syrian nationalisms, each evolving in its local context. Some would play a larger role than others.

CLAIMING THE MANDATE

France completed the occupation of Syria in 1920. One of the new colonial government's first acts was to divide the mandated territory into a series of regional units, based on sectarian difference and the perceived interests of France. The coastal regions of Mount Lebanon, the areas of greatest traditional French influence, became the state of Greater Lebanon, intended to maintain a Christian Uniate, or nominally Catholic, majority. The state of Greater Lebanon, while tiny as compared with most independent countries, was several times larger than the special administrative district, the *mutaṣarrifiyyat jabal lubnân,* which the Ottoman state had set up after the war of 1860 to ensure intersectarian peace and limit European interference in Ottoman affairs. French colonial functionaries drew the borders between Greater Lebanon and the state of Syria specifically to favor members of the Uniate rites, the only reliable French clients, with a state of their own. The border zigged and zagged from mountain to valley, sometimes spiking 15 kilometers or more, in a surreal effort to divide regions, districts, and even villages by religious sect. Still, the new state of Lebanon included many Muslims and Christians alike who preferred to be part of a larger mixed state centered on Damascus. From the state of Lebanon, the mandate power turned its attention east, to inland Syria and Damascus.

Resistance to mandate rule began before France had fully occupied inland Syria. Many Syrians, with fresh memories of the Great War, had resisted Fayṣal's attempts to conscript them into the army. But when French forces advanced east from Beirut, thousands of Syrian men and women, some armed with no more than sticks, went to stop them at the pass of Khân Maysalûn in the Anti-Lebanon mountains, 25 kilometers west of Damascus. While Damascenes were not universally persuaded by Fayṣal's calls for national sacrifice, army veterans, quarter bosses *(qabaḍâyât),* local religious leaders, and merchants found scores of volunteers in each Damascus neighborhood when they started to organize resistance. More than a few of these local leaders did not survive the battle of Maysalûn, though almost all of those who did survive took part in the uprising of 1925.[1] Ḥawrân Druze forces under Sulṭân al-Aṭrash did not arrive in time to join the battle.

French forces easily defeated Syria's ragtag army at Khân Maysalûn, but the defeat was the beginning of resistance rather than the end. A series of relatively uncoordinated resistance movements emerged in the north of mandate Syria, led by Shaykh Ṣâliḥ al-ʿAlî in the north coastal Alawite (ʿAlawî) mountains and later by Ibrâhîm Hanânû, an Ottoman-trained lawyer and former Ottoman army officer. While they both received material assistance from Turkish and Arab nationalists, Ṣâliḥ al-ʿAlî's revolt remained locally focused on conditions for the Alawites in their mountains, and Hanânû turned toward the new Turkish state for inspiration. Hanânû's revolt took place in the countryside surrounding Aleppo; and for the former army officers who played the most important roles, it was a dress rehearsal for the uprising of 1925. When the French agreed to withdraw from Cilicia in what became southeastern Turkey, the Turkish resistance was forced to curtail support for both Ṣâliḥ al-ʿAlî and Hanânû. Their movements died out; but Hanânû's revolt, at least, had lasting effects. The uprising brought together people who would continue to fight European occupation for years. Former Sharîfian officers who had deserted the Ottomans, like Ramaḍân Shallâsh, rejoined those who had remained with the Ottomans until the end of the war, like Hanânû himself.[2] Local resistance emerged sporadically in Ḥawrân and Jabal Ḥawrân as well.

Regional resistance led to regional partition. Besides Greater Lebanon, the new government divided the mandatory territory into the state of Syria (including Damascus and later Aleppo), the Alawite state of the northern coastal regions, and, after 1922, the state of Jabal Druze.[3] The policy of separation aimed to exploit divisions in Syrian society and break Syria into easily managed geographically and religiously separate pieces. The architects of this policy were French colonial officers, most with North African experience and with a particular right-wing, pro-Catholic political bent. The colonial policy that they designed in Morocco and brought to Syria mixed indirect rule, through co-opted traditional elites, with a heavy measure of unself-conscious paternalism. It favored traditional elites over those with modern education and nationalist ideas, the countryside over the city, Uniate Christians over Orthodox Christians and all Christians over Muslims, and minorities over majorities generally and sought to emphasize divisions within society and to develop each segment independently of others, thereby facilitating colonial rule and curtailing organized challenges before they could emerge. At the base of the conception of colonial rule was a romantic notion of timeless and changeless "Oriental" society, best governed with fatherly "love" for the colonial citizens. Combined with paternalistic love was an emphasis on the material and economic advantages of colonial rule.[4]

Colonial bureaucrats believed that these policies served the interests of both France and the colonized country. While the notion of common interests may have been functional in Morocco, it was not functional in Syria. In 1920 Syria had a well-defined nationalist movement, many leaders with modern education and ideas, the collective experience of nominally independent rule under Fayṣal, and a large number of unemployed military officers who had resisted the colonial occupation. France was widely blamed for the overthrow of Fayṣal's government and for a crushing economic crisis. The paternalism of colonial rule was probably unworkable in the end, particularly given the meager benefits the mandate brought to Syria, but the policy was not to remain constant in any event.

At the beginning of 1925 the third French high commissioner for Syria and Lebanon arrived in Beirut. Unlike his predecessors and the architects of France's policy in Syria and Lebanon, General Maurice Sarrail was a republican anticlericalist freethinker and a darling of the French Left. He also differed from his predecessors in that he had a total lack of colonial experience. Sarrail abandoned the idea of paternalistically guided indirect rule for direct military rule. He was a general who courted controversy, and his military staff was divided along political lines. The rightist officers were skeptical of Sarrail, and he was suspicious toward them; but he trusted his fellow leftist mandate officers wholeheartedly. One of these men was the governor of Jabal Ḥawrân, Captain Gabriel Carbillet.

General Sarrail had received the office of high commissioner in Syria because he was the most famous leftist general in France. In 1925 the Left had just taken power. The Right already had its colonial general in Marshal Louis-Hubert Lyautey, the resident-general in Morocco, architect of indirect rule in North Africa, and inspiration for the original conception of paternalistic indirect rule in Syria. As a republican radical with no knowledge of Syria, Sarrail unequivocally and enthusiastically supported the "reforms" of his fellow leftist officer Captain Carbillet, designed to break the back of the Druze "feudal society." Reforms included punitive measures such as forcing Jabal community leaders, and even religious shaykhs, to break stones in their villages as punishment for noncooperation with the mandate reform program.

GOVERNING JABAL ḤAWRÂN

In 1922 the mandate government had signed an agreement with some of the Ḥawrân Druze shaykhs, usually called the "Druze Charter of Independence." This agreement guaranteed an elected council or *majlis* and an elected Druze governor under French military supervision. The agreement was not universally popular, and the anti-French camp felt it made too many concessions to the mandatory power. They referred to it derisively as the Abû Fakhr document because of the preponderance of the Abû Fakhr family among its signatories.[5] Salîm al-Aṭrash was the first governor under the agreement. When he resigned and died in mid-1923, he was replaced as governor, on a supposedly temporary basis, by the mandate advisor to the governor of the state of Jabal Druze, Major Trenga. A few months later Captain Carbillet replaced Major Trenga and ignored calls for an election of a native governor. Carbillet, like Sarrail, was a republican reformer and an enthusiastic bearer of French civilization. He combined zeal and ambition with the paternalistic "love" of his mandate predecessors. As governor, he became the effective ruler of Jabal Ḥawrân; but more than ruling, he sought to alter the foundations of Druze society by mobilizing those he perceived as oppressed serfs against their feudal and despotic lords.[6] In lieu of taxes, which the mandate government had promised the Ḥawrân Druze they would not have to pay, Carbillet instituted a policy of public works based on conscripted *corvée* labor. His government conscripted mostly peasants, but shaykhs were sometimes required to work too, usually as punishment. They built paved roads and canals, among other projects. He explained that these projects would improve life for the inhabitants of the Jabal, but neither those he identified as oppressed peasants nor those he saw as feudal lords appreciated his efforts. Carbillet and his supporters in France attributed this opposition to the fact that the peasants were too backward to recognize their best interests and the shaykhs were too self-interested to support reforms that would erode their power. He and his superiors were constantly concerned with limiting the influence of outside agitators in the Jabal, particularly Sharîfians and Damascene nationalists. Quite apart from any outsiders, however, there was plenty of opposition to Carbillet's rule among the residents of Jabal Ḥawrân. Sulṭân al-Aṭrash led the opposition, while a few of his Suwaydâ' relatives, Fâris Sa'îd al-Aṭrash foremost among them, supported Carbillet.

The Druze shaykhs tried to convey their complaints against Carbillet to General Sarrail as soon as he arrived in Beirut. Carbillet successfully limited access to the high commissioner; and when Ḥamad, Nasîb, and 'Abd al-Ghaffâr al-Aṭrash finally met Sarrail, Carbillet had already briefed him on their grievances. They produced the Charter of Independence and demanded their right to elect a native governor to replace Carbillet. Sarrail, in an act his many critics later seized upon as proof of his incompetence, proclaimed that the agreement had no validity and was nothing more than a scrap of paper for the archives.[7] Sarrail continued to ignore protests and petitions and more than once refused to see Druze delegations that had traveled to Beirut to meet him.

In late spring 1925, with trouble brewing in Jabal Ḥawrân, Carbillet was ordered to return to France for a vacation. His temporary successor, Captain Antoine Raynaud (a member of the more numerous right wing among the French officer corps), was more popular with the Druze; but his alarming reports to the high commissioner were viewed by Sarrail as part of a conspiracy to remove Carbillet permanently. Encouraged by Raynaud's more accommodating attitude, a Druze delegation of twenty-nine local leaders traveled to Damascus on 15 June 1925 to present a petition to a visiting French senator.[8] The petition shows evidence of growing Syrian nationalist sentiment among the independence-minded Ḥawrân Druze shaykhs. It demonstrates the commercial basis for relations with the capital from the perspective of Jabal Ḥawrân. The Ḥawrân Druze were conscious that their grain fed Damascus. They presented the petition to Senator August Brunet "in cognizance with the wishes of the whole of the Syrian nation" *(lil-wuqûf 'alâ maṭâlib al-umma al-sûriyya jam'â')*. It stated that "the Jabal Druze is an integral part of

Syria through deeply ingrained common language, common nationality, and common economic relations. Damascus gets its food from the Jabal and the Jabal procures all its supplies from Damascus. These relations between them date from the distant past."[9] The petition goes on to cite ties between the Jabal and the desert and to request a basic law, an end to arbitrary judgment and imprisonment, the guarantee of personal freedom, and freedom of speech and finally to request the permanent replacement of Carbillet with Raynaud. Sarrail refused to act on the petition, and a second delegation to Beirut was met by his complete refusal to receive them.[10]

The petition is significant in view of the themes that introduced this chapter. It demonstrates with crystalline clarity both national consciousness and regional specificity. The petition blended the unambiguous language of Syrian nationalism with specific local goals and grievances. While Jabal Ḥawrân and its inhabitants were an integral part of the Syrian nation and the signatories sought general guarantees of the rule of law, legal freedoms, and rights, they had concerns that were unique to Ḥawrân and centered on the replacement of Carbillet with Raynaud. As there was tension among the Druze between inclusive nationalism and regional autonomy, there is tension in the petition; in June 1925 popular Syrian nationalism was a way to gain freedom from the harsh rule of the mandate government. It was not a way to lose regional autonomy to the politicians of Damascus. There was not one Damascene among the petition's signatories.

Later that same month, many of the same people formed a group that they called *al-Jam'iyya al-Waṭaniyya* (the Patriotic Club). Sulṭân al-Aṭrash took a leading role in both the delegation and the formation of the new organization.[11] The initial meeting of the club drew more than 400 men and resulted in a list of aims and policies, which focused primarily on retaining Raynaud as governor, preventing the return of Carbillet, and asserting a measure of advisory control over the pro-French members of the elected council. At a second meeting, at the house of Ḥusayn Murshid Riḍwân, the members of the new organization resolved to attend the next representative council meeting and call upon the council to serve its community and prevent the return of Carbillet. Sulṭân al-Aṭrash claimed that the main intention of the planned demonstration was to galvanize and mobilize the Jabal population against Carbillet and to prevent the council from disregarding their wishes.[12]

At ten o'clock on the morning of 3 July Sulṭân al-Aṭrash headed a group of mounted men to the council building in Suwaydâ'. According to Ḥannâ Abî Râshid, 400 men arrived, mostly on horseback. They swept into the square in front of the government building and began what he described as a peaceful protest of shouting traditional songs and slogans. Sulṭân al-Aṭrash noted that they sang war songs, and some fired their guns in the air. It was a feast day, and the square was already crowded with people. Inside the building, the council was in session under Raynaud and included Muḥammad 'Izz al-Dîn al-Ḥalabî, 'Alî 'Ubayd, and Ḥannâ Abî Râshid, among others. The protesters outside the building called on the council in the name of al-Jam'iyya al-Waṭaniyya and the future of the Jabal to depose Carbillet and to promote Raynaud.[13]

The protest did not remain peaceful. Abî Râshid claimed that Lieutenant Maurel, whom he called a spy and provocateur for Carbillet, propelled the Jabal into revolt.[14] Fâris al-Aṭrash, who was a pro-Carbillet member of the council, came into the square and denounced the demonstrators as "traitors to the homeland, and enemies of France."[15] Abî Râshid exclaimed in his chronicle, with perhaps unintentional irony, that it started as "a demonstration more peaceful than those in the heart of France, or America, or Beirut, and this among men of war and of the sword." Sulṭân al-Aṭrash, dictating his memoirs fifty years later, appears to have read Abî Râshid shortly before meeting his interviewers. Each mentions 400 men, and while Sulṭân al-Aṭrash too insists on a *peaceful* demonstration, he proceeds to mention firing in the air, singing war songs, abusing pro-French Druze, and generally raising a ruckus. He recounts driving the gendarmerie back with a shower of stones and wounding several among them, including Maurel. Salâma 'Ubayd wrote that Maurel ordered the gendarmerie to disperse the demonstrators without consulting Raynaud; after dispersing them, they continued to pursue the demonstrators, until the protesters retaliated by throwing stones and drove the soldiers back.[16] The demonstrators retreated from the square in front of the government building, fifty meters down the street, and into the second square of Suwaydâ', at the foot of which sat the Aṭrash guesthouse or *maḍâfa*. During the confusion, Ḥusayn Murshid fired his revolver at Lieutenant Maurel and missed. Maurel fired back but also missed; and the Druze chiefs intervened, offering an immediate apology to Maurel for the "regrettable mistake."[17]

Raynaud adjourned the council meeting and came on the scene. He called on the Aṭrash leaders of Suwaydâ' in the guesthouse of 'Abd al-Ghaffâr al-Aṭrash to demand apologies and discuss punishment for Ḥusayn Murshid and the inhabitants of Suwaydâ' generally. According to Abî Râshid, 'Abd al-Ghaffâr offered an abject apology and twenty Suwaydâ' youth for immediate detention, including his eldest son, Yûsuf.[18] Raynaud left the Aṭrash guesthouse and returned across the town square to the government building. At two o'clock that afternoon he summoned the community leaders for his judgment.

The punitive measures were harsh. The people of Suwaydâ' were commanded to pay 100 Ottoman gold pounds and to give up twenty of their youth for detention. Raynaud ordered Ḥusayn Murshid's family to be expelled to Ṣalkhad and his house to be destroyed. Ḥusayn Murshid had meanwhile evidently escaped to Transjordan, and the fine was levied in his absence.[19] Raynaud had dispatched the gendarmerie to Ḥusayn Murshid's house before the meeting. As the shaykhs learned of the punishment, troops were already arriving at Ḥusayn Murshid's house. While the Druze shaykhs indicated their willingness to comply, they protested the destruction of Ḥusayn Murshid's house and claimed that such action would result in an immediate uprising.[20]

Confident of surprise, Maurel and a troop of soldiers immediately went to destroy the house of Ḥusayn Murshid. When the soldiers arrived, however, it was they who were surprised. The Murshid family and their neighbors greeted Maurel and his troops with defiance, and a large group of armed men was already present. Fifteen minutes before, Sulṭân al-Aṭrash had arrived with armed horsemen.[21] Salâma 'Ubayd wrote: "Ḥusayn Murshid and his family refused the destruction of their home out of fear that [if they did not resist] it would become customary [punishment]. Their indignation and sense of outrage increased until they were joined by nearby villages who were prepared to help."[22] They forced the French soldiers to back down. A French report on the causes of the revolt found Sulṭân al-Aṭrash's arrival on the scene, and his ability to face down the mandate power, one of the most important elements in the beginning of the revolt. As he alone challenged the mandate power and opposed what all viewed as injustice, his popularity increased; and those who sought accommodation with the French and Druze independence from Damascus national politics were pushed to the sidelines.[23]

High commissioner General Sarrail received the news from Suwaydâ' the same day. Despite the humanistic claims of the colonial mission, calls for justice and due process brought heavy-handed repression. Sarrail resolutely refused to meet with or consider the petitions or complaints of Druze leaders, considering them ungrateful troublemakers rather than representatives of their communities.[24] He ignored the warnings of his own staff and suggested that Raynaud, the interim governor and a member of the more numerous right wing among the French officer corps, did not know what he was talking about when he warned of imminent revolt.[25]

Sarrail recalled Raynaud and appointed Major Tommy Martin, Damascus chief of the Service des Renseignements (Intelligence Service), as interim governor. Sarrail also instructed Martin to investigate the complaints against Carbillet pending Carbillet's return to the Jabal. Meanwhile Druze shaykhs sent a petition enumerating thirty-five specific grievances against Carbillet and the mandate government. Despite Martin's ongoing investigation and the continued efforts of the inhabitants to voice their grievances, Sarrail had decided on his course of action. On the same day that he issued orders for the return of Carbillet, he ordered the French delegation in Damascus to summon five Druze chiefs to Damascus. Ḥamad, Nasîb, Mitʿib, ʿAbd al-Ghaffâr, and Sulṭân al-Aṭrash were invited for a discussion of their grievances, but the actual intent was their capture and imprisonment.[26]

Just a week and a half after taking his post, Tommy Martin wrote to his colleague and friend Major Henri Dentz, predicting an uprising and expressing his wish to leave Suwaydâʾ as soon as possible. Martin refrained from directly criticizing Sarrail, but he wrote that an uprising had become inevitable and that military repression was the only option at that late point. He pointedly refused to take responsibility for the inevitable and, most particularly, refused to guarantee the safety of Carbillet, whose return Sarrail had ordered. Martin did not get his wish to vacate Suwaydâʾ. Instead, he was forced to remain in the citadel of Suwaydâʾ under siege until September. He dated his letter 17 July 1925, two days before the uprising began.[27]

Keeping his own counsel, Sarrail decided that setting a trap to arrest and imprison the most prominent Druze leaders would best prevent an uprising. He issued an invitation to negotiations to five Aṭrash chiefs. While Sulṭân refused and Mitʿib claimed illness, Ḥamad, Nasîb, and ʿAbd al-Ghaffâr were seized at their hotel in Damascus. In the arrest order Sarrail wrote: "I request you to summon the leaders to Damascus . . . under pretext of hearing their claims. You will tell them that I hold them responsible for any disorder that may occur in the Djebel, and shall hold them as guarantors in obligatory residence at a place you will designate."[28] The place of obligatory residence turned out to be the prison at Palmyra. In justifying Sarrail's actions, his secretary, Paul Coblentz, wrote: "It was not without reflection that this procedure was adopted. The annals of our Colonial, and our African, services would provide any number of analogous examples." Normally such action would be the purview of the Intelligence Service, "where certain methods used in dealing with notorious bandits or agitators are certainly not always comparable with the methods used in similar cases in Europe."[29] Sarrail apparently distrusted his Service des Renseignements subordinates and chose to deal with the matter personally. According to Coblentz, this was due to his deep sense of personal responsibility.[30]

The reaction in southern Syria was immediate. As the three men were arrested, their relative Ḥasan al-Aṭrash rushed from Damascus to Suwaydâ' by car to spread the news.[31] Damascus was already abuzz with rumors of an uprising. The following day the British consul in Damascus reported the seizure and wrote:

> The Druze situation has been manifestly mishandled by French colonial officialdom, which, apart from its inability to adapt itself to the particular conditions of the mountain, has, during the last six months, been afflicted by incoherence not at all in keeping with the logical realism of French colonial methods. It now appears decided to return to its traditions and solve the problem by force.[32]

ORGANIZING FOR RESISTANCE

It took more force than anyone could have imagined. Upon receiving confirmation from Damascus, Sulṭân al-Aṭrash, who had spurned the summons and feared a trick, immediately began to mobilize resistance. After ignoring the call to Damascus, Mitʿib and Sulṭân had retreated to the village of Rassâs, midway between Sulṭân's village of al-Qrayâ and Suwaydâ', the provincial capital. They first returned to al-Qrayâ and assembled relatives and close allies. Then they moved south toward the frontier with Transjordan and east up into the mountain, stopping at the villages of al-Kafr, Bakâ, Umm al-Rummân, al-Ghâriyya, Mashqûq, Milaḥ, and finally ʿUrmân, as they skirted all the villages surrounding Ṣalkhad, the second city of the Jabal and the site of a French gendarme garrison. Some villages refused to participate. They put banners on the roofs of their houses to show that they would not join and wanted no confrontations between insurgents and mandate troops in their villages.[33]

At each village the insurgents stopped and called on the male villagers to join them. They articulated the call to arms in traditional terms and consciously echoed the uprisings against the Ottoman government in the previous century. Their goals may have extended beyond their mountain, but they utilized the language of Druze honor and Druze particularism. They rode into a village, assembled in the square, and began to sing war songs.

> It's no secret, the wars have begun
> In the years past, the rebellion has lain
> Hidden in the depths of the valleys

Finally today, it is known
To the peaks of the mountains.[34]

Sulṭân al-Aṭrash "captivated the determined, decided the reluctant, menaced the resistant, and confronted all with the decisive argument, 'The French are only 7,000 in all of Syria. With the support of Damascus, which will rise up, we will liberate our homeland from the foreigner.'"[35] Without question, the homeland he referred to meant different things to different people. To many villagers it surely meant no more than their mountain, and perhaps no more than their village. To many of the larger farmers, village shaykhs, and those with Damascene commercial connections, it meant all of southern Syria, especially the grain-producing Ḥawrân, which they had dominated for generations. To a few former Ottoman officers and recipients of military education, like Muḥammad 'Izz al-Dîn al-Ḥalabî or others who had been committed partisans of Amîr Fayṣal, it meant the whole of Greater Syria, from the Red Sea to the Taurus mountains.

On 19 July, when they reached the village of 'Urmân, they were 250 horsemen. As they entered 'Urmân, a pair of reconnaissance airplanes circled the group. The insurgents fired on the airplanes, and one was hit and forced down in the nearby village of Mitân. Though the airplane crash-landed, its pilots survived and were taken by 'Alî Muṣṭafâ al-Aṭrash (who was thirteen years old) to his family house, where he gave them refuge under his protection. Within about three hours villagers burned the unguarded airplane and tore it to pieces. Captain Narcisse Bouron, writing a few years later, explained this incident by claiming that the villagers of Mitân were friends of France and that *other* villagers destroyed the airplane. It seems likely, however, that Bouron failed to give young 'Alî Muṣṭafâ al-Aṭrash and his fellow villagers their due. While 'Alî protected the French aviators from angry villagers and insurgents until a prisoner exchange a month later, he joined the uprising immediately after. The French later exiled this same 'Alî Muṣṭafâ al-Aṭrash until 1930 for his role in the revolt. It seems that while Bouron was writing down the story of this young "friend of France," 'Alî Muṣṭafâ was actually in exile. In 1935 'Alî Muṣṭafâ became the Ḥawrân representative for the Central Committee for Aid to the Children of the Desert, which was the organization providing aid to the exiled rebel refugees living in Saudi Arabia. Ḥannâ Abî Râshid quoted 'Alî Muṣṭafâ as saying, "If I had loved France, my cousins and the sons of my homeland are [even] more hallowed." It seems to me that personal kindness and traditional hospitality shown to French aviators could quite easily have coexisted with burning resentment at French power and its symbols of oppression—a surveillance airplane, for example.[36] In the following weeks, as French airplanes ceased surveillance and began bombing all Jabal villages, the residual loyalty of friendships with individual Frenchmen faded.

The following day the insurgents entered Ṣalkhad. As in all of the villages before, they rode into the square and called on the inhabitants to join them. Many from Ṣalkhad did join them, but that day their help was unnecessary. The French garrison of about forty officers and mandate employees surrendered without a fight. The rebels burned and pillaged the buildings and archives of the French delegation and the police.[37] On 21 July the insurgents moved north back up the mountain. They were joined by villagers from al-Kafr and by members of the bedouin tribes who lived on the agricultural fringes of the mountain and whom the Druze referred to as *ʿarab al-jabal.* Like the Druze, they were mixed horsemen and foot soldiers, mostly armed with German and Ottoman rifles left over from the war, but some were armed with nothing but swords. They carried the banners of their villages.[38]

Neither the rebel leaders nor the mandate authorities had a clear conception of the direction and seriousness of the uprising at this early point. ʿUbayd argued that while Sulṭân al-Aṭrash's immediate goal was the release of the seized chiefs, the French in Suwaydâʾ continued to consider the uprising a local disturbance.[39] On 20 July Commandant Tommy Martin sent a column of between 150 and 250 men under Captain Normand out from Suwaydâʾ.[40] They were ordered to march south toward Ṣalkhad, retrieve the wounded pilots, and restore order generally. On the twenty-first Sulṭân al-Aṭrash sent emissaries to meet Normand at his encampment alongside the road near al-Kafr between Ṣalkhad and Suwaydâʾ. The emissaries accused the French of treachery over the arrests and proposed that Normand return to Suwaydâʾ, where the rebels would enter negotiations over the release of the prisoners.[41]

Normand had his orders; and for whatever reason, he refused the offer of negotiations and prepared for an attack. At first light on the morning of 22 July the Druze and bedouin rebels swept down from the surrounding hills and up from the valley and decimated the French camp. The battle was short: it was all over in thirty minutes. It is unclear how many people were involved. French sources claim more than 1,000 insurgents, while Arab sources indicate much smaller numbers; but the results were not disputed: the battle was bloody, and only a few among the French camp survived to straggle back to Suwaydâʾ. A number of rebels were killed as well, including Sulṭân's brother Muṣṭafâ.[42]

The next day the insurgents rode into Suwaydâʾ, where they occupied the city and besieged the citadel, a siege that would last two months. While the mandate authorities and their families holed up in the citadel, French airplanes bombed the surrounding city from the air.[43] Both the Druze of the mountain and the mandatory power in Damascus now realized that the uprising was more serious than they had first thought. The success of the battle at al-Kafr brought those Druze chiefs who had been initially reluctant over to the side of the rebels.[44] The entire Jabal was now at war.

The news of the battle traveled quickly. In Damascus and throughout the southern countryside the dramatic French defeat became common knowledge overnight. The Damascus bazaars were abuzz with excited rumors.[45] The French closed the roads and severed all communication from Suwaydâʾ; as the result, "the most fantastic rumours [were] in circulation," as the British consul claimed.[46] But what he called fantastic rumors turned out to be true. Damascenes quickly learned of the defeat of the Normand column; and news circulated that the Druze, in collaboration with the Sardiyya and al-Slûṭ bedouin tribes, had control of all the Jabal and had moved onto the plain to threaten the Ḥijâz railway line at al-Mismiyya, only 50 kilometers south of Damascus. The consul dismissed the likelihood of Druze-bedouin cooperation; but like French authorities, he was apparently unaware of the complex social and commercial relations among the Druze, bedouin, Ḥawrânî peasants, and Damascene merchants. As the uprising grew, the importance of these relations came to the fore.

While a total news blackout prevailed, communication reverted to the old standby of rumor, the operative mode of any insurgency and the operative mode of a population under military occupation.[47] Authorities threatened Damascus newspapers with immediate closure and the court-martial of their publishers if they printed any mention of the uprising. Meanwhile the French Delegation issued a press release and ordered it run in all newspapers. It asserted that the propaganda of Sulṭân al-Aṭrash did not reflect the actual feelings of the inhabitants of the Jabal and that the delegation had received many letters "proclaiming absolute loyalty to our cause." Despite the language of this press release, no one, especially mandate civil servants, seemed to know precisely what the mandate cause in question represented. If the cause was only the attainment of the modest and idealistic aims of the League of Nations Permanent Mandates Commission, it was unclear how martial law; press censorship; bans on free association, political parties, and public gatherings; the spectacle of public hangings; the deportation under death threat of political leaders; and the aerial and artillery bombardment of innumerable villages, including the eventual bombardment of Damascus itself, would serve these modest and laudable aims.[48] The press release went on to promise that numerous acts of banditry committed by the rebels against the population who refused to take part in revolt would be answered by many tons of explosives visited upon the centers of dissidence. It concluded on a gloating note, informing readers that Muṣṭafâ al-Aṭrash, brother of Sulṭân, was dead and ʿAlî, another brother, was gravely wounded.

The positive effect of such notices on the mandate populace is doubtful, particularly since they contradicted the news that people received every day in the bazaars and in their neighborhoods. While the European consuls concentrated on, and publicized, the plight of Christian refugees from the Ḥawrân, the populace of Damascus was excited and frightened by the possibility of the spread of revolt. And while the mandatory power and the British consul emphasized the divisiveness of revolt and the sectarian nature of what they characterized as Druze pillage and plunder, the revolt involved Druze villagers, Muslim bedouin, and at least a few Christian villagers from the beginning. An example is the Orthodox Christian *mukhtâr* (village head) of the Ḥawrân village al-Kharbâ, and friend of Sulṭân al-Aṭrash, ʿUqla al-Quṭâmî.[49] He was in jail until mid-August, when the Druze chiefs negotiated his release as part of a prisoner exchange, at which point he returned to the Ḥawrân and immediately joined the insurgents. French authorities, apparently unable to credit that Christians could rally behind the enemies of the mandate, claimed that ʿUqla al-Quṭâmî was the bastard son of Maḥmûd Shiblî al-Aṭrash and thus the cousin of Sulṭân.[50]

There were many cases of pillage of Ḥawrân villages, and many villages suffered at the hands of both the insurgents and the mandate power. But the claim of a simple sectarian dichotomy is false and is in essence the core of colonial justification. France was the self-proclaimed protector of the "Oriental Christians." If Christians, Muslims, and Druze could unite in resisting the mandate, the mandate mission itself would be rendered meaningless. The importance of sectarian and ethnic conflict was central to the role of France in Syria and was in practice and theory a matter of policy, manifested by the active recruitment of sectarian and non-Arab ethnic minorities (especially impoverished Armenian and Circassian refugees) to serve as shock troops in rebellious villages and later in the neighborhoods of Damascus.[51]

Villages menaced by insurgents appealed to mandate authorities for help. Mandate authorities, however, had limited resources, and rural security was less a priority than keeping train lines open, for example. In consequence, the mandate government provided weapons to Christian and especially Uniate villages so that they could defend themselves. Even without this policy, rebels perceived Uniate villages as French allies. The fact that a policy of arming Uniate villages aggravated sectarian tensions was actually beneficial for French interests. French public sources claimed repeatedly, in self-justification, that only the mandate power prevented massacres of Christians. And while Christian villages did suffer at the hands of the rebels, colonial methods of repression in rebellious villages, including Christian villages on occasion, were far more violent.

By contrast, many villages welcomed the rebels and willingly supported and provisioned them, as allowed by their resources. The appearance of even-handedness was particularly important to the Druze because of their status as a minority sect, uncomfortably situated on the fringe of Islamic society. Sulṭân al-Aṭrash wrote at least one letter to the Greek Orthodox Patriarch of Damascus, calling attention to mandatory government crimes, apologizing for rebel misdeeds, promising to compensate losses, guaranteeing security in the name of the insurgent government, and pledging to eliminate further problems.[52] It also bears mention that the mandate authorities actively sought to provoke and emphasize sectarian division between the Muslim majority in Damascus and the Druze. This task was rendered easier by a long history of animosity involving the Druze, the Ottoman state, and the governors of Damascus. Since the Druze were known for heresy and perennial resistance to outside authority, there is little doubt that some Syrians, particularly elites, viewed them not as heroes but as troublemakers.

On 25 July General Roger Michaud, commander of the Armée du Levant, came to Damascus from Beirut with orders to assemble a punitive force to restore order in southern Syria. The French estimated 8,000 to 10,000 rebels and intended to put a heavily armed column of 3,000 troops under Michaud into the field. The rebel numbers, which British consul W. A. Smart received from French sources, were certainly exaggerated at this early point. The contrast between these figures and the public notices mentioned above is ironic. While the mandatory government was busy proclaiming that the revolt was unrepresentative of the population and made up of only a few troublemakers, it was simultaneously reporting wildly exaggerated rebel numbers in its accounts of military engagements. The estimated 10,000 rebels would represent nearly 25 percent of the total population of Jabal Ḥawrân in the 1920s.[53]

As General Michaud assembled the column in Damascus, the rebels were busy making his job more difficult. The rumors of attacks on the Ḥijâz rail line were confirmed, and a train headed from Damascus for Darʿâ on the southern border in the Ḥawrân turned back due to destroyed track at al-Mismiyya.[54] From the railhead at Azruʿ, between Darʿâ and al-Mismiyya, there was a paved road to Suwaydâʾ. As of 29 July the rebels had destroyed a section of the rail line and parts of the new paved road between Azruʿ and Suwaydâʾ.

The mandate government had recently built this road with *corvée* labor. Along with other improvement projects, Carbillet counted these roads among his reforms. They were built with forced unpaid labor—one of the most hated innovations of mandate rule and a grievance that came up repeatedly in complaints during and after the revolt. "Peasants resented the excessive amount of road work they were forced to do in lieu of taxation far more than they appreciated the advantage of roads available for wheeled vehicles which they did not possess."[55] In consequence, the destruction of these roads was both tactically important and symbolically significant. Mandate authorities told the inhabitants of the Ḥawrân that the roads were built for their benefit. With the best interests of villagers in mind, it was only fitting that they be forced to provide the labor; but the hollowness of this altruistic claim was clear to all at the first sight of an armored car or troop-laden wagon speeding along a recently completed road.

Destruction of the rail line and the road slowed the progress of Michaud's force of 3,500 men. Nonetheless, on 31 July the column began its march from Azruʿ to Suwaydâʾ. The first stop was Buṣrâ al-Ḥarîr, where (owing to drought) the spring was dry. The midsummer heat was unbearable, but the column (which consisted of five battalions of infantry, three squadrons of cavalry on the flanks, and armored cars and artillery at the rear) pressed on for a march of 25 kilometers and finally halted at al-Mazraʿa on 2 August. Al-Mazraʿa is an agricultural village on the plain at the base of the Jabal about 12 kilometers from Suwaydâʾ. It lies in open country with little vegetation and little topographical variation. The view is clear from the slopes of the mountain, including Suwaydâʾ, and movement on the plain is visible from many kilometers away. As the column halted, 500 Druze and bedouin horsemen attacked, killing and wounding a number of French troops. The French force eventually drove off the attack.

Early the following day, rebel attacks forced a supporting ammunition column at the rear to retreat to Azruʿ. Under August sun, with little water and no rear support and suffering continuous low-level attacks, Michaud decided to abandon the short advance on Suwaydâʾ and make the lengthier return to Azruʿ. Once the rebels saw that the column was retreating, they attacked with full force and routed the column in its entirety. Michaud was in full retreat; and his second in command, Major Jean Aujac (commander of a Malagasy unit, which he had reported to Sarrail was unfit for combat), was left behind to cover the retreat. The Malagasy unit was destroyed, its survivors panicked and fled, and Aujac shot himself in the field.[56]

The rebels gained 2,000 rifles with ammunition and supplies, a number of machine guns, and some artillery. But they also gained something else: the breathless attention of the entire country. The inhabitants of Damascus knew of the defeat of Michaud's force overnight. Much of the capital and the surrounding countryside soon joined the revolt. In the following months the revolt spread to include nearly all the territories under French mandate. Disentangling the events of those months, and the people who took part, is the concern of the following chapters.

CHAPTER 4

Mobilizing the City

Appeal from the Women's Society to Damascus

O Arabs, descendants of glorious ancestors, we appeal to you to awake in these critical times of great tragedy under the government of France. There is nothing left to us but to mount a vigorous attack and expel this government from our country.

O People, this is an auspicious moment, we must not let it pass. To Arms! To Arms! The time has come to realize what you have promised to yourselves.

O People, your brother Arabs of the countryside have made an appeal to your courage. Unleash your arms before the enemy who has invaded our homes, set fire to our temples of God, and tread on our sacred books . . .

—*Excerpt from a notice distributed in the Damascus bazaar, 3 August 1925*[1]

Notices like this appeared in Damascus repeatedly during August 1925. Such appeals demonstrate the existence of a sophisticated but not necessarily widespread nationalist consciousness. Despite repeated entreaties, the notices seemed to have little effect. The language, or perhaps the medium of transmission, failed to incite Damascenes to rise against the mandate power. The nationalist leadership of Damascus produced a number of such documents, but the same leaders were unwilling or unable to lead the armed revolt that they invoked so passionately. While the popular quarters of Damascus would eventually rise against mandate rule, they would not do so behind the nationalist elite of the capital but rather behind armed villagers and militants from their own quarters.

Damascus remained generally quiet through August, but the French population was deeply demoralized. Military resources were woefully inadequate to suppress the uprising in the countryside; there were few reinforcements on the immediate horizon; and despite French insistence that disorders were the work of a small number of Druze criminals and bandits, the actions of the mandate power betrayed a well-founded suspicion of the whole of Syrian society. The Ḥawrân Druze were rumored to be collaborating with and receiving supplies from the bedouin, the nationalists, the Hashemites, the Turks, the Russians, and the English.[2] There was little coordination of mandate policy and enforcement. When Captain Huguenot, the officer in charge of the Ḥawrân garrison at Darʿâ, ordered all European women to evacuate the Ḥawrân for their safety, Sarrail sacked him for causing a panic.[3] Sarrail himself ordered Damascus streets strung with barbed wire and the government buildings encircled with it.

Agitation and resistance also increased outside Damascus during August. Attacks took place on the roads leading from Damascus; and intelligence sources claimed that Zayd al-Aṭrash, brother of Sulṭân, planned to invade the region of Damascus and burn the airfield in al-Maza.[4] Attacks by unnamed bandits began in the region of Ḥumṣ to the north and continued throughout Ḥawrân. In Ḥumṣ inflammatory nationalist tracts appeared, urging the "nation to rise and throw off the chains of tyranny." The mandate authorities arrested four teenaged boys, two of whom were sons of Hâshim al-Atâsi, nationalist politician and former partisan of Amîr Fayṣal.[5] Rumors flew of imminent attacks on Damascus and the swelling of the insurgent ranks with bedouin horsemen from the major tribes of Greater Syria, the Banî Ṣakhr, and the Ruwalâ. Sulṭân al-Aṭrash was reported in Damascus, in Amman, and in his village. The French authorities panicked and blamed all disturbances on the Druze, a pattern that was to continue throughout the rebellion. British diplomatic dispatches noted that the bands that had appeared in the countryside "are always accused of being Druses, but they are probably many kinds—Druses, bedouins, villagers, deserters from the Syrian Legion, bad characters from the towns. The universal misery, caused by the present disastrous economic situation . . . is everywhere arming the people against authority."[6]

Meanwhile the nationalist elites of the capital tried to decide what to do. The mandate government had legalized political parties only months before. Damascene nationalists had formed a new party, Ḥizb al-Shaʿb (the People's Party), and emerged into the open for the first time since the defeat of Fayṣal's government five years before. French intelligence reports show that the party counted some of Damascus' most prominent and wealthy citizens among its members. And yet very few of the landowning elite took part in the revolt or were arrested by the mandate government. Those few of the younger generation of the elite who did take part (men like Nasîb al-Bakrî, Shukrî al-Quwwatlî, and Jamîl Mardam Bek) were pardoned almost immediately after by the mandate government, and their confiscated property was returned. Most members were understandably hesitant to jeopardize the small breathing space that they had so recently gained. They spent the month of August debating a course of action; while a few advocated a path of militant action, most were uncomfortable with the risks of such a course—a concern that turned out to be well founded. Those who eventually took part in the revolt were mostly merchants, intellectuals, and journalists; and while the former military officers among them urged militant resistance alongside armed peasants, such prospects could not have been appealing to many. After the revolt and the exile of its leaders, the landowning elite of the capital and the truly wealthy who had stood apart from the revolt would form the National Bloc and take up positions of leadership and moderate opposition to the mandate.

In the weeks leading up to the revolt, national leadership belonged to the members of the People's Party. The meaning of national leadership was clearly contentious, however, as many argued for caution, and a few (who were of similar background and age as the rebels of the countryside) argued for armed opposition. French intelligence records indicate a clear split between party members. Older members of the landowning elite advocated negotiation and accommodation and tried to diffuse the increasingly volatile situation by recourse to the French government, the Senate, and the League of Nations, while younger men, often of more modest mercantile or military background, sought a more militant response. In the end, events forced the situation. This chapter outlines the halting first steps of an unprecedented union between city and countryside, as the nationalist leaders of Damascus tried hesitantly to breathe life into a movement they could not control. When militant resistance finally emerged, most of the nationalist elite of Damascus was forced to follow rather than to lead.

DAMASCUS

The old city of Damascus is oval and enclosed by ancient walls. Its narrow ends face west and east. The limestone mountain that looms over the city, Jabal Qâsyûn, is 3 kilometers to the northwest. Along the lower slopes of the mountain lie several modern neighborhoods, including ʿArnûs and al-Ṣâliḥiyya. The French military headquarters and artillery batteries were in these neighborhoods. Farther up the slopes of the mountain lie neighborhoods settled by immigrants and refugees in Damascus during the nineteenth century, including al-Muhâjirîn, al-Sharkassiya, and al-Akrâd. West of the city, and next to the mountain, the Baradâ River, the source of Damascus' water and the life-spring of 8,000 years of human settlement, emerges from a narrow winding valley that cuts through the Anti-Lebanon mountains. The railroad and auto route to Beirut follow the river. The river splits off into six streams that flow through the city and along its walls, watering its gardens and public fountains. Once outside the city, its streams irrigate dense gardens and orchards on the north, east, and south. This area is the Ghûṭa, and its orchards and villages provided sustenance for the insurgency of 1925.

South of the old city, the medieval neighborhoods of Bâb Muṣallâ, Maydân Fawqânî, and Maydân Taḥtânî (upper and lower Maydân) stretch along the road south like a finger pointing from the hand of the city. The road extends to Ḥawrân and Transjordan and to the Ḥijâz beyond. In the centuries before air travel and national borders, pilgrims to Mecca traveled the road each year, and farmers and merchants traveled the road each day as they brought Damascus its food. When farmers and merchants became armed insurgents, they continued to use the road to transmit news, information, and weapons and to enter and exit the city. For two years the neighborhood of Maydân, which flanks the road, was the heart of the rebellion in Damascus. Maydân was the neighborhood with the closest cultural and geographical ties to Ḥawrân, and the principal business of Maydân was the distribution and export of Ḥawrânî grain.

The tattered remains of Michaud's force passed through the southern neighborhoods of Maydân in retreat. Sarrail blocked news of Michaud's defeat from both the Paris and Damascus newspapers. News leaked out slowly over the coming month as Paris newspapers learned of the disaster, first from the English papers and later from reports trickling in from Syria and from Sarrail's many enemies in the army and Foreign Ministry.[7] After a series of taciturn telegrams claiming that the situation was calm and under control, the Foreign Ministry at the Quai d'Orsay demanded a fuller accounting from Sarrail.[8] In spite of the news blackout, word of the destruction of Michaud's force reached Damascus instantly. Merchants in the bazaars spread the news of the defeat and failure of the French military, and Damascenes passed written notices from hand to hand. Damascus was already restive in any case; the appeal reproduced at the head of this chapter circulated in the market on the same day as the defeat of Michaud's column and before any news from the south could have arrived.

THE PEOPLE'S PARTY

Meanwhile the nationalist People's Party held both public and closed meetings at nearly daily intervals. The closed meetings were supposedly secret, though they took place in the same party headquarters as the public meetings did. French intelligence reports contain detailed minutes of both sorts of meetings. Although a few of the eventual urban rebels and political leaders emerged from the party, its nationalist fervor was necessarily lukewarm, as reflected in the reports of its public and secret meetings in early August. Members debated such things as illegal acts committed in their name, including the distribution of anti-mandate nationalist tracts, popularly believed to originate with the party. They also sought French metropolitan and League of Nations intervention to diffuse the situation in Syria.

The intelligence records of the Party meetings pose a puzzle. The innocuous content suggests either that the People's Party was far less militant than many members later claimed or, alternately, that meetings served to camouflage the party members' secret activities, perhaps even from one another. There may have been more than one party: a public party and one or more secret cells within it. Spies infiltrated public meetings and closed meetings, but there were also secret sessions at the houses of party members.

The members of the People's Party already had long experience in loosely organized secret organizations. The first underground meetings of the party had coincided with the arrival of Sarrail as high commissioner in January 1925; but Dr. ʿAbd al-Raḥman al-Shahbandar, the party president, and other party members had organized secret political organizations under Ottoman rule. Many had supported the Arab Revolt during the First World War and took jobs in Fayṣal's government after the end of Ottoman rule. Generally they were not among the Damascene elites who had opposed Fayṣal's government, and most of them remained friendly with the Hashemites.[9]

In June they emerged as an officially condoned political party. The opening celebration for the party took place on 5 June 1925, and at least 1,000 attended.[10] The opening ceremony, like the public meetings, professed general goals of Syrian sovereignty, unity, freedom, civil rights, and protection for Syrian trade and industry. In actuality, the People's Party centered around two related issues: the independence and the unity of Syria within its natural borders, by which they meant the geographical area stretching from al-ʿAqaba to the Taurus Mountains, under British and French mandate in Transjordan, Palestine, Syria, and Lebanon. Arguably, the Syrian public understood and supported these goals, though in public speeches and proclamations the party leaders were more circumspect.[11]

Independence was the central goal of the party, but few members expected to be the ones personally to expel the French from Syria. Most, though not all, were content to hold secret meetings and debate and strategize endlessly:

while they were the radicals among elite Syrian urban society, few were militants. The single aim that most agreed on was independence, and any further goal or program risked disunity and division. Political mobilization was based on slogans and not on detailed programs. Party life was stunted by the day-to-day reality of military occupation and geographical partition, and the vague policies and lack of party formation around common interests were much less a symptom of political immaturity than a result of colonial domination. A party based on the goals of social transformation would have been the site of contentious negotiations, while most segments of Syrian society could agree on independence and unity. Still, both aims, explicitly stated, were anathema to the mandate power; and Syrian political leaders knew well that to be effective they had to avoid exile and prison.

The French had already imprisoned Shahbandar, the party president, for a year and a half, releasing him in mid-1924. A military court sentenced him to twenty years in prison for his vocal opposition to the mandate and for suspicious foreign contacts.[12] After his release, he traveled to Europe and America to build support for Syrian independence. Back in Syria, and at the head of a new party made up of leading nationalist Damascenes, Shahbandar tried to keep his head down. While keeping a low profile, he and other party members cultivated secret ties with nationalist-minded Druze in the southern countryside. Shahbandar and his colleagues had limited experience as members of a legitimate political party, but they had years of experience as members of a secret opposition. While they held public party meetings with open doors, and closed meetings under party auspices as well, there were also meetings held under strictest secrecy at various locations. They met at the houses of members both inside and outside Damascus.[13]

MAKING CONTACT WITH THE COUNTRYSIDE

At the beginning of May 1925 Amîr Ḥamad al-Aṭrash, the displaced popular choice as Jabal governor, traveled to Damascus and met Shahbandar at the house of Qâsim al-Haymânî, publisher of the Damascus newspaper *al-Fayḥâ'*.[14] Shahbandar later wrote that they discussed igniting an uprising. Several more meetings followed at Shahbandar's house in the Damascus neighborhood of 'Arnûs, which was, and is, a modern quarter situated along the lower slopes of Jabal Qâsyûn, 3 kilometers away from the higher-density medieval neighborhoods of the old city. A number of Druze leaders and nationalist politicians attended the meetings, including many of those later of central importance in the revolt. Shahbandar listed 'Abd al-Ghaffâr al-

Aṭrash, Mitʿib al-Aṭrash, Nasîb al-Aṭrash, Abû Ḥamdî Sayf al-ʿAysmî, Saʿîd Ḥaydar, and others.[15]

Shahbandar recorded that their discussions focused on sparking armed revolt throughout mandate Syria. While this may have been true—and all of the men he listed later willingly opposed the mandate with armed force—there were apparently other, perhaps more pressing, matters under discussion. Though most participants in the revolt (and later Arab chroniclers) were loath to admit it, the notion of Syrian unity and independence was often a hard sell among the Druze, for whom independence had usually meant independence from any central authority—Ottoman, French, or Damascene. Shahbandar makes it clear that their concerns were often purely local and focused on their opposition to the French administration in the Jabal, rather than on the wider issues of unity and opposition to French occupation generally. The meetings were an opportunity for nationalist and integrationist-minded Druze leaders to call on charismatic Damascene nationalists to help sway their less convinced brethren to accept the need for integration into the larger Syrian polity. References to prerevolt meetings appear in a number of sources. With few exceptions, recent historians ignore these meetings and fail to explain precisely the contacts between nationalist politicians and the countryside.[16]

The meetings were part strategy sessions, part nationalist education sessions. Sulṭân al-Aṭrash and a small number of Druze chiefs had formed strong ties with Damascene nationalists in the years surrounding the First World War. Beginning in the 1860s, the Druze in Jabal Ḥawrân had been in the forefront of a new and expanding agricultural export trade. They forged ties based on commerce in grain with a number of prominent and emerging merchant families in Damascus. It was the Ḥawrân Druze who, sometimes acting as war profiteers, supplied the British-funded Arab army during the war with bread. They also fed thousands of refugees and gave Arab fugitives from the Ottoman government sanctuary in the safety of their mountain. The wartime governor of Syria hanged a number of suspected nationalists, and many sought refuge in Jabal Ḥawrân on their way out of the country.

Meetings between Druze leaders and Damascene nationalists before the revolt helped foster growing nationalist sentiment in Jabal Ḥawrân. The Druze petition of 15 June 1925 shows evidence of increasing Syrian nationalism among the normally separatist and independent-minded Druze. The petition was concerned with the whole of the Syrian nation and advocated the total integration of Jabal Ḥawrân with Damascus and Syria generally. It cited economic ties based on agriculture and trade as well as the commonality of language and history.[17] The petition continued to cite ties between the Jabal and the desert and to request a basic law, an end to arbitrary judgment and imprisonment, the guarantee of personal freedom and freedom of speech, and finally, and of course most importantly, the permanent replacement of Carbillet with Raynaud. This petition, unsuccessful though it was, led to the formation of al-Jamʿiyya al-Waṭaniyya (the Patriotic Club) in the Jabal, a name with solid nationalist associations despite its local membership, horizons, and goals.[18] The signatories of the petition and the members of the club were all residents of Jabal Ḥawrân; no Damascenes were involved. The signatories coincide closely with the men that Shahbandar claimed visited him at his home in May and June 1925.

The relationship between the southern countryside and Damascus was mutual. The petition of Druze notables indicates that they envisioned the union of the countryside with the city as one between equals based on historical trade relations. They did not expect to be dominated; and as Damascenes entered the uprising, they willingly cooperated with the Druze rebels. When the revolt began, Sulṭân al-Aṭrash made the first contacts. After the destruction of the Normand column at al-Kafr, Sulṭân al-Aṭrash sent letters to Nasîb al-Bakrî and Shahbandar. Bakrî was a member of the People's Party, a friend of Sulṭân al-Aṭrash, and Amîr Fayṣal's envoy to Jabal Ḥawrân between 1917 and 1920.[19] He appears rarely in the French reports of party meetings, but among the party members he was one of the most committed to armed revolt. Bakrî received letters dated 23 July 1925; and a meeting followed at the Bakrî house in their village of al-Qâbûn just outside Damascus in the Ghûṭa, at which time the Bakrîs decided to join the revolt. Nasîb al-Bakrî then delivered Sulṭân al-Aṭrash's letter to Shahbandar. After some contemplation, Shahbandar committed the People's Party to the insurgency. He wrote: "We are ready for death, all of us, in the cause of raising the beacon of the nation and the homeland. We will share in the uprising and join the Jabal al-Durûz. And from today onward, we will appeal to Syria's leaders to join the revolution."[20] While Shahbandar clearly saw his role as propagandist and spokesman, a few Damascene nationalists were committed to armed struggle and went to the Jabal within days to join the Druze in battle against the French. The Damascene jurist and historian Ẓâfir al-Qâsimî, drawing on French court judgments, demonstrates that young Damascenes Saʿîd Ḥaydar, Ḥasan al-Ḥakîm, Aḥmad ʿUmar, and Tawfîq al-Ḥalabî were in the Jabal for the battle of al-Mazraʿa and defeat of Michaud's force on 3 August 1925.[21]

Meanwhile party members still resident in Damascus were involved in a complicated double game between the insurgents and the mandate authority. For a month between late July and late August, they served as the rebels' liaison to Damascus, while walking a thin line with the French, a restive populace, and Damascus' traditional landowning notable leadership, both inside and outside the party. There is no doubt that the greater part of Damascus' traditional landowning elite, particularly those of the older generation, had little enthusiasm for popular politics or armed revolt and was more comfortable negotiating with French civil servants than plotting collaboration with armed peasants. Even among People's Party members, there was no consensus on a course of action. The most committed of Damascene nationalists were reluctant armed insurgents. Most had significant material and social interests to consider, and they only acted decisively when they had no other choice. The few who were ready for armed resistance went and helped to convince the Druze to keep fighting. Most of the rest, including Shahbandar, stayed in Damascus. They acted when they had to: when the police came in the night, and they scattered under threat of arrest and imprisonment. Before the arrests of late August, they held a series of meetings, which the Service des Renseignements meticulously observed and documented. The meetings' minutes read like exquisitely choreographed disinformation sessions—sessions perhaps aimed at the French or perhaps aimed at one another within the party.

The meeting of 6 August is representative.[22] After some general discussion of the precarious financial situation, someone makes terse mention of the defeat of French troops in Jabal Druze. There is little discussion of this obviously earthshaking news, and the conversation quickly turns to what the party can do to *calm* inflamed spirits. A speaker mentions the necessity of learning the names of people and tradesmen fomenting unrest in the bazaars in the name of the People's Party and advocating closing the markets to protest the mandate government. Luṭfî al-Ḥaffâr, a prominent merchant, speaks up and declares that the principal provocateur is a small merchant named ʿUmar Hâshim, who is approaching bankruptcy owing to the financial crisis. He is a member of the Syrian Unity Party (Ḥizb al-Waḥda al-Sûriyya), the pro-mandate puppet party set up by mandate authorities as a counterweight to Ḥizb al-Shaʿb. ʿUmar Hâshim has claimed that the People's Party advocates closing the markets. The party president, Dr. Shahbandar, interrupts and insists that they must be certain that ʿUmar Hâshim is guilty before they denounce him to the authorities. Luṭfî al-Ḥaffâr declares that he speaks for the merchants of Sûq Midḥat Bâshâ, who have been solicited by ʿUmar Hâshim to close their shops in accordance with a directive of the People's Party. One does not need much imagination to suppose that the very purpose of this exchange was to denounce ʿUmar Hâshim to the authorities.[23]

The so-called secret meetings were hardly more subversive. They focused on internal party matters, and particularly on the conditions in the markets and the conditions for trade in Damascus. The reports demonstrate that inasmuch as the People's Party represented any particular constituency, it was the merchants of Damascus, who were accustomed to extensive trade with the southern countryside and who had been gravely hurt by drought and by the continued inflationary slide of the Syrian currency, pegged to the French franc. The merchants continually protested the actions of mandate government by mass-closings of their shops. Whether or not the party orchestrated such protests, it had to give the impression that it did not condone them. On 30 July, in a closed party meeting, Luṭfî al-Ḥaffâr noted that he sought to "counsel [his fellow shopkeepers] to stay open, but he knew that a significant number of small merchants are creditors to the Druze. They serve as banks to their debtors, and they rely upon their payments. Therefore they are required to close their shops [to show solidarity with their principal customers]."[24] A few days later al-Ḥaffâr reported that he had been detained and questioned by the police in connection with the distribution of propaganda in the bazaars. He claimed that he protested to the contrary, that he had actively urged his friends to keep calm and avoid trouble.[25]

The connections among merchants, journalists, and rebels were important, and the French understood this too. Intelligence officers had a number of merchants under surveillance, in addition to Luṭfî al-Ḥaffâr, including ʿAbduh al-Nûrî, a Maydânî grain merchant who was said to be an intimate friend of Sulṭân al-Aṭrash and a frequent visitor to Jabal Ḥawrân. He was later reported to have evaded surveillance and joined the rebels.[26] Merchants and journalists made up the most militant members of the People's Party, and both groups were deeply involved in the uprising from its earliest stages. Damascenes got their information from the newspapers or in the markets; and merchants and journalists played a central role in popular resistance and agitation in Damascus. By late August the newspapers still in print were publishing the most innocuous fare imaginable; the mandate power shut down the best newspaper in Damascus, *al-Muqtabas,* on 18 August. Its editor, Najîb al-Rayyis, was soon jailed along with other People's Party members.[27] Damascus was alight with fantastic rumors; while Syrians waited with anxiety and excitement for events to unfold, the entire French population was gripped by panic and fear.

ḤAWRÂN PEACE NEGOTIATIONS

The desperate situation drove the French to seek peace negotiations. The first efforts at negotiations failed, and the rebels refused to talk with the Lebanese Druze delegation sent by the French. Sarrail then authorized ʿAbdallâh Najjâr, former public education director in the Jabal, to test Druze opinion and secure the exchange of prisoners.[28] On 11 August Najjâr returned to the French garrison at Azruʿ with the Druze request that former Jabal governor Captain Raynaud accompany him and open peace talks with the Druze leaders.[29] Sarrail had sacked Raynaud on suspicion of intriguing against the return of Carbillet after the disturbances of early July; but desperate times called for desperate measures, and Sarrail authorized his return as chief negotiator. The following day Raynaud and Najjâr returned to Umm Walad, where the exchange and talks would take place.

A group of five Druze shaykhs representing the five most powerful families met with Raynaud, Najjâr, and Yûsuf Shidyâq. According to Raynaud, Sulṭân al-Aṭrash was not directly involved. Negotiations began with an exchange of prisoners. The mandate authority asked for the return of all military prisoners, the right to bury the dead still on the field from the battles at al-Kafr and al-Mazraʿa, the cessation of hostile acts, and the evacuation of fifty civilians from the citadel of Suwaydâʾ. The Druze delegation asked for the release of ten prisoners from the Suwaydâʾ citadel detained since 3 July, in addition to the Druze shaykhs seized at Damascus and imprisoned at Palmyra. Some of those present protested the absence of Ḥamad al-Aṭrash, the popular leader of the Druze community (Raynaud noted that "the majority of the Druze chiefs called [him] Amîr Ḥamad"). The following day he joined the negotiations.

On 14 August they exchanged prisoners at the Ḥawrân village of Umm Walad. The Druze released fifty-three military prisoners, including six French *métropole* soldiers and one officer. There were some difficulties, as Ḥamad ʿÂmr appeared with three hundred armed horsemen and demanded to know why there was not a one-to-one exchange of prisoners. Raynaud claimed that his personal intervention calmed the potentially volatile situation. Following the exchange of prisoners, the Druze returned to the village of ʿArâ, where the non-Arabic-speaking Raynaud described a scene of buccaneer bacchanalia, as more than two thousand Druze horsemen—wearing swords and revolvers and slinging bandoliers—celebrated the return of their jailed chiefs with songs and revelry. It is certain that no one translated the songs for Raynaud, for they could not possibly have been complimentary to France. He noted that the celebration lasted all through the night and that it was impossible to continue negotiations.[30]

The negotiations continued in the following days. Raynaud's report is comical and tragic in its efforts to show how highly the Druze honored him and how sincerely they entered into the negotiations. Both he and the Druze

FIGURE 4. Ḥawrân rebel celebration after the release of several detained insurgents. Man on horseback is Hilâl al-Aṭrash, shaykh of the rebellious Jabal Ḥawrân village of Rassâs. 14 August 1925. Courtesy Archives du Ministère des Affaires Etrangères—Paris, Fonds iconographique.

negotiators evidently expressed deep regrets at the "grave misunderstanding" that had befallen the region owing to the tyrannical despotism of Raynaud's various predecessors and superiors—especially, of course, Carbillet. Druze peace conditions for the mandate power ran to twelve items and included a demand to keep their weapons and the freedom to enter union with the state of Syria, understood to mean Damascus. Two accounts of the negotiations are extant: that of Ḥannâ Abî Râshid and that of Raynaud. Each lists the same demands, but Abî Râshid makes no mention of the condition that Raynaud be reinstated as governor of the Jabal. It figures prominently in Raynaud's list of demands.[31] Raynaud's military superiors could not have been well disposed to a smug subordinate who reported commiserating with enemies of the mandate about "grave misunderstandings" that had left more than a thousand French colonial soldiers dead and, more importantly, had already destroyed several military careers. After further discussion the Druze delegation declared that the French conditions for submission were acceptable with the exception of a few minor points, most particularly the indemnity of 5,000 gold Turkish pounds. They expected eventual agreement on all points and recessed for the allotted thirty-six hours.[32] Raynaud returned to Damascus with the Druze demands.

The Druze exceeded by a day the thirty-six hours allotted to them. Raynaud's worry and exasperation are clear from his report. What had started as a cordial discussion of misunderstandings and self-reported lavish praise of Captain Raynaud was spinning out of his control. When he returned to the negotiation table after a number of stalls and false starts, he had begun to distrust his interpreter, 'Abdallâh Najjâr, and had begun to worry about "foreign influences" destroying the good work that they had already accomplished and leading the Druze astray. After the close of the day's talks, Raynaud visited Sulṭân al-Aṭrash, who, Raynaud claimed, was sincere in his desire to make peace but who respectfully requested a further delay until the next meeting. Meanwhile Raynaud reported the shadowy presence of "foreign elements" (by which he meant any non-Druze) on the fringes of the meetings and among the people he met, including a bizarre and mysterious doctor, who, he reported, was a Jewish journalist for a German newspaper. For Raynaud, a right-wing member of the French officer corps, the presence of this man was the most unfavorable sign imaginable.[33]

Raynaud broke off negotiations in disgust on 20 August. He declared that he had no further interest in useless meetings and that the negotiators had insufficient force of will to prevent the ignorant masses of their community from being fooled and dragged into hostilities by the People's Party, all of whom were Francophobes and most of whom were simply xenophobes.[34] He seems not to have realized that it was perhaps he who had been fooled by providing ten days without aerial bombardment of Ḥawrân and Jabal Ḥawrân. In the following days Raynaud reported aerial reconnaissance showing the massing of rebels in the region. While a few Damascene members of the People's Party joined the rebels in the Jabal, bedouin from the Banî Sakhr tribe and the Banî Ḥasan arrived as well. Muḥammad al-Zu'bî, Muslim shaykh of the Ḥawrân village of al-Masayfra, also arrived with horsemen; and Sulṭân al-Aṭrash was said to have sent special envoys to insure smooth relations between villagers and rebels in the northern Jabal villages around Shahbâ, where they assembled. Bedouin rebels had moved their tents near Jabal villages, and the emissaries made sure that relations between villagers and their bedouin guests remained trouble-free.[35]

Raynaud had recorded the presence of Damascene nationalists at the negotiations of 18 August. Tawfîq al-Ḥalabî, Zakî al-Durûbî, and As'ad al-Bakrî, all People's Party members, had arrived and met with Sulṭân al-Aṭrash two days earlier, on 16 August, at Shahbâ on the northern edge of the Jabal. It is unclear who was persuading whom; but, during a notably successful negotiation, they agreed to meet before dawn on the morning of 24 August at the village of Ḥawsh al-Matbin outside Damascus with a mixed force of Damascenes, Druze, bedouin, and Ḥawrânîs. Shahbandar, ʿUbayd, and Raynaud each claimed that the Damascenes persuaded Sulṭân al-Aṭrash to sabotage negotiations with Raynaud.[36] The evidence for Damascene persuasion and Druze reluctance is formidable, and yet each writer had good reasons to emphasize the role of Damascenes and downplay the role of the Druze in spreading the revolt. Shahbandar was trying to unify disparate forces behind his leadership and had every reason for emphasizing the contribution of Damascus to a struggle that appeared to many to be sectarian and local. ʿUbayd may have sought the same goal and perhaps wished to shield the early leaders of the revolt from criticism for the retribution that the French visited upon the Ḥawrân. Raynaud had the most powerful reasons of all to show the Druze had been duped by the nationalists, rather than admitting that he had been duped by the Druze. The actions of the rebels during and before negotiations belie the contention that they were seduced to continue their fight against the mandate power.

The most militant members of the People's Party were ready to drive the French from Syria. Tawfîq al-Ḥalabî, Zakî al-Durûbî, and Asʿad al-Bakrî had come to stay with the Druze shaykhs during negotiations. They were more committed to armed revolt than most Damascene nationalists. But they were also younger and less likely to be convincing as true national leaders, like ʿAbd al-Raḥman al-Shahbandar, or the few others of towering nationalist stature. Of the three, only Zakî al-Durûbî survived the uprising. Durûbî was a former Ottoman and Arab army artillery officer and a graduate of the Damascus military school and the Ottoman military college. He was the son of an army officer from Ḥumṣ, but he was born in Anatolia. He had sought refuge in Jabal Ḥawrân during the war, served in Fayṣal's government, and fought at Maysalûn. Since 1920 he had worked under the *qâʾimmaqâm* of Zabadânî outside Damascus. Other sources indicate that the *qâʾimmaqâm* he served was Druze insurgent leader Muḥammad ʿIzz al-Dîn al-Ḥalabî, who graduated from the Ottoman military college the same year. Tawfîq al-Ḥalabî was born in the Qaymariyya quarter of Damascus and worked as a journalist. He fled Jamâl Bâshâ's hangings of suspected nationalists during the war with Dr. Shahbandar and, like Durûbî, spent time in the safety of Jabal Ḥawrân with Sulṭân al-Aṭrash. He was in Cairo for most of the war, returned to Damascus with Fayṣal in 1920, and was immediately jailed by the French. He was killed fighting in the Ghûṭa in 1926. Asʿad al-Bakrî was Nasîb's and Fawzî's younger brother, and he too was killed during the revolt. All three were young and outwardly similar to those among the Ḥawrân Druze most committed to armed struggle. Durûbî and Ḥalabî, like almost all the revolt leaders, were born within a few years of 1890. They had both come of age during the First World War and the collapse of the Ottoman state.[37]

The militants in both camps dragged and cajoled their more cautious comrades behind them, and it is reasonable to suppose that an actual dialogue took place between the militant nationalists and the Druze leadership.[38] A good amount of evidence supports the notion that the nationalists and the Druze, inspired by dizzying success in defeating mandate forces, persuaded one another. According to all the Arab sources, Sulṭân al-Aṭrash contacted the Damascene nationalists before they contacted him. ʿUbayd, in listing the reasons behind the common decision to bring the rebellion to Damascus, undermines his own contention that the Damascenes sold the reluctant Druze on expansion.

A. They wanted to popularize the revolt and split apart the French forces between them and take the revolt to victory after victory throughout the country.

B. They lacked confidence in French promises and guarantees.

C. They had to satisfy the opinion of the majority of rebels who wanted to throw the French into the sea![39]

During late August the most radical among the nationalists and the Druze leaders resolved to bring the revolt to Damascus. In keeping with the generally vague goals of the People's Party itself, there was apparently little discussion of what would follow the French withdrawal; but the idea that France could be defeated and forced to abandon its mandate was widely held. The British consul in Damascus reported that "men's minds at Damascus are being exercised by what is to happen if the French decide to retire to the coastal regions." He recorded an encounter with someone he called a moderate nationalist, who asked: "What should we Arabs do after the French leave Damascus?"[40]

Conversations like this evidently occurred many times and inevitably were reported by British officials. Gertrude Bell, in a secret report that found its way into the French archives, opined that the French would abandon Syria and that "it is the Druze who will enable his brother Syrians to evict the French."[41] British consul Smart, on another occasion, reported meetings with Amîr Saʿîd al-Jazâʾirî, during which the *amîr,* "like many other Syrians, seems inclined to the belief that France's day in Syria is coming to an end."[42] The fact that British officials received such confidences supports the persistent French notion of British and Sharîfian intrigues against the French mandate. Raynaud was not alone in perceiving anti-French treachery in every quarter. The attitude permeated all of French mandate officialdom. But as the failure of Raynaud's negotiations amply demonstrates, his paranoid worries were more than simple delusions.

On the same day as his meeting with the nationalists, Sulṭân al-Aṭrash sent emissaries to a number of Ḥawrân villages to ask for horsemen.[43] After organizing the disparate forces, Sulṭân al-Aṭrash sent a letter on 23 August to invite Raynaud to resume talks the following day. It was the final gesture of the negotiations and a final attempt to trick the mandate power before the attack on Damascus of 24 August.[44] The attack was already planned, and the letter could only have been an attempt to catch the French off guard. Raynaud himself (the scales finally slipping from his eyes) opined that the letter might have been a deceitful gesture.

The negotiations represent the final phase in the transition from local to national rebellion. They were symbolic of what Philip Khoury calls the transitional character of the revolt as a whole, and they played out as an apparent debate over two weeks or so within the Druze community about their collective future. Despite the debate among the community members, they had agreed immediately on some previously contentious issues. The conditions that the Druze shaykhs submitted show that they were serious about union with a larger Syrian state and that the Druze had accepted the *language* of nationalism, at the least. The question remains: was the entire negotiation a ruse to gain the release of rebel chiefs and delay the inevitable French counterattack?

Shahbandar echoed Raynaud's contention that Damascene members of the People's Party had stiffened Druze resolve at a critical moment. Raynaud contended that except for outside agitators the Druze would have submitted. Among the Druze, some sought an end to hostilities and an end to the nearly continuous aerial bombardment they had suffered for a month. Nevertheless, men allied with Sulṭân al-Aṭrash carefully manipulated Raynaud and the French negotiators and probably manipulated conservative members of their own community. The strategy of manipulation did not simply evolve during the course of the negotiation but was planned from the beginning.[45] While the Druze negotiated with the French, the nationalists were engaged in a process of negotiation over the role of Damascus in the uprising. Armed revolt was not universally appealing to the merchants, journalists, and politicians who made up the membership of the party. In both Damascus and the Jabal, the militants prevailed. All five of the men directly involved in the

Druze negotiations immediately participated in the rebellion. Muḥammad 'Izz al-Dîn al-Ḥalabî, graduate of the Ottoman Military Academy, former officer, and employee in Fayṣal's government, led rebel bands all over southern Syria and was in exile under death sentence until 1937. Hâyl 'Âmr had joined Amîr Fayṣal during the Arab Revolt; and though he did surrender to the French after the Great Revolt, it was not until 1927.[46] On the eve of the first attack on Damascus, the militants in both camps had reached a critical mass and had succeeded in bullying the less committed into acquiescence.

The attack on Damascus was not successful. The Damascene force, promised as 500 horsemen, turned out to be only about 100. Yaḥyâ al-Ḥayâtî and Zakî al-Durûbî, both former Ottoman army officers and graduates of the Ottoman Military Academy, led the Damascenes. The Druze, bedouin, and Ḥawrânî force numbered more than 1,000 people, led by Zayd al-Aṭrash and Muḥammad 'Izz al-Dîn al-Ḥalabî. While the two groups were organizing and their leaders were arguing, a French airplane spotted them and immediately launched an attack. The air attack was fierce; and more airplanes joined the fight shortly, dropping bombs and scattering the insurgents with machine-gun fire. A Moroccan cavalry troop charge immediately followed the air attack.[47]

The French were relieved, but the rebel setback was slight. A single insurgent was killed, while several French Moroccan Sipahis and one officer were killed.[48] The insurgents scattered; some returned to Jabal Ḥawrân, and some returned to the Ghûṭa, the gardens surrounding Damascus. Their losses were small, but there was a valuable lesson in the aborted attack: rebel forces would not again engage the French in large numbers in daylight in open country. Nighttime attacks and guerrilla warfare would dominate. Nationalist agitation in Damascus continued unabated.

On the night of 23 August, immediately before the aborted attack, circulars signed by Sulṭân al-Aṭrash appeared all over Damascus.

> *TO ARMS! SYRIANS:*
>
> At last the day has come when we can reap the harvest of our struggle for liberty and independence. Let us arouse ourselves from our torpor and disperse the dark clouds of foreign oppression which weigh heavily on our land. For ten years we have struggled for the cause of liberty and independence. The written and spoken word no longer avails us; let us pursue the struggle with the sword.
>
> A right claimed with sufficient persistence must be conceded in the end. Syrians, experience has proved that rights are never given, but

must be won. Let us arise then and wrest these rights from the usurpers at the point of a sword. Let us seek death that we may win life.

Syrians, remember your forefathers, your history, your heroes, your martyrs, and your national honor. Remember that the hand of God is with us and that the will of the people is the will of God. Remember that civilized nations that are united cannot be destroyed.

The imperialists have stolen what is yours. They have laid hands on the very sources of your wealth and raised barriers and divided your indivisible homeland. They have separated the nation into religious sects and states. They have strangled freedom of religion, thought, conscience, speech, and action. We are no longer even allowed to move about freely in our own country.

To arms! Let us realize our national aspirations and sacred hopes.

To arms! Sons of the nation.

To arms! Confirm the supremacy of the people and freedom of the nation.

To arms! Let us free our country from bondage.

The usurper has ignored our rights and broken his plighted word.

We disavow before God all responsibility for this conflict to which the greedy and insatiable foe has driven us. The blood of the innocent victims of this mass rising in defense of the sacred rights of the nation will be on the heads of those who caused it to flow.

Insult and injury have pursued us to our very homes. We have only asked of the oppressor that an inhuman French Governor may be replaced by another of the same race. Not only has our prayer not been answered, but our envoys have been driven away like sheep and cast into prison.

The cup is full to overflowing. To arms! Let us wipe out this insult in blood.

The die is cast. Our war is a holy war.

We have drawn our swords and will not sheathe them until our demands are fulfilled. These are our demands:

1. The complete independence of Arab Syria, one and indivisible, sea-coast and interior;

2. The institution of a Popular Government and the free election of a Constituent Assembly for the framing of an Organic Law;

3. The evacuation of the foreign army of occupation and the creation of a national army for the maintenance of security;

4. The application of the principles of the French Revolution and the Rights of Man.

To arms! Let us write our demands with our blood, as our fathers did before us.

To arms! God is with us.

Long live independent Syria!

Sulṭân al-Aṭrash
Commander of the Syrian Revolutionary Armies[49]

The manifesto first appeared in the neighborhoods of Damascus, but it soon found its way into newspapers in other Arab countries, the French press, and the archives of the League of Nations and Great Britain. It was not the work of Sulṭân al-Aṭrash alone. French intelligence surmised that it was written by Samî al-Sarrâj, a nationalist from Aleppo who had traveled to Jabal Ḥawrân to join the revolt. He had been active in nationalist causes since the reign of Fayṣal and, as a journalist, had been responsible for a number of fiery tracts.[50]

It is, by any standard, a radical and sophisticated document and an interesting mix of local politics and militant nationalism. It could only have been a collaboration between the Druze and the nationalists. Though the manifesto was aimed at all Syrians, and those beyond Syria as well, the reference in the final paragraph is clearly to the trap set by Sarrail to capture Druze notables before the revolt. This paragraph did not appear in all the versions of the tract, and the versions published outside Syria did not have it. The episode was probably not familiar to most of the intended audience of this manifesto. An obscure reference to a matter of purely regional Druze politics in an avowedly nationalist tract is a reminder that the revolt started as one type of political action and evolved into another. Whoever wrote it, the signature at the end proclaims to all that the leader of the movement is not an urban notable, not a member of the nationalist elite, not a privileged recipient of a modern education, but a rural shaykh and farmer from a rebellious sectarian minority.

By late August armed bands had begun to form in the neighborhoods of Damascus and the surrounding villages. Later on the same day of the attack on Damascus, Nasîb al-Bakrî gathered armed men from the various neighborhoods of Damascus, including al-Shâghûr, inside the city walls; Bâb Muṣallâ, just outside the walls; Maydân; and the nearby Ghûṭa village of Jaramânâ.

Though he gathered 260 men before heading south to the Jabal that evening, intelligence reports noted with satisfaction that some villagers in Jaramânâ had refused to join him. The reluctant villagers of Jaramânâ soon felt the effects of the uprising anyway, since by the end of September French bombs had flattened their village. Saʿîd Ḥaydar went into the Anti-Lebanon mountains above Damascus with men from his town of Baʿlabak, 65 kilometers northeast of Damascus in the mandate state of greater Lebanon. They planned to destroy the railroad lines out of Damascus. Armed bedouin had robbed travelers on the roads in all directions leading from Damascus, and the roads were no longer considered secure.[51]

Insurgent emissaries visited Ḥawrân villages and the villages surrounding Damascus in the final days of August. Five or six Ḥawrân villages were known to have joined the rebellion, and bedouin swelled the rebel ranks.[52] The small tribes of the Jabal, the *ʿarab al-jabal,* had been with the rebels from the beginning; and a major Transjordanian tribe, the Banî Ṣakhr, had joined the rebellion as well. In late August the Service des Renseignements intercepted copies of a letter addressed to Ḥamad and Sulṭân al-Aṭrash and all the shaykhs of the Jabal from the shaykhs of the Ruwalâ tribe. The Ruwalâ was a very large, fully nomadic tribe that ranged from central Syria to the Arabian Peninsula. In the mid-twenties it numbered several thousand tents and at least 3,000 armed men.[53] The Ruwalâ shaykhs claimed that they were concerned that their help might bring trouble upon the Druze, presumably by alienating their other bedouin allies and causing pillage. Nevertheless, they went on to say: "From fathers to sons we have always walked hand in hand, and as our fathers were with your fathers and our grandfathers were with your grandfathers, so too we are with you. You and us, we are alike. Tell us what we must do for you."[54] Despite the crucial role the Ruwalâ played in the Arab Revolt, this letter is based entirely on traditional relationships, without a single echo of nationalist sentiment. The same intelligence report that contained the letter mentions that mandate authorities had invited Nûrî al-Shaʿlân, *amîr* of the Ruwalâ, to organize a bedouin security force to patrol the roads. He had not signed the letter to the Druze. Nûrî al-Shaʿlân took no chances. Soon after, he sent a three-line telegraph to the president of the French Republic, the president of the Senate, and the deputies. "The Druze insurrection [is] provoking general indignation in the house of the great Ruwalâ tribe. On this occasion, [we] renew [our] sincere sentiments of sympathy for glorious France. We are ready to spill our blood under the noble tricolor flag."[55] The intelligence report noted that Nûrî had assumed his habitual political attitude and that he was in constant contact with the insurgents.

The Damascus members of the People's Party continued their meetings, propaganda, and debates, but the mandate power was closing in. On the night of 27 August, after a secret meeting at the house of a Damascene merchant, ʿUthmân al-Sharâbâtî, the clampdown came. The meeting had been another debate on the role of the Party in the rebellion. After the conclusion of the meeting the secret police seized al-Sharâbâtî in his house and all the other members who had returned to their own houses. They arrested lawyer Fâris al-Khûrî and merchant Tawfîq Shâmiyya, both prominent Orthodox Christians, who (like Shahbandar and Nazîh al-Muʾayyad al-ʿAẓm, who both escaped) were graduates of the American University of Beirut and former officials in Amîr Fayṣal's short-lived government. Police also seized Najîb al-Rayyis, the editor of the banned nationalist newspaper *al-Muqtabas,* and Fawzî al-Ghazzî, a nationalist notable from a prominent family of religious scholars.[56]

When police stormed Shahbandar's house in ʿArnûs that night, they found him missing. He—along with Asʿad, Nasîb, and Fawzî al-Bakrî, Yaḥyâ al-Ḥayâtî, Nazîh al-Muʾayyad al-ʿAẓm, Jamîl Mardam Bek, Nabîh al-ʿAẓma, and Saʿîd Ḥaydar—escaped the dragnet. Some of those who escaped arrest had already taken part in attacks on mandate troops in Ḥawrân and outside Damascus. Those who escaped capture scattered in the early morning hours after the arrests. Most would later turn up in Jabal Ḥawrân or outside mandate Syria. The arrests did not pass unnoticed in Damascus; 28 August was a Friday, and the bazaars were closed.

Notices circulated directing merchants to "respond to the appeal of the Party and close your shops for three days" in protest.[57] After Friday noon prayer, an angry crowd gathered at the Umayyad mosque in the center of the old city. The mosque is the grandest and oldest building in Damascus and the historical epicenter of antigovernment protest. The main bazaar, Sûq al-Ḥamîdiyya, leads directly to the front door of the mosque.[58]

A young man identified as Lûṭfî al-Yafî mounted the pulpit and spoke: "The government has imprisoned and expulsed the notables and intellectuals who were working for our independence. We must demonstrate before Sarrail to protest this act." The crowd moved out from the mosque, and at some point a man identified as Khâlid Barkawî from al-Shâghûr quarter fired some shots. The police moved in and erected barricades and machine-gun posts at the entrance to Sûq al-Ḥamîdiyya, about 400 meters from the mosque. The police dispersed and chased the demonstrators out of the bazaar, arresting about twenty. The remaining protesters moved out of Sûq al-Ḥamîdiyya into the al-Shâghûr, Bâb Muṣallâ, and Maydân quarters, where the police claimed they originated. Demonstrations and sporadic gunfire continued all day and into the night in the neighborhoods.[59] Neither Damascus nor its nationalist leaders had taken the uprising seriously until they were forced into jail or into the countryside to seek the protection of the rural insurgents. The revolt was soon to evolve into a full-blown guerrilla war.

CHAPTER 5

The Spread of Rebellion

URBAN AGITATION

Protests and agitation continued into September 1925 and gradually spread to all the cities of mandate Syria. Mme. Shahbandar immediately assumed the mantle of her fugitive husband and engaged in a series of meetings with the wives of exiled and jailed Damascene nationalists and with other prominent women. She organized women's marches and decried the lack of courage among the men of Damascus and the failure of merchants to close the bazaars completely.[1] French intelligence opined that the house of Mme. Shahbandar was "a hotbed of anti-mandatory propaganda."[2] Still, the devoted attention that she received from French intelligence came from a general lack of more threatening activity. She held meetings at her house and drafted petitions to the League of Nations. Twenty or thirty women routinely attended and represented the most accomplished and publicly visible Syrian women. They included several school and orphanage directors and teachers and at least one lawyer. Like the male members of the People's Party, they met at the Shahbandar house and the house of jailed merchant ʿUthmân al-Sharâbâtî. They also met at the Damascus-American Girls' School in al-Ṣâliḥiyya.[3]

Agitation continued in the countryside too. Nasîb al-Bakrî toured villages throughout southern Syria seeking support and making contacts. Sulṭân al-Aṭrash sent various letters to villages and towns all over the countryside in the name of "independence, liberty, fraternity, and equality," declaring that all Druze, Sunnîs, ʿAlawîs, Shîʿîs, and Christians were sons of the Syrian Arab nation. As there was no difference between them, there was only one enemy before them: the unjust military authority and the foreign colonizer. As leader of the Syrian Arab revolutionary army, he asked all to help:

> Ensure harmony between all communities.
>
> Guard the tranquility of their villages and towns and allow entry of rebel troops [into their villages] in order to speed the flight of the colonizers.

> Allow patrols . . . loyal to the homeland to blend in among the inhabitants, in order to take possession of the villages in good order, and to safeguard the inhabitants and their belongings against pillage and all aggression.
>
> Recruit volunteers in the towns and villages [to welcome] the detachments of the patriotic rebels with chants of enthusiasm.[4]

Intelligence agents recovered this tract in al-Qunayṭra, a city mostly populated by Circassian Muslim refugees settled by the Ottoman government after the defeat of 1878. The implied threat in the third point reflects the realities of guerrilla warfare and the historically poor relations between the Circassians and the Druze. Despite the fine language and inclusive nationalist sentiments, villagers were responsible for the consequences if they resisted the insurgents. Circassian villages in Ḥawrân had long resisted Druze domination more fervently than other communities in the Ḥawrân. Druze migrants resented the more recent Circassian migrants to a frontier region that they had fought to dominate. As refugees resettled by the Ottoman state, the Circassians also had a deeper identification with the central government than most of their neighbors did. This loyalty apparently carried over to the mandate. Circassians, along with Armenian refugees from Anatolia, constituted the majority of locally raised French colonial troops during the revolt.

A few days before this tract appeared, rebels, reported to be Druze, engaged Circassian gendarmes in the Ḥawrân village of Durîn. When the gendarmes pursued the rebels into the formerly peaceful village, the villagers themselves fired on the gendarmes. Soon after, aerial bombardment destroyed the village, and the villagers abandoned their homes. The report affirmed that Circassian troops were widely disliked and that many had quit the gendarmerie or requested reposting elsewhere.[5] The League of Nations Permanent Mandates Commission charter explicitly prohibited the use of locally raised troops outside their states of residence. Since Syria and Lebanon had been partitioned into Greater Lebanon, the state of Syria surrounding Damascus, the state of Jabal Druze in Ḥawrân, and the state of the Alawites in the northern coastal regions, Circassian and other locally raised troops protested that they could not be sent outside their home regions.[6]

Muslims and Christian villages in Ḥawrân also had difficult historical relations with the Ḥawrân Druze. The Druze shaykhs, particularly the Aṭrash, had long bullied the Ḥawrânîs (plural Ḥawârna), and some resisted the uprising.[7] A few Ḥawrân shaykhs aided the French to the extent possible without exposing themselves and their villages to insurgent retribution. Nevertheless, the new nationalist call that accompanied the revolt was compelling for many, and a number of Ḥawrân shaykhs did join the uprising. While the Druze had many traditional enemies, the nationalist component of the uprising and the illegitimacy of mandate rule had altered these relations; and some of those among the Christian communities most favored by France trenchantly criticized the mandate government. Authorities intercepted a tract circulating in Beirut and addressed to the "defenders of humanity." It was signed by a self-identified Maronite Christian of Dayr al-Qamr in Mount Lebanon. He wrote: "The government of France has decided to punish those they call the rebels and bandits of the Jabal Druze." As a member of the human race, he protested the violation of human rights and claimed: "The French army has employed poison gas against the Druze, which affirms French will to exterminate an entire people." Finally, the writer called upon the League of Nations and the noble spirit represented by many French people to preserve the human rights of the mandate population.[8]

Damascus remained the center of urban resistance, but agitation emerged from Beirut too, and this tract was widespread there. The possibility exists that it was phony, produced by someone other than the signatory. The roots of Druze-Maronite animosity in Mount Lebanon were deep and emerged before the 1860s. The identity of its writer as a Maronite would have confounded the mandate authorities. French claims to the mandate in the first place were based on its relationship with its historical clients, the Maronite and other Uniate Christians. The creation of a separate mandate for Maronite-dominated Greater Lebanon was a manifestation of this commitment. Anti-mandate voices from within that community consequently had special resonance. It is generally true that members of the Catholic rites were better disposed toward the French mandate than other sectarian groups in Syria and Lebanon. Just as there were pro-mandate Druze, however, it should be no surprise that there were anti-mandate Christians. Ḥannâ Abî Râshid, the preeminent contemporary chronicler of the uprising in Ḥawrân, fierce foe of colonial occupation, and Maronite Christian, is a good example. Fâris al-Aṭrash is an example from the opposite pole. He spent the revolt in the Ḥawrân town of Darʿâ under French protection from his relatives. Still, mandate authorities and apologists searched much more assiduously for "friends of France" among the Druze than they searched for enemies among the Christians. The sources reflect this. The tract differs substantially from rebel tracts. It appeals not to nationalism, martyrdom, or blood spilling but to human rights and general humanity. Since it differs so greatly from the tone of insurgent tracts, and appeals to humanity and not to violence, perhaps it was the call of a single anguished conscience.

Other letters and tracts circulated in Beirut. Some were the work of the local Communist Party; and hundreds, perhaps thousands, of Arabic-language tracts were mailed to Syria and Lebanon by the French Communist Party. At the beginning of September mandate authorities seized hundreds of tracts postmarked from all over France. They usually came in envelopes marked "Touring-club de France," and they turned up in every village and town, addressed to local journalists, teachers, and notables. Mandate authorities translated the single text at least fifty times, until the Service des Renseignements finally reported it to all mandate offices.[9] The Central Committee of the Communist Party of Syria and Lebanon soon distributed notices as well, which were, however, much better attuned to the situation than those of the French Communists. Bulletins mailed from Beirut to various towns and cities and addressed "to soldiers and workers" called on all Syrian Arabs and all sectarian communities to join their Druze brothers and fight for liberty, freedom, and honor. They made a special appeal to the Armenians, "the sons of the oppressed, and victims of the imperialists' war, not to join the imperialist oppressors."[10]

Meanwhile meetings took place among the insurgent leaders (Druze, Ḥawrânî, and Damascene) in the villages high on Jabal Ḥawrân. They held a meeting at al-Qanawât above Suwaydâ' on 28 August and resolved to advance on Damascus after ten days.[11] A few days later a much larger meeting took place at the house of Salmân Kaylânî, shaykh of the remote Jabal village of Nimra. A hundred or so Ḥawrânî Druze and other rural shaykhs were joined by fifty or more Damascenes, mostly from Maydân, and various others, including former army officers. Some of the Druze reportedly upbraided the Damascenes for their broken promises of help and military assistance. "We in the Jabal have been deceived and ruined. We did not make peace because of your promises that Damascus would stand alongside us. But the Damascenes came only for their self-interest."[12]

Shahbandar and Jamîl Mardam replied by recounting their recent journey in search of support in Transjordan. They reported a meeting with ʿAlî Riḍâ Bâshâ al-Rikâbî, who would send weapons, ammunition, troops, and even airplanes to help further the cause.[13] Rikâbî was King ʿAbdallâh's prime minister. He was a Damascene, a former ranking Ottoman officer and a former high official in Amîr Fayṣal's government. The former officers and the pro-Hashemite Druze held Rikâbî in high esteem, but it is doubtful that anyone besides paranoid French intelligence officers could have credited the story that such reinforcements were coming from Transjordan. In fact, it is doubtful that Shahbandar—his credibility with the Druze already strained—would have made such outlandish promises.

Intelligence officers purchased this information from a Syrian who was there. It is self-evident that informants tell the stories that their paymasters want to hear, but the revolt leadership was eventually concerned enough about informers to discuss and document penalties for treason. Sulṭân al-Aṭrash drafted a letter to the chief of police of the rebel government, Ḥusnî Ṣakhr, a Damascene who had occupied the same position under the mandate government in Jabal Druze, prescribing the amputation of the hands of informers (but with anesthesia and under a doctor's supervision). Ḥusnî Ṣakhr began his career as an Ottoman military officer and took part in an Ottoman mission to the World's Columbian Exposition in Chicago in 1894, when he was fifteen years old.[14]

Whether the supply and reinforcement journeys to Amman were fruitful or not, someone began operating the cannons captured at the battle of al-Mazraʿa.[15] Artillery pieces were placed at various locations guarding Suwaydâ' and were reportedly manned by "Sharîfian" artillerymen. They periodically fired on the citadel at Suwaydâ', with its French garrison still holed up after two months and in radio contact with Damascus, though apparently without great effect.[16] Shahbandar, Ḥasan al-Ḥakîm, and some members of the Bakrî family returned to Amman to obtain Egyptian passports. Muḥammad ʿIzz al-Dîn al-Ḥalabî brought eight cases of rifle ammunition from Amman and was reportedly detained there by a police officer who found him listed on an arrest warrant. An unnamed police commissioner released him and reprimanded the arresting officer severely.[17] Preparations continued for the inevitable French counterattack.

The Military Command in Paris had replaced General Michaud, the disgraced commander of the column destroyed at al-Mazraʿa, with General Maurice Gamelin. When Sarrail resisted removing Michaud after his defeat, Paris went over his head to remove the general and appoint another, though Sarrail was given the latitude to choose Michaud's successor from a short-list of six.[18] Gamelin arrived in mid-September along with several thousand reinforcements, including Foreign Legion troops. The advance toward Suwaydâ' began a few days after his arrival.

As Gamelin's column left Damascus, another meeting took place at ʿArâ on the lower slopes of the Jabal between Suwaydâ' and al-Qrayâ. The insurgents knew of the departure of the new force to al-Musayfra and resolved to intercept its advance units there or on the way to Suwaydâ'. French intelligence received a report of the meeting from a Ḥawrânî shaykh who had been present and knew of rebel plans for a large attack at al-Musayfra. Rebels planned to assemble at the village of ʿArâ and call the inhabitants to arms and then proceed to al-Qrayâ; from there around 2,500 men would attack the citadel at Suwaydâʾ. If it turned out well, they would immediately attack the approaching French column. They planned to set traps for armored cars and tanks on the roads and camouflage the traps so that they could capture the vehicles.[19] Reportedly, many of the Druze at the meeting were tired of fighting and were ready to surrender. But among those claimed by the informant to be ready for submission was Muḥammad ʿIzz al-Dîn al-Ḥalabî, who later fled to al-Azraq in Jordan in 1927 with the last of the insurgents and continued to fight the French in cross-border raids until 1930, when the insurgents and their families were finally expelled by the British.[20]

Agitation in Damascus and sympathetic dispatches in European newspapers did little to stop the daily rain of bombs on villages all over the southern countryside or to help the Druze when the inevitable French force returned to the Ḥawrân. While Gamelin assembled his force in Damascus, an advanced group of Foreign Legionnaires and heavy infantry under Colonel Charles Andréa reached al-Musayfra. The advance troop numbered six hundred or eight hundred seasoned soldiers. Al-Musayfra had accepted the mandate government and had evidently paid taxes since the beginning of the uprising. Willingness to pay taxes was the general standard by which the French measured submission or rebellion.[21] The villagers of al-Musayfra had paid taxes and later harbored rebels. The acceptance of rebels made this a "treasonous" village, subject to the harshest punitive measures, which meant summary execution of most male villagers and demolition of their houses.[22]

The choices available to such Ḥawrân villages at this time were limited. The region was not completely under the control of either the French or the rebels. Tax collectors came with a complement of several hundred armed troops, and troops looted and burned villages that refused to pay. Soldiers executed villagers who did not flee immediately on the spot. Sometimes they were shot while they fled.[23] Villagers fared marginally better at the hands of the rebels. Those who refused entry to insurgents had to be prepared to defend themselves and would end up pillaged if they failed to drive the insurgents away. Rebels usually stole animals and agricultural goods, though in many cases villagers freely gave all that they had to give to support rebels. French forces also took animals and foodstuffs, both from villages in rebellion and from those that had submitted. Pillaging insurgents might well leave villagers destitute, but rebels did not demolish villages and seem not to have executed villagers even if they had joined the French. Monsignor Nicolas Cadi, Greek Catholic archbishop of Ḥawrân and Jabal Druze, made a claim for compensation to the mandate authority in September 1925. He listed the theft of around 3,000 sheep and 800 cattle, but not one human death. He noted that cold and starvation could follow and claimed that the majority of pillaged villagers were Catholic. Even the villages securely under rebel control and protection and not reachable by French forces were subject to nearly continuous bombing from the air whether they were Druze, Christian, or mixed.[24]

Foreign Legion troops and Andréa's Eighteenth Tirailleurs occupied al-Musayfra on 15 September. The troops expelled and killed the remaining inhabitants of the village and immediately built strong fortifications surrounding it.[25] They strung barbed wire, dug trenches, and built a series of walls from earth and stone. The fortifications were guarded by machine guns. The insurgents knew that Gamelin's main force was coming and resolved to attack the smaller advance guard. At four o'clock in the morning on 17 September they attacked in a wild charge. Machine-gun fire cut down the charging rebels, but they continued the attack. The battle raged for hours, but the insurgents did not break through the fortifications in large numbers. After the sun came up, French airplanes bombed the rebels twenty-seven times in three hours as they retreated. Three hundred to four hundred were killed. Among them was Shaykh Salmân Ḥamza of the village of Rassâs, who was killed along with his four sons. "When their mother found out, she died too," wrote Salâma ʿUbayd.[26]

Colonel Andréa lauded the performance of his troops and claimed that the attack had been a surprise. Intelligence documents and the memoir of Bennett Doty indicate without question that Andréa and his troops expected and prepared for an attack. Andréa also claimed that the rebel force numbered 10,000.[27] French intelligence and his own men knew better; the rebel force was no more than 2,500. After the battle, Andréa ordered the captured insurgents put to work stacking the bodies of their dead comrades and the dead of al-Musayfra in front of the village as an example. After they finished the job, he ordered the prisoners executed.[28] He failed to report these last details in his memoirs.

Documentation of such policies is rarely found in the mandate archives. The private memoirs of its soldiers and lower functionaries are often more candid.

The strange memoir of Bennett Doty is the best example. Doty was an French Foreign Legion volunteer of American origin who later deserted with John Henry Harvey, a Foreign Legion volunteer of English origin, who also wrote a memoir. Each blames his desertion on the other. Doty's book seems more reliable and has more verifiable information. Harvey's book is more horrifying and fantastic and contains fewer names, dates, or locations. It also contains overt anti-French sentiment. Both men were veterans of the First World War, and both memoirs are inexplicably well written. Such books were apparently very popular in Europe and America, though some were clearly written by people who never served in or even visited Syria.[29]

Doty used the name "Gilbert Clare" in the Foreign Legion. Documents from the mandate archives indicate that he was indeed wanted by the French authority for desertion. Desertion was a major problem for the French forces, particularly the colonial legions. North African and Syrian Legion troops regularly deserted and joined the rebels, and sometimes German Foreign Legion soldiers changed sides too. Foreign Legion troops deserted en masse on more than one occasion, usually fleeing for Palestine, sometimes accompanied by their junior officers.

Gamelin arrived at al-Musayfra two days later. The column of 8,000 traveled by rail to Azruʿ and marched to al-Musayfra. They joined Andréa's exhausted troops and stayed at al-Musayfra for two additional days before marching on Suwaydâʾ. The march and occupation of Suwaydâʾ provoked only minimal opposition. The rebels had retreated to the more remote villages; many had sent their families over the border to Transjordan. By the time the French reached the town it was deserted, and water sources had been destroyed. They relieved the garrison in the citadel, burned everything still standing after two months of continuous bombing, and returned to al-Musayfra. The countryside around Suwaydâʾ was denuded, the water supply was ruined, and the hills were insecure. Gamelin decided that due to lack of water and the difficulty of holding the town without provisions he had to retreat to Ḥawrân.[30]

Despite months of agitation in Damascus, the Druze had faced the French onslaught alone. They had suffered a painful defeat, but Gamelin's retreat from Suwaydâʾ made defeat look like victory. The mandate government had filled the few Damascus newspapers still in print with loud predictions of the end of the uprising. When the massive French army evacuated Suwaydâʾ after one day, the effect on public opinion in Damascus and the Jabal was predictable; the Druze had once again defeated the French. A few Druze chiefs made submissions to the mandate government in the days after al-Musayfra, but the submissions quickly dried up when it was clear that the French could not hold the Jabal.[31] The Paris press finally had something to celebrate, but the celebration was short.[32]

The nationalists of Damascus had failed to help the Druze repulse the French advance. They distributed fiery tracts in Damascus and traveled between the Ḥawrân and Amman trying to gain support from outside. Although meetings continued and new tracts appeared in Damascus, few were willing or able personally to mobilize or lead armed resistance, and the militant masses had yet to materialize.[33] The Druze, confounding the claims of later social scientists that they conform to the expectation of a "compact minority," continued to lead resistance and maintained their hard-won role as masters of the Ḥawrân and full partners (commercial and otherwise) with Damascus.[34] Insurgent leaders celebrated what they called the "final evacuation of the Jabal by the French."[35] New groups of rebels would soon emerge, but they would neither follow nor even acknowledge the leadership of Damascene politicians. They would take their inspiration from the Druze of Jabal Ḥawrân.

REBELLION IN ḤAMÂH

On 4 October an insurgent force of hundreds occupied the central Syrian town of Ḥamâh. In 1925 it was mandate Syria's third largest town, with 80,000 inhabitants. Ḥamâh lies in a fertile valley along the Orontes River, 200 kilometers north of Damascus. It was a market center for the agricultural produce of the valley and the surrounding regions. The town was known for the beauty of its river and parks and the medieval wooden waterwheels that raise river water to irrigate its gardens. It was also known for Islamic conservatism and fierce opposition to French rule.

A renegade captain in the French-Syrian Legion led the uprising. Fawzî al-Qâwuqjî was a former Ottoman army officer and Ottoman Military Academy graduate. Qâwuqjî was born in modest circumstances in Tripoli, in what became Greater Lebanon, in 1890. He attended the Ottoman Military Academy in Istanbul and was there at the time of the Unionist (Young Turk) revolution in 1908. He later wrote that while he waited for an assignment in Istanbul an officer came and announced that the army was free and that freedom, justice, equality, and brotherhood would reign. Meanwhile he heard that the Arabic language would be relegated to the status of Chinese in the school. Shortly after, the students from different regions grouped together with their compatriots and began to quarrel and fight based on their regional, linguistic, or ethnic identification. Qâwuqjî graduated from the Harbiye in 1912, at the relatively advanced age of twenty-one or twenty-two. He immediately went to Libya to fight the Italian invasion of that Ottoman province. During the war of 1914–1918, Qâwuqjî remained with the Ottoman forces. He later ridiculed the Hashemites and wrote that Ottoman rule, for all its iniquities and injustices, was far better than partition and domination by the European imperialists. In 1925 he was a cavalry commander of a Syrian unit based in Ḥamâh.[36]

Qâwuqjî had watched events in Ḥawrân closely and sought to coordinate his efforts with those in the south. He and other former officers and religious leaders had formed a local party, Ḥizb Allâh, as a secret focus for resistance to the mandate.[37] Ḥamâh was a town of significant outward Islamic religiosity, and religious sentiment was more widely expressed in public there than in Damascus. In his memoirs Qâwuqjî wrote that though the party's goals were nationalism and independence they chose the name to gain the support of the religious establishment in Ḥamâh and to confuse the mandate authorities. In an earlier account of the party's formation Qâwuqjî was more ambivalent about the religiousness of the party and about its nationalist orientation. In any event, the name apparently did not deceive mandate authorities, since their documents referred to Ḥizb Allâh as the People's Party in Ḥamâh. Qâwuqjî wrote in his memoirs that he had contacted Dr. Shahbandar months earlier, seeking formal union with the People's Party in Damascus. He also sought advice about armed rebellion against the mandate. Shahbandar refused to sanction subsidiary organizations and told Qâwuqjî that armed resistance against the mandate was dangerous and detrimental to the situation in Syria.

Qâwuqjî published his memoirs in 1975. In an introduction to a friend's memoir published in 1935, he was both more oblique and more damning about his relations with Damascene nationalists. Less than ten years after the revolt he wrote that he had made contact with some leaders in Damascus (whose names he could not mention) to ask if they could help in an uprising or if they would take part or provide support for the undertaking and that they replied that they would never consider such a thing. There is little doubt that the people he refused to name in 1935 were Shahbandar and members of his party.[38] Qâwuqjî attacked the nationalist elite elsewhere too. Munîr al-Rayyis quoted him as complaining about their lack of commitment to the cause of expelling France and exclaiming: "Who will rise in armed revolt in Ḥamâh? Will the nationalists do it, the majority of them of the cultured classes who refuse to carry arms and who do not know how to fire a rifle?"[39]

It turned out, however, that the assessment of the nationalist leaders that Qâwuqjî cursed was correct; armed struggle was detrimental to Syria, and the French response led to the deaths of thousands and the destruction of much of the country. Qâwuqjî, Shahbandar, and many of their comrades were in exile until 1937. Whether or not the nationalists (in their reluctance to lead) were responsible for the failure of the revolt—as both Qâwuqjî and his former Ottoman army comrade Sa'îd al-'Âṣ charged—is another question.

In seeking help, Qâwuqjî received no such reticence from the Druze insurgents in the south. After the beginning of the revolt in Ḥawrân, Qâwuqjî sent emissaries to Sulṭân al-Aṭrash. He had already contacted Nasîb al-Aṭrash in Damascus before the revolt; and after the battle of al-Musayfra he sent Maẓhar al-Sibâ'î and Munîr al-Rayyis. He charged them with the following:

1. To convey their numbers and strength.
2. To request that the Druze keep the pressure on Gamelin's forces in early October in Ḥawrân, to facilitate and expand their scope of operations in the region of Ḥamâh.
3. To appoint one trusted man to serve as the link between them.
4. To advise of any needs or pending operations, and to convey information and instructions *[ta'lîmât]* orally only—not one word written.[40]

Munîr al-Rayyis and Maẓhar al-Sibâ'î were fitting emissaries. They were young (both born in 1901) and committed to armed resistance. Sibâ'î was born in Ḥumṣ, attended the Damascus military secondary school, and was in one of the last classes to attend the Ottoman Military Academy in Istanbul during the war. After the war he joined Mustafa Kemal fighting in Anatolia in the Turkish war of independence and later joined Ibrâhîm Hanânû in northern Syria against the French. After the end of Hanânû's revolt he was in jail for a year and ended up in Ḥamâh in 1925, when he was still only twenty-four years old. Munîr al-Rayyis was educated in Damascus as well, though in the civil system rather than the military system. He took a degree in literature from the Syrian University and worked as a journalist and agitator his entire life. While Sibâ'î was killed in the Ghûṭa early in 1926, Rayyis fought in the Syrian revolt until 1927, in Palestine in 1936, and in Iraq in 1941, each time with Fawzî al-Qâwuqjî. He chronicled each experience and published three volumes in the 1960s and 1970s.[41] Qâwuqjî chose them as emissaries to Sulṭân al-Aṭrash for their reliability and commitment.

Qâwuqjî had carefully planned and prepared the town for an uprising. He knew the activities and habits of the French military command, and he knew the importance of secrecy. He claimed that most of the people of Ḥamâh were members of his organization or sympathizers. The French knew that they had no support in Ḥamâh, but their intelligence failed them; they were unprepared when Qâwuqjî mutinied with the entire cavalry troop he commanded and occupied the city with the help of bedouin irregulars from the Mawalî tribe. Qâwuqjî knew that the French army was stretched thin in Syria. The French empire was engaged in a guerrilla war in Ḥawrân and facing a major colonial war in the Rîf in Morocco at the same time. Qâwuqjî planned to force open a second front in Syria and compel France to abandon the mandate. He had been busy making friends among the religious establishment, the local bedouin, the police, and merchants, and it seemed that everyone but the French knew that a revolt was coming. Qâwuqjî argued for a holy crusade with the religious leaders of Ḥamâh. With the bedouin and the ordinary people of Ḥamâh, he emphasized the riches held in the offices of the government and its banks that the imperialists had stolen from the people, who would share it after their defeat.[42]

Ḥamâh's population opposed French rule and readily joined Qâwuqjî, but his writing from the 1930s contains precious little that could be defined as normative nationalism. He regarded the nationalist leaders of mandate Syria with undisguised contempt and variously referred to them as high-class nationalists, traitorous aristocrats, or worse. Dr. Shahbandar's reply to Qâwuqjî's prerevolt entreaties reveals that the nationalists did not care for Qâwuqjî either. Shahbandar was resolutely secular, liberal, and nationalist, and it is not surprising that he chose not to sanction a supposedly nationalist party in Ḥamâh with a name like Ḥizb Allâh. Ḥamâh was a city with a reputation for the type of Islamic conservatism that western-oriented nationalists viewed with deep concern. Still, Qâwuqjî's vision was compelling. While the People's Party in Damascus distributed artfully written appeals to national revival and resistance, which had little impact apart from worrying the mandate power, Qâwuqjî's theoretically untidy mix of religion, anti-imperialist agitation, and class warfare evidently mobilized the majority of Ḥamâh's citizens.[43]

At seven in the evening on 4 October the insurgents struck. They cut the telephone lines, blocked the roads, attacked the government *sérail* (palace), captured the few French officers who did not escape, and opened the jail. By 11:30 that night the battle was over, and Ḥamâh was in rebel hands.[44] The following morning, however, the French struck back. They subjected the town to continuous aerial bombing from first light until early afternoon. The bombing laid waste to most of the town bazaars and several of the houses of its leading citizens.

Ḥamâh had long been the political and economic preserve of three notable families. The Barâzî and the ʿAẓm were the most important landholding families and controlled most high secular offices, and the Kaylânî family was preeminent in the control of religious offices.[45] Qâwuqjî had reached agreements with members of these families in the banks and in the offices of the government held by Syrians.[46] As Qâwuqjî had planned, Gamelin's troops were occupied in Ḥawrân. Qâwuqjî had several hundred armed bedouin, the mutinous Syrian Legion, and virtually the entire population of Ḥamâh behind him.

The mandate government rushed two companies of reinforcements from Rayaq and Aleppo.[47] The critical element in ending the uprising, however, was the role played by Ḥamâh's leading families. Early the morning after the uprising—amid burning buildings, smoldering ruins, and still falling bombs—Farîd al-ʿAẓm, scion of Ḥamâh's most prominent family, joined Najîb al-Barâzî, the mayor of Ḥamâh, to call on Commandant Coustillère of the besieged French garrison in his headquarters. The two sought an end to the bombing of Ḥamâh and, according to Qâwuqjî, an end to the uprising. The three men struck a deal in which the mandate government would stop the bombardment and not hold the town's notables responsible, if they persuaded the insurgents to evacuate the town. Through unclear means, Barâzî convinced Qâwuqjî and his forces to leave. Years later Qâwuqjî was still angry over the betrayal of the "people's hopes by the wily and hypocritical aristocratic class," specifically Najîb al-Barâzî. He accused them of selling out to the foreigners and destroying the prospects of a plan sure to defeat the French and force their evacuation from all of Syria.[48] Qâwuqjî and the bedouin left Ḥamâh the following day and met up with a group of rebels led by another former Ottoman officer, Ramaḍân Bâshâ Shallâsh, who had come from Transjordan late the previous month.

Despite the bombardment's short duration, deaths and damages in Ḥamâh were considerable. The citizens filed petitions to the League of Nations in which they reported that the repression had taken 344 lives, mostly civilians (many of them women and children). Mandate authorities—responding to the charges—reported that 76 were killed, all insurgents; but contemporary internal intelligence documents and reports from the commander of the Ḥamâh garrison claimed more than 100 killed. Property destruction was also great. Besides the public buildings besieged by the rebels, bombs and mandate troops destroyed several large houses and two bazaars, including 115 shops.[49] Whatever the cost in lives and property, mandate authorities considered it cheap, and the *Bulletin de Renseignements* of 10 October commented with self-satisfaction on "the excellent impression produced by the energetic manner in which order was restored during the events in Ḥamâh. The prestige of France is vastly increased . . ."[50]

REBELLION IN DAMASCUS

The mandate power blocked the news from Ḥamâh. Once again press censorship proved worse than futile; bands of insurgents had begun to form all over central and southern Syria. Still, mandate officials considered Ḥamâh a victory. General François Soule, commander of the garrison at Damascus, remarked darkly—and with chilling prescience, in light of the devastating bombardment of the capital ten days later—that "he wished the Damascenes would give France a chance of dealing with them as the Hama rebels had been dealt with."[51] While the details of the repression of Ḥamâh were unknown to foreigners in the capital, it was clear to everyone that the countryside of mandate Syria was rapidly passing out of even nominal government control. Separate bands emerged in the countryside of Damascus and began a loosely coordinated guerrilla campaign on all sides of the capital.

The French response was ineffectual. In the first week of October mandate authorities sent a group of sixty Syrian gendarmes into the countryside against the band of Ḥasan al-Kharrâṭ, a former chief night watchman of al-Shâghûr quarter. The troops proceeded to the eastern Ghûṭa village of al-Malayḥa, where they spent the night. During the night, a mixed band of insurgents from Damascus, Jabal Ḥawrân, and the Ghûṭa captured the gendarmes in the house of the *mukhtâr* of the village, Abî ʿUmar al-ʿÎsâ. They killed one gendarme, disarmed the rest, and sent four officers to Jabal Ḥawrân as prisoners and the men back to Damascus, stripped of their belongings. Sulṭân al-Aṭrash released the officers when he learned they had not resisted the rebels.[52]

It was certainly gentler and more artful treatment than captured rebels could expect at the hands of the French army. At about the same time the British consul protested (via an intermediary) the rebel theft of forty goats belonging to a Palestinian-British subject resident in the countryside of Damascus. The insurgents replied to the consul (through the intermediary) that they were sorry, but they had already eaten the goats.[53]

Two principal bands had emerged: that of Ḥasan al-Kharrâṭ, mostly in the eastern Ghûṭa, and that of the ʿAkâsh brothers from Dummar in the Baradâ River valley, northwest of the city. As the fifty-year-old night watchman of al-Shâghûr quarter, Kharrâṭ knew the city and its environs well. Al-Shâghûr was a quarter dominated by the Bakrî family, and Kharrâṭ had close ties to the family and especially the brothers Nasîb and Fawzî. According to Sa'îd al-'Âṣ, Kharrâṭ's band was formed under Nasîb al-Bakrî's urging after the meetings of August with Dr. Shahbandar at the house of 'Uthmân al-Sharâbâtî. In his telling, Kharrâṭ was practically a Bakrî family employee and served as their link to, and enforcer in, the quarter of al-Shâghûr. Kharrâṭ was in an ideal position to form a band. With a local following of young men, notoriety outside the quarter, good connections, and a reputation for toughness, Kharrâṭ and his men operated very effectively. Kharrâṭ formed a partnership with a Damascene Ṣûfî shaykh, Muḥammad al-Ḥijâz; al-'Âṣ claimed that they brought a distinct tinge of Islamic crusade to the band, which he did not approve of.[54]

No one claimed influence over the 'Akâsh brothers' band. Indeed, with a strong scent of criminality emanating from their band, they are practically absent from the Syrian sources. Contemporary European sources, however, particularly intelligence reports, attest to their astonishing effectiveness. Sa'îd 'Akâsh was the leader of the band, which operated out of their village of Dummar just outside Damascus in the Baradâ River valley. They hid in caves along the sides of Jabal Qâsyûn (above Damascus) and above the valley, from which they attacked trains and automobiles passing through the valley on the Beirut auto road and railroad. By mid-October mandate authorities had accused them of killing a gendarme, wounding the *mukhtâr* of their village, killing at least one of their fellow residents in Dummar, and pillaging any number of automobiles on the Beirut-Damascus road, sometimes killing the occupants. They would later manage to destroy train lines and mount attacks on trains.[55] It is also notable that while Ḥasan al-Kharrâṭ and his son Fakhrî died martyrs and were thus easily eulogized (their faults and sometimes not very patriotic behavior forgotten), most members of the equally humble 'Akâsh family survived the revolt to cause even more trouble in their native Dummar. While Sa'îd al-'Âṣ found Ḥasan Kharrâṭ's Islamic fervor troubling, the 'Akâsh brothers and their friends seem to have identified with a much smaller community; they fought for Dummar.[56]

As pressure built on the French forces inside Damascus, military reaction ratcheted up from the comically ineffectual to the staggeringly brutal. Mandate forces tried to deal with Kharrâṭ first. On 12 October a strong force supported by aircraft, tanks, and artillery moved into the Ghûṭa with a plan to encircle the rebels in the region of al-Zûr, which was a heavily wooded area along the river in the eastern Ghûṭa. Peasants from al-Malayḥa warned the insurgents of the approach of the French column. The French first pursued Kharrâṭ's band along the banks of the river; though they drew continuous sniper fire, they were unable to bring any rebels into the open. In frustration, they backtracked to the village of al-Malayḥa, which they looted and burned. The justification for this, intelligence claimed, was that a small boy of the village had alerted the insurgents of the visit of French troops a week earlier.[57] The complicity of the villagers had thus facilitated the capture and humiliation of the earlier French force.

The French then marched to the village of Jaramânâ, which they also looted and burned, though aerial and artillery bombardment had mostly destroyed it already. Although they never engaged Kharrâṭ's band in the open, troops executed nearly a hundred villagers in the Ghûṭa, many of them in their fields and orchards. Mandate soldiers brought their corpses to Damascus as trophies, and they brought a number of prisoners as well. Some of the young male prisoners were publicly shot in Marja Square, the central square of Damascus. Mandate authorities left sixteen mutilated corpses on display in a row for most of the rest of the day. The dead were "brigands," and the demolished villages where they had lived were destroyed for the crime of harboring brigands. French troops openly sold their plundered loot in the bazaars.[58]

Anonymous Syrians avenged the killings and the spectacle in Marja Square a few days later. The government newspaper *La Syrie* had called the display of dead villagers a "splendid hunting score," but the next morning the mutilated bodies of twelve Circassian soldiers appeared outside Bâb Sharqî, the eastern gate to the old city and entry from the eastern Ghûṭa.[59] Meanwhile Nasîb al-Bakrî was organizing insurgents inside and outside Damascus for a much bigger attack. He planned the infiltration of Damascus and the capture of the massive Ayyubid citadel at the western end of the old city. French military forces and artillery batteries were concentrated at Fort Gourard, in the northern suburb of al-Ṣâliḥiyya, and at the citadel. Insurgents also learned that General Sarrail would be lodging at the high commissioner's residence in the old city, at the eighteenth-century house of Damascus' most famous family, the ʿAẓm Palace. The French government had acquired the house for use as the Institut Français d'Art et d'Archéologie Musulman. A modern apartment was built for use of the high commissioner. The rebels wanted to capture Sarrail and knew that he would be there on the nights of 17 and 18 October. Nasîb al-Bakrî formulated the plan and wrote to Sulṭân al-Aṭrash, seeking his help. Aṭrash wrote back to say that he was busy with operations in the Ḥawrân but that the whole of his force would come as soon as possible and told Bakrî to wait for them at their base at the house of the prominent grain merchant family al-Mahâynî in the Damascus neighborhood of Maydân. The letter was delayed, and Bakrî did not wait for the reply. Fawzî al-Qâwuqjî and Ramadân Shallâsh were on their way from east of Ḥamâh too. Neither they nor the Druze force arrived in time.

Nasîb al-Bakrî decided there was no time to wait. He had two groups of insurgents, Kharrâṭ's band and a mixed band made up of Druze and men from Maydân and Ghûṭa. The Druze were particularly anxious to avenge the outrage of Jaramânâ.[60] They assembled at the al-Mahâynî house. On the morning of Sunday, 18 October, forty men with Ḥasan al-Kharrâṭ entered the city from the cemetery just outside the southern city walls into al-Shâghûr quarter through the Bâb al-Saghîr, shouting: "The Banî Ma'rûf [Druze] have arrived!" The crowds in the streets greeted them with wild applause, and many joined them.[61] They disarmed and took over the police station in al-Shâghûr and proceeded north to the 'Aẓm Palace. Ramadân Shallâsh along with twenty bedouin arrived and came along. When they entered the 'Aẓm Palace, they found that Sarrail had already left for a journey to Ḥawrân and a meeting in Dar'â. They pillaged and burned part of the grand house in any case. Though it held no tactical importance, it certainly held symbolic importance as the historical seat of economic and political power in Damascus, now usurped by the French and totally undefended.

Meanwhile Nasîb al-Bakrî, his brothers, and 200 others worked their way up from Maydân, stopping along the way to murder a number of Armenian refugees in a camp in al-Qadam. The rebels claimed that the Armenians had taken part in the pillage of Ghûṭa villages as French armed irregulars. They entered the city hours later, at Bâb al-Jâbiyya, after proceeding through the quarters of Bâb Muṣallâ and al-Qanawât, outside the city walls. In each neighborhood they disarmed and pillaged the police stations and increased in number, as Damascenes joined them.

The police and gendarmes laid down their weapons and abandoned their posts in all the neighborhoods of Damascus. Insurgents roamed the city at will. They occupied the city without serious opposition. The French military had ceased foot patrols and sent only armored vehicles, firing randomly, into the quarters. Rebels shouted the Islamic statement of faith and various religious slogans, along with "the Banî Ma'rûf are coming!"[62] Residents in all the quarters built barricades from torn-up paving stones and fed and encouraged the insurgents. Muslim *qabaḍâyât* (quarter youth gang leaders) went to the Christian and Jewish quarters to insure that rebels and rioters left residents unmolested. "These Moslem interventions assured the Christian quarters against pillage. In other words it was Islam and not the 'Protectrice des Chrétiens en Orient' which protected the Christians in those critical days," wrote the British consul in Damascus.[63]

FIGURE 5. Damascus under bombardment. Courtesy Archives du Ministère des Affaires Etrangères—Paris, Fonds iconographique.

The mandate authority had decided on its response before the uprising had begun; and when Sarrail returned from the Ḥawrân that afternoon, he merely approved the plan to shell and bomb the city before departing for Beirut.[64] The bombardment of the city began at around five o'clock on Sunday afternoon. The authority gave no warning to anyone and withdrew the few remaining mandate troops immediately before the shelling began. At first they fired blank shells; but at some point they switched to live ammunition and shelled every quarter where insurgents had been reported.

The bombardment lasted two full days. Entire quarters of Damascus were flattened. Nearly 1,500 were killed.[65] When the insurgents left on Tuesday morning, several Damascene notables immediately contacted the French command, securing a promise to end the bombardment that afternoon. General Gamelin held a meeting with them after the bombardment ceased. Amîr Saʿîd al-Jazâʾirî led the notable delegation, composed of Shaykh Muḥammad Taj al-Dîn al-Ḥasanî (a prominent Damascene cleric) and members of the al-ʿAẓm family and the al-Muʾayyad al-ʿAẓm branch of the same family. Gamelin first demanded 200,000 Turkish gold lira, quickly reduced to 100,000, and 3,000 rifles.[66] Members of the delegation disavowed responsibility for the uprising; but after lengthy negotiation—or "discussions" as French intelligence termed them—they approved the measures, subject to the acceptance of the population. The fine was due on Saturday, 24 October; otherwise the bombardment would resume.[67] The mandate command, probably under orders from Paris, realized that it could not resume bombardment; and eventually the state's puppet government, led by Ṣubḥî Barakât, paid the fine.

Sa'îd al-Jazâ'irî, who led the delegation, was a grandson of Amîr 'Abd al-Qâdir al-Jazâ'irî, the exiled leader of opposition to the French colonization of Algeria. The Jazâ'irî family, along with hundreds of friends and retainers, entered comfortable exile in Damascus in 1856, supported in part by a large French subsidy. Hundreds and perhaps thousands of Algerian refugee followers of the *amîr* were settled in villages granted to him by the Ottoman state in Ḥawrân and what became the British mandated state of Palestine. 'Abd al-Qâdir won further fame as the protector of Damascene Christians during the riots of 1860. His grandson Amîr Sa'îd evidently tried to play this role during the uprising in Damascus in October 1925, after French troops withdrew. He went to the Christian quarter in Bâb Tûmâ, where he first made contact with the European consulates and then situated his followers in prominent places to help protect the Christians from attack.

By the 1920s the Jazâ'irîs had long been one of the wealthiest families in Damascus. They had extensive agricultural holdings in villages throughout southern Syria, including the regions under British mandate.[68] They had been involved in the Ḥawrân for years and had negotiated with the Druze, the bedouin, and the Europeans on behalf of the Ottoman government at various times during the late nineteenth and early twentieth century. Amîr Sa'îd was born in 1881 and educated at Maktab 'Anbar (Damascus' elite preparatory school) and later in the Galatasaray school (Mekteb-i Sultanî) in Istanbul. He was ambitious and had worked hard to further his goals since the Ottoman withdrawal from Damascus, when the departing authorities left him in charge of public order. He appointed himself president of the Syrian Arab government; and when Amîr Fayṣal arrived, he went into opposition. The British, supporting their client Fayṣal, helpfully exiled Amîr Sa'îd to Palestine. When the French exiled Fayṣal in 1920, Amîr Sa'îd came back. During the revolt of 1925, he maintained relations with the French, the British, and the insurgents. According to British consul Smart, Amîr Sa'îd had casually offered his services as prince of a united Palestine and Transjordan in the spring of 1925, since, in his words, King 'Abdallâh's incompetence was plain to see. Like many, he expected the revolt to expel the French from Syria, and he thought that Britain would step in.[69] His close relations with the British evidently paid off modestly: when the French jailed his cousin Amîr Ṭâhir (the famous shaykh and Arabist) immediately after the uprising in Damascus, British intervention got him released. Still, no one suggested that Amîr

Saʿîd, his cousin Ṭâhir, or any other members of Damascus' landowning elite, with the exception of Nasîb al-Bakrî, had participated in the uprising in any significant way.

The attack on Damascus had failed to dislodge the mandate power. Two days later, on 22 October, mandate authorities captured and eventually executed Fakhrî Ibn Ḥasan al-Kharrâṭ. They transcribed a ten-page interrogation, in French translation, before his death. The issue of waiting for more rebel fighters was contentious and clearly hotly argued at the time, particularly after the failure of the attack on Damascus and the apportionment of blame. Fakhrî al-Kharrâṭ claimed confusedly that the Druze who were already with them brought news that Sulṭân al-Aṭrash and a large force would soon join them. The following day Nasîb al-Bakrî told Fakhrî's father, Ḥasan al-Kharrâṭ, that he had received a letter from some unnamed Druze of the Jabal, refusing to come and join them. Fakhrî al-Kharrâṭ reported immediately thereafter that Nasîb and his father decided not to wait for Sulṭân al-Aṭrash. It bears mention that this was an interrogation transcript, translated from one language to another, and probably extracted under torture or at least threat of torture.[70]

Surviving insurgents criticized Nasîb al Bakrî's role in the attack. Saʿîd al-ʿÂṣ bitterly denounced him for not waiting when he knew that Sulṭân al-Aṭrash's force was coming and for trying to take Damascus with tiny, poorly coordinated forces without a clear plan. Al-ʿÂṣ claimed that Nasîb wanted the glory for himself and decried the folly of trying to take Damascus with 250 men. The British consul documented that the Druze band, numbering at least 1,000, eventually showed up under the command of Zayd al-Aṭrash, Sulṭân's brother.[71]

Damascus had finally risen. Its rallying cry was not the eloquent and impassioned appeals of its nationalist politicians, but the surprising call of ordinary Muslim Damascenes, "The Druze are coming!" Damascus' nationalist leadership had not inspired or led the uprising. Many of the nationalist elite had been forced to flee the city in any case. The city's traditional notable leadership and the members of its great families disavowed any role or responsibility for the uprising and were concerned with ensuring the security of their property against marauding rioters and later from French bombardment. Only a few of Damascus' leading citizens—mostly grain merchants from Maydân, and only one from the higher reaches of Damascene society (Nasîb al-Bakrî)—were directly involved in the uprising in Damascus. The major grain merchant family al-Mahâynî played a central role in facilitating the revolt by providing a meeting place and entry into Damascus from Maydân. Even they eventually begged the insurgents to leave before the French destroyed the city. The Mahâynîs were different from other Damascene notable families, however, in that their wealth was based almost entirely on the grain trade in Ḥawrân and not on the ownership of land. They were also unusual in that they exercised their considerable local power primarily in their quarter, Maydân (which they dominated, together with the grain merchant Sukkar family), and not in city or nationalist politics more generally.[72] Ṣubḥî al-Mahâynî and 'Abd al-Qâdir Sukkar would both lead bands of insurgents in the Ghûṭa and in the city itself in the following months. The uprising had spread throughout southern Syria.

CHAPTER 6

The Politics of Rebellion

> The strength of the movement is in the middle and lower classes, who, indeed, reproach the notables for their lack of co-operation . . . What constitutes the difficulties at Damascus is universal popular support for the rebels . . . The guerrilla [war] in the city is rendered possible by the universal complicity of the humbler inhabitants, who are not far from regarding the rebels as heroes. My barber, for instance, did not hesitate to compare them to "Antar," the hero of popular Arab legend, much to [his] disadvantage, who, he pointed out, never had to fight against artillery, tanks and aeroplanes.[1]

The bombardment of Damascus changed the direction of the uprising. The nationalist leadership of Damascus had fled abroad or to Jabal Ḥawrân. Some were in jail. Impassioned and artful appeals to patriotism and nationalism nailed to shop doors and passed from hand to hand in the bazaar stopped too. Still, the insurgency expanded every day in the region surrounding Damascus. Intelligence records show that thousands of Syrian men and women took part in the revolt during these months. The documents of their enemies are the best and in some cases the only written record of their actions. Many of their names are recorded nowhere else. This chapter reads these records backward, in direct contradiction to what mandate chroniclers intended, to uncover the consciousness of the mandate's enemies in its own records. And while there is a collective consciousness hidden in negative relief in the records of resistance and suppression, these same traces show that the elements that made up this collective consciousness differed from region to region and from person to person.

The mandate authorities collected letters and directives passed between rebels and between other Syrian citizens. The letters speak in the name of the Syrian Arab nation and deal with matters both patriotic and venal. Memoir accounts also add to the composite picture of an insurgent consciousness and emerging national identity, made up of sometimes wildly disparate and seemingly inconsistent elements. This inconsistency could be a source of strength for the insurgents, however; because while rebels agreed on common membership in a Syrian national community, they remained free to articulate and imagine independently what membership meant. The debates over the membership and meaning of national community were contentious. Some insurgents argued that the evolving nation should be secular and nonsectarian, while others argued for Islamic symbols of identity that excluded minorities. In this chapter I have not tried to impose order and consistency where little was evident. Instead, I have tried to let these fragmentary sources speak to demonstrate the uncompromised vitality of a subaltern nationalist insurgency.

France continued to fight the rebellion on a variety of fronts. The bombardment of Damascus and the resulting international outcry led to a shakeup in Paris and the recall and replacement of General Sarrail. His successor was Henry de Jouvenel, a prominent journalist and the first civilian high commissioner of the mandate. Meanwhile French intelligence officers carefully recorded all ongoing rebel activity—while doggedly arguing that all resistance was the work of bandits and outlaws. Disturbances were also blamed on a variety of outside elements, since French political leaders wished to avoid acknowledging the tremendous opposition to French rule among ordinary Syrians.

Mandate forces continued to bomb and shell numerous villages, neighborhoods, and suburbs in the region of Damascus. Typically troops and armored vehicles entered only after intensive bombardment. Having learned the lesson of late October, and the fate of General Sarrail, mandate forces avoided shelling the areas of Damascus where foreign embassies and missions resided. Christian villages in the mountains were compelled to swear allegiance to France and to accept weapons to fight against insurgents. Oaths of allegiance were solicited and received from major urban notables in Damascus and Ḥamâh and from leaders of the various bedouin tribes. French intelligence and political agents cultivated spies and politicians among the Syrian population in an endless search for "friends of France." Such people often made proclamations of undying loyalty to France and the colonial mission, which figured prominently in intelligence documents prepared for Paris and the new high commissioner, Henry de Jouvenel.

Despite months of agitation and countless pamphlets and proclamations, the French bombardment of Damascus ended any organized mobilization in the city. The city's destruction indelibly underscored the inability of the urban elite to lead resistance. But the effects of the bombardment were not what mandate authorities had hoped. Resistance shifted back to the Ghûṭa and the surrounding countryside. The destruction of their city failed to pacify the population with fear and led to an outraged expansion of rebel activity, especially among the more humble inhabitants. Guerrilla bands soon gained control of the countryside on all sides of the city. They continually cut the lines of communication by road, telephone, and train, on all sides of the city. Damascus went days on end virtually cut off from outside contact. Large areas of the old city were in rebel hands night after night. Contemporary sources document that the southern region was completely under the control of the insurgents. It took more than a year, and massive reinforcements of troops and equipment, for the mandatory power to regain effective control of the countryside of Damascus.

INSURGENTS IN THE COUNTRYSIDE OF DAMASCUS

On 2 November 1925 the Druze finally advanced on Damascus. Zayd al-Aṭrash, younger brother of Sulṭân, approached the city with at least 1,000 men. But before they arrived, ʿAbd al-Qâdir Sukkar and Ṣubḥî al-Mahâynî—two Maydân quarter leaders, grain merchants, and close associates of several Ḥawrân Druze shaykhs—went and advised them not to enter the ruined city but to carry the attack to mandate forces in the countryside. Both ʿAbd al-Qâdir Sukkar and Ṣubḥî al-Mahâynî had been in contact with the insurgents for weeks. Mahâynî had provided his house for a meeting point during the first foray into Damascus. Both soon organized bands to fight inside and outside the city; but days after the bombardment they spoke with an authority that the Ḥawrân Druze insurgents evidently respected: the cost of French vengeance was too high. Zayd al-Aṭrash replied that they would gladly fight in the open, and they left to attack French installations in the southern Anti-Lebanon mountains.[2]

By the end of the first week of November at least three or four major bands were active in the area around Damascus. Former army officers and Damascene quarter toughs led mixed bands of Ghûṭa villagers and city youth. Zayd al-Aṭrash and Muḥammad ʿIzz al-Dîn al-Ḥalabî led bands of Druze and demobilized soldiers and spoke for secular Syrian Arab nationalism. Ḥasan al-Kharrâṭ, former night watchman from al-Shâghûr quarter, led Damascene and Ghûṭa villagers and mixed popular religion and patriotic banditry. Ramaḍân Shallâsh led bedouin and mountain villagers and also mixed religion, patriotism, and banditry. The ʿAkâsh brothers' band dominated the Baradâ River gorge near their native Dummar and were principally interested in banditry. Apparently their enthusiasm for pillage sometimes attracted rebels from other bands to join them and leave their original comrades.[3] 'Abd al-Qâdir Sukkar, the Maydânî grain merchant who had urged the Druze to stay out of Damascus early in November, soon led a large band from his quarter.

'Abd al-Qâdir Sukkar was born in 1867 and was almost sixty years old in 1925. He was a legend in the quarter of Maydân. The Sukkar family had come to prominence in Maydân in the late nineteenth century due to its involvement in the Ḥawrân grain business. Sukkar had organized fighters for the battle of Maysalûn in 1920 and fed the poor in the quarter. Members of the family had served on the Ottoman *majlis al-baladî* (local council) but had not been considered part of the notable elite of Damascus. As in the case of the other grain merchant families, their educational and class background limited their political influence to Maydân.[4] 'Abd al-Qâdir and his younger brothers Muḥammad and Muṣṭafâ and various nephews and cousins, along with members of the grain merchant Mahâynî family, prevented the assertion of French control of the Maydân and the surrounding Ghûṭa into 1927. French forces eventually destroyed their quarter, and Sukkar and his brothers were in exile until the declaration of general amnesty in 1937.[5] Sukkar collaborated closely with the Druze and former officers and spoke with both religious and nationalist authority.

The bands' sphere of operations ranged from al-Nabk in the north along the Ḥumṣ road at the edge of the desert to the Ḥawrân in the south and the Anti-Lebanon mountains west of Damascus. Intelligence reports from early November 1925 show their activities in meticulous though often contradictory detail. The bands each had a village or quarter base, but they frequently joined forces for operations in neighboring areas. They funded their activities by levying men, weapons, and money from villages and landlords. French sources estimated 5,000 armed rebels in the countryside of Damascus.

Muḥammad 'Izz al-Dîn al-Ḥalabî, former Ottoman officer and Druze shaykh, led the largest and best-organized group in the Ghûṭa. 'Izz al-Dîn al-Ḥalabî enjoyed good relations with other graduates of the Ottoman Military College and former military officers such as Ramaḍân Shallâsh, Sa'îd al-'Âṣ, Fawzî al-Qâwuqjî, Zakî al-Durûbî, Zakî al-Ḥalabî, Yusûf al-Ḥayâtî, and many others. Sulṭân al-Aṭrash's twenty-year-old brother Zayd was often at his side. The Druze operated with men from Maydân under the command of 'Abd al-Qâdir Sukkar. Maydânîs in the grain business and Druze shaykhs of Jabal Ḥawrân cooperated closely and easily as they had during the Great War and for decades before. Mandate authorities collected a series of letters addressed to wealthy merchants of Maydân from late November and December.

FIGURE 6. Muḥammad ʿIzz al-Dîn al-Ḥalabî *(center)*, leading insurgents in the Ghûṭa. Courtesy Markaz al-Wathâʾiq al-Târîkhiyya.

The letters document efforts to levy support for the insurgency and the politics behind the revolt. They show that rebels also agreed conditionally on the meaning of Syrian Arab nationalism and on the goal of the armed struggle. In their letters, national survival and the immediate demands of waging war preempt carefully crafted arguments for independence. They assumed broad agreement on Syrian nationalism and patriotism, and the rebels did not see the need to defend or explain the existence of a national community requiring patriotic sacrifice. It is hard to imagine that such assumptions could have been made only ten years before in the midst of World War I.

The bombardment of Damascus ended direct elite engagement in the revolt. People's Party members who had drafted articulate appeals to patriotism and nationalism had fled. Most of the remaining members of the landowning and mercantile elite of Damascus were not interested in armed confrontation with France. The rebel leaders of the countryside continued to create documents, however, and they directly addressed the ideology of revolt and the lack of cooperation of wealthy Syrians. When ʿAbd al-Qâdir Sukkar wrote to his neighbors in Maydân demanding support, he knew the recipient of his letters. Letters differed substantially in tone, depending on whether they sought insurgent recruits from a humble village, material support from a merchant of Maydân, or vast sums of money from major landowners notoriously aligned with the mandate government. Intelligence officers usually received letters from addressees who petitioned the mandate power in vain for protection from insurgent demands. Villages and neighborhoods were sometimes split between those families that went over to the rebels and those families that aligned with the government. Even today Syrians continue to trace neighborhood and village feuds to the tumultuous months of 1925 and 1926.

To Sayyid Abû Tawfiq al-Ḥakîm and all members of his family:

Greetings.

You know that the question of the homeland is foremost for all, and its deliverance from the hands of the enemies will not be realized without money. After discussion with the shaykhs and amîrs, the Commander imposes on you a payment of 200 Turkish pounds, and warns you to pay promptly. Salutations to those who serve the cause of the Arab Nation.

22 November 1925
The Commander in Chief
'Abd al-Qâdir Sukkar[6]

Honored Notables of Maydân:

Greetings.

You are surely aware of the honorable goals for which the nationalist revolutionaries struggle. There is no other aim than to deliver the homeland from the yoke of tyranny and to imitate the history of our ancestors. The nationalist revolutionaries struggle heroically for the cause of Syria and to force the enemy's expulsion.

Despite repeated nationalist victories with the help of God, and despite your perfect familiarity with our struggle for the national cause, and the complete independence of Syria, we notice your negligence in assisting the nationalist mujâhidîn.

You have not contributed men or money. This makes us doubt the patriotism and the good faith of some among you. We call on you to show your good intentions, and present a positive example of the national cause to all the world, as did your ancestors.

Arab national zeal and your religious duties obligate you to unite with us and support us with your men and your finances. You must not allow the triumph of those who speak for the colonizers. No one else has the right to address the Syrian question on behalf of the Syrian Revolutionaries.

We ask that you send 1500–2000 ʿabâʾas *[cloaks], of the bedouin style, and funds to allow the purchase of rifles, cartridges, wheat, and barley. Do not delay.*

We send our salutations to all the world.

3 December 1925
Commander in Chief of the region of Ghûṭa, Muḥammad ʿIzz al-Dîn al-Ḥalabî, Mujâhidîn ʿAbd al-Qâdir Sukkar, and Muḥî al-Dîn Ḥabâb[7]

To Sayyid Abû Jamîl bin Ismâʿîl al-Aktaa [sic]:

Greetings.

You know well that the national cause cannot be realized without money. Consequently, the regional commander requests that you send 200 Turkish pounds, 10 ʿabâʾas *[cloaks], 2 German rifles, and two full cases of cartridges.*

Attention: we warn you, do not delay.

Salutations to all who serve the Syrian national cause.
4 December 1925
Commander ʿAbd al-Qâdir Sukkar[8]

Despite the claims of the French and the protests made by the recipients of such letters, the demands were not simple extortion. The writers of these letters believed in their uprising and quite clearly believed themselves to be at the forefront of a national struggle. Sukkar and ʿIzz al-Dîn al-Ḥalabî spoke for a subaltern national uprising, but they also invoked consultations with elite Syrians, in the form of shaykhs and *amîrs*. The letters repeat the assertion that the rebels possess the right to speak and act for the nation.

The guerrilla war required money and material assistance. The quarter's humble inhabitants provided foot soldiers, shelter, and intelligence. Wealthy notables were almost invariably called upon to provide Mauser rifles and bedouin clothing for the rebels. Mauser rifles, of German or Turkish licensed manufacture, were left over from the war and used smokeless powder and a bolt-action mechanism. The rebels had some similar rifles of British manufacture, also left over from the war. Older Ottoman Martini army rifles were

FIGURE 7. Rebels in Maydân *(front row, left to right):* ʿAbd al-Qâdir Sukkar, Saʿîd al-ʿÂṣ, Shaykh Muḥammad al-Ashmar. Courtesy Markaz al-Wathâʾiq al-Târîkhiyya.

widely used, but the rebels vastly favored the modern technology for its greater effectiveness. They carried swords and captured grenades and light machine guns from the French.

Rebel dress had important symbolic significance. The widespread adoption of rough traditional dress (typically of the style worn by bedouin and the rural Druze) and the total absence of elite Ottoman trappings (such as fezzes and frock coats among the rebels) indicate unambiguously the rural and non-elite character of the revolt. Nationalist intellectuals and elites like Dr. ʿAbd al-Raḥman al-Shahbandar and Nasîb al-Bakrî adopted bedouin headgear and cloaks when they were photographed among rebels of the countryside. The adoption of peasant and bedouin dress by elites represented a symbolically significant inversion of the status quo. The emphasis on traditional rural dress and the accompanying cultural and national symbolism was notable in later revolts against European rule too, including Palestine in 1936, which ultimately gave the Palestinian national movement its enduring symbol, the checkered *kûfiyya* head scarf.[9]

The aims of the insurgents were clear: the expulsion of France and the independence of Syria. Night after night they engaged mandate forces in battle in Maydân and the surrounding orchards and gardens. Entire villages were reported to have joined them for attacks, such as the attack on the night of 5 December when 2,000 rebels descended on the barracks at al-Qadam on the railroad south of Damascus. Khalîl Bassâlî, *mukhtâr* of the large village of Dâryâ, brought hundreds of men from his village to join a force described as Druze, bedouin, Damascenes, Maydânîs, and peasants from five listed villages. Leading the attack were Sukkar, ʿIzz al-Dîn al-Ḥalabî, Zayd al-Aṭrash, and Ḥasan al-Kharrâṭ. While intelligence reports claimed very large numbers of attackers, they also provided assured numbers of wounded and dead rebels. Reports indicated that each band miraculously had regained its former strength by the following night.[10]

The band of Jumʿa Sawsaq, a former *mukhtâr* from the Anti-Lebanon mountain village of Rankûs, ranged from the region of al-Nabk on the edge of the desert to around Rankûs and south to Zabadânî. He was accompanied by his friend Ramaḍân Shallâsh, bedouin horsemen, and local peasants in numbers reported to range from 600 up to 1,000 men, some of whom did not have rifles. In early November Sawsaq and Shallâsh began to call themselves (with sanction from Sulṭân al-Aṭrash) joint commanders of a unit of the National Army. The French viewed this development with horror, since, as an intelligence officer noted, it was likely to "attract young nationalists, and xenophobic partisans of all classes. It is feared that this organization, if consolidated, would be reinforced and funded by foreign pan-Arab committees."[11]

A few days later intelligence officers reported that Ramaḍân Shallâsh and Jumʿa Sawsaq had visited a number of villages in the region of al-Nabk, in the mountains north of Damascus. Typically they arrived in secret at night, gathered some of the villagers, and captured and disarmed the local gendarmerie. After taking over a village and pillaging government offices, and perhaps the homes of pro-mandate villagers, Ramaḍân Shallâsh often spoke publicly in the center of the town. According to mandate intelligence, Shallâsh would call the villagers to arms by announcing that they were all engaged in a struggle like that of Ghazi Mustafa Kemal and telling the villagers that their village was like Ankara in 1920. This was apparently wildly popular among Muslim and Christian villagers.[12]

Mandate intelligence also collected and preserved Ramaḍân Shallâsh's letters. He wrote nearly daily demand letters to the *mukhtâr*s of various villages and to big landlords of the same regions. The letters differ dramatically based on their intended audience. Like the appeals of Fawzî al-Qâwuqjî in Ḥamâh, Shallâsh's appeal to villages mixed patriotism, popular religion, and tribal honor. When he wrote to landlords, he relied upon threats of violence.

To the mukhtârs *and shaykhs of the village of Quṭayfa,*

Greetings and blessings of God.

We need you to gather your mujâhidîn *and leave one part to guard your village from the [French] troops and bring the other part to Yabrûd tomorrow for the greater glory of the religion of Islam. If you bring them late, you will be responsible before God and before the partisans. If you do not respond to this appeal, and assemble [the* mujâhidîn*] today, we will come and take them tomorrow.*

14 October 1925
General Ramaḍân Shallâsh

To our brothers, the notables and the shaykhs of the village of Quṭayfa,

Greetings.

We have written previously to you on the subject of sending your mujâhidîn *to cooperate with your brothers the* mujâhidîn *of Jabal Qalamûn. But unfortunately we have not received a response from you.*

Brothers, if you are among those who wish to deliver the country from the yoke of the colonizers, and save the honor of the Arab nation, as well as the honor of its women, hasten to gather and send your mujahâdîn *to ʿAsâl al-Ward. If you do not intend to respond to this request, we will know.*

3 December 1925
Ramaḍân Shallâsh, Jumʿa Sawsaq[13]

Shallâsh used a different approach to Saʿîd Bey Shîshshaklî, principal landlord and notable of Dûmâ. The Shîshaklîs were the richest family in the fertile agricultural town of Dûmâ, and Saʿîd's son Wadîʿ had served in the French-sponsored administrative council since 1922.[14] Shallâsh wrote in the name of the Arab army and complained that earlier letters had been delivered to the "enemy of the nation," the French army—which, he pointed out, made Shîshaklî an enemy too. In consequence Shîshaklî now had a choice between the destruction of his house and the immediate payment of 250 gold pounds. Shîshaklî apparently did not pay the extortion demand; because a month later, on 29 November 1925, Shallâsh wrote again, this time demanding 2,000 Ottoman gold pounds. In his second letter Shallâsh dispensed with calls to national duty and utilized exclusively religious language, including a religious injunction: "God requires Muslims who follow Him and his Prophet to make *jihâd*, 'Undertake *jihâd* with your possessions and your person'; it follows then that you should conform to the requirements of God and that you should send 2,000 for the maintenance of the army of the *mujâhidîn*."[15] Shallâsh was more successful in his request to the village of Quṭayfa, since mandate intelligence noted that a number of village men soon joined him. He was also eventually accused by his fellow insurgents of criminal extortion against the *people* of Dûmâ, about which more will be said shortly.

Like other rebel leaders, Ramaḍân Shallâsh had a long history of militant resistance to the mandate. He was born in the region of Dayr al-Zûr along the Euphrates River in the late 1880s. He was the son of a locally influential bedouin chief from the Bûsarâya tribe, and while he was a teenager he traveled to Istanbul to attend the Tribal School.[16] Shallâsh later attended the Ottoman Military Academy, served in the Ottoman army in Libya and the Balkans, and joined the Arab Revolt with Amîr Fayṣal in 1917. He fought alongside Ibrâhîm Hanânû against the French in the early 1920s. The mandate power had condemned him in absentia, and he had been living in exile in Transjordan. Shallâsh had long been friends with Muḥammad ʿIzz al-Dîn al-Ḥalabî, ʿAlî Fâris al-Aṭrash, Saʿîd al-ʿÂṣ, Fawzî al-Qâwuqjî, and other former Ottoman officers among the insurgent leadership. He had come from Transjordan to Jabal Ḥawrân early in September 1925, accompanied by a small number of armed horsemen.

Other bands were active all over the region of Damascus. Ḥasan al-Kharrâṭ operated in the Ghûṭa and relatively close to his base in the al-Shâghûr quarter. Kharrâṭ was active in the eastern Ghûṭa, especially in the heavily wooded marshland of al-Zûr. He and his band made many forays into Damascus itself under cover of night. During one of these nighttime raids, shortly after the bombardment of Damascus, mandate forces captured Kharrâṭ's son, Fakhrî al-Kharrâṭ. They promised to spare his life if Ḥasan would surrender; but he refused, and Fakhrî al-Kharrâṭ was publicly executed in Marja Square early in 1926.[17]

Ḥasan al-Kharrâṭ also signed demand letters to prominent Syrians. Unlike the others, however, several of his original letters were preserved. The wide variations in the handwriting of Kharrâṭ's letters indicate that he dictated them and suggest he was probably illiterate. Kharrâṭ did not let his modest background and educational attainments stand in the way of his political agitation, and he communicated to newspapers and posted open letters to the Syrian population. In the letter that follows he calls for a general strike but also issues a blood-chilling and prescient threat to Damascene elites. No one, he states categorically, may associate with Jouvenel or negotiate with French authorities on behalf of the rebels. All the insurgent leaders clearly dreaded betrayal and marginalization by Syrian elites, fearing that the elites would force them into exile, or capture, in collaboration with the mandate authority. Kharrâṭ and his comrades recognized and intended that the popular mobilization and armed revolt should present a threat both to the mandate power and to Syria's elite politicians. Their fears turned out to be well founded, though Kharrâṭ was killed rather than captured or exiled. He remains a folk hero in Damascus today.

To all the Population of Syria:

The French High Commissioner will arrive shortly in Syria and visit Damascus. All inhabitants must, as a sign of protest against French colonialism, abstain from associating with him, and not engage in talks with him, so that he knows that the French Government is totally unacceptable to us, and so that they will leave this country and leave us to govern ourselves.

Anyone who disregards this directive will be severely punished, and his house will be destroyed. We have Damascus under surveillance in order to reveal those who do not conform to this directive.

5 December 1925

Commander of mujâhidîn of Ghûṭa — *Ḥasan al-Kharrâṭ*

Shaykh of Islam — *Muḥammad Ḥijâzî Kilânî*[18]

Shortly before his death on 25 December Kharrâṭ dictated demands to a prominent Greek Orthodox Christian of Damascus, Amîn Mamlûk. Kharrâṭ's letter begins by assuring Mamlûk that the letter pertains to matters patriotic and has nothing to do with religion. He then immediately demands 800 Ottoman gold pounds within twenty-four hours or, as a substitute, fifty rifles with ammunition and thirty Christian men under arms. Kharrâṭ evidently expected the demand for men and weapons to be taken seriously, because he goes on to list qualifications for the men. They must be from the Patriarchate, which is to say they must be Greek Orthodox. Further, Kharrâṭ lists the neighborhoods from which they may come. "Reassure their families that they will be safe [with us]," he says, "but if you fail to pay this levy, you and your family will be killed and your house destroyed." After details of proposed meetings and invocations of God and independence, he again reassures the addressee that this is not a matter of religion by stating that similar demands will be made of the Muslims and Jews. He signs as "the patriot Ḥasan al-Kharrâṭ."[19] The unmistakable impression is that Kharrâṭ sought men more than money and wanted to include Christians among his rebels.

This short letter challenges two central claims made by mandate chroniclers. It demonstrates, first, that—contrary to claims of sectarian fanaticism of Damascene Muslims against their Christian neighbors—even the uprising's most humble leaders attempted to expand the revolt to include Syria's non-Muslims and sought to appear even-handed toward them. It demonstrates, second, that—contrary to ceaseless mandate claims of banditry and pillage as the principal aim of the rebels—their primary aim, at least some of the time, was to further the albeit vaguely stated cause of the revolt itself. But some bands were more interested in pillage than patriotism.

Saʿîd ʿAkâsh and his band operated west of Damascus in the Baradâ River valley, winding up into the Anti-Lebanon mountains.[20] They menaced the train and auto route to Beirut with devastating and fearless effectiveness through 1925 and 1926. They apparently did not much differentiate among French soldiers, European civilians, wealthy Syrian merchants, and certain rival bands, attacking and robbing all with equal enthusiasm. They took part in some of the operations in the Ghûṭa as well. Saʿîd ʿAkâsh's younger brothers, Aḥmad and ʿAbdû, sometimes seem to have cooperated with other bands for individual attacks; but the ʿAkâsh were generally characterized by fierce independence and lawlessness. In late 1925 ʿAbdû ʿAkâsh killed the insurgent leader of the Kurdish al-Ṣâliḥiyya band, Aḥmad al-Malaʾ al-Kurdî. Kurdish rebels soon retaliated and killed ʿAbdû in the Wâdî Baradâ village of Qudsiyyâ.

The feud between the Kurds and the ʿAkâsh threatened to do serious harm to the revolt; early in 1926 insurgent leader Abû ʿUmar Dibû Aghâ from the Ghûṭa village of Ḥarastâ convened a truce between the two warring parties. The truce, however, did not hold; and they continued to kill each other more fervently than they killed mandate soldiers. Saʿîd ʿAkâsh was in exile under death sentence until the late 1930s, and he was continually passed over for amnesty, since the mandate government claimed that he was a common criminal and murderer. Saʿîd, Muḥammad, and ʿAbdallâh ʿAkâsh were members of two tiny groups denied amnesty in the final amnesty decree of 1937. The first group, which included Fawzî al-Qâwuqjî and six others, was permanently condemned for political crimes. The second group, which included the three ʿAkâsh brothers and four others, was permanently condemned for common-law crimes. Shortly after he finally returned to Damascus in 1941, Saʿîd ʿAkâsh was assassinated by a Kurd named Marʿaî al-Bârâfî in the vegetable market adjoining Marja Square in central Damascus.[21]

In addition to Ghûṭa and mountain villagers, large groups of bedouin frequently joined one band or another and appear in intelligence reports. The bedouin were often under the command of Ramaḍân Shallâsh.[22] He was sometimes joined by his friend, "le Capitaine déserteur," Fawzî al-Qâwuqjî. They were usually accompanied by other men from the region of al-Nabk, including Khalâṣ al-Naḥîr, Khâlid al-Nafawrî, and Tawfîq al-Ḥaydar, a younger brother of Sa'îd al-Ḥaydar, a member of Dr. Shahbandar's Ḥizb al-Sha'b. Sa'îd al-Ḥaydar had gone to prison in 1922 with Shahbandar and fled to the Jabal Druze with him early in the revolt.[23] These men appear repeatedly in the reports and clearly cooperated with any number of other rebels in nearly every region.[24]

The insurgents, with limited outside supplies, lived off the land and took from villagers and quarter dwellers what they needed for sustenance. They called their levies revolt taxes. French sources inevitably called such levies pillage. Typically the rebels demanded recruits, guns, cloaks, food, or gold. As the letters above illustrate, the notion of pillage does not begin to explain the range of these activities. In the first place, villagers often willingly supported the rebellion as their resources allowed, including passing intelligence to insurgents, housing them, feeding them, actively spreading disinformation about the rebels, and finally simply joining their ranks. In the second place, many of the most serious examples of pillage and property destruction involved French troops and not rebels. Insurgents extorted money, supplies, and involuntary recruits from uncooperative villages; French forces indiscriminately pillaged and razed villages and shot inhabitants who were perceived to oppose mandate rule—even if their only crime was refusal to pay taxes or the suspicion that they had harbored rebels, voluntarily or involuntarily.[25] Finally, in the Ghûṭa and the regions north of Damascus in the mountains on the way to Ḥumṣ there was no government presence from November 1925 until the following summer. In regions where there was little government presence, mandate officials gave weapons to pro-mandate villagers in order to fight against the rebels. Rebel leaders knew of the policy and aimed to seize these weapons. Insurgents demanded vast quantities of weapons from the most humble villages. The mandate power armed Greek Catholic and Maronite peasants against their neighbors all over the Anti-Lebanon mountain range between Ḥumṣ and the border with Palestine.

One of these villages was Ma'alûlâ in the mountains north of Damascus. In November 1925 Ramaḍân Shallâsh wrote a letter to the inhabitants of Ma'alûlâ, demanding:

Ottoman gold pounds
140 rifles

10 cases of rifle cartridges
10 sacks of rice
100 sheep
5 revolvers
100 grenades
20 sacks of flour
20 sacks of cracked wheat
10 flasks of ?
5 mules[26]

Maʿalûlâ was and is a medium-sized village in an arid region, and these demands would have been wildly optimistic under normal circumstances. The village sits in a deep Y-shaped limestone gorge; and its buildings, churches, and mosques perch along the walls of the gorge in picturesque fashion. It is famous throughout Syria for the fact that its mixed Muslim and Christian villagers speak Aramaic and for its two early Christian monasteries, one of which, Mar Sirjûs, converted to Greek Catholicism in the eighteenth century. Maʿalûlâ suffered heavy insurgent demands, as many villagers went over to the rebellion and others, especially Uniate villagers, helplessly and futilely called on the French for protection.

The officer who reproduced this demand letter for mandate intelligence failed to explain why a village like Maʿalûlâ would be so prodigiously armed. Other sources, however, were more forthcoming. British consular reports from November 1925 indicate that French authorities had provided rifles and ammunition to Christian young men in a number of mountain villages. The acting British consul general in Beirut wrote of this policy: "At best it was a confession of weakness. It laid the mandatory Power open to the dangerous suggestion that, perhaps without realizing the consequences, they had encouraged not only civil but also religious war . . . it never occurred to anyone that the volunteers would be anything but Christians."[27] Other contemporary reports were less credulous about the ultimate intentions of France's policy of arming Christians and about French knowledge of the policy's possible consequences. The United States consul at Beirut likewise reported the wholesale arming of Christians, but he believed not only that mandate authorities understood the dangers of inciting one religious community against another but that they actively sought to exacerbate sectarian divisions.[28] Mandate authorities claimed that sectarian cleavages were endemic, and only France could protect the Christians of the East from the predations of their neighbors. Insurgent documents tell a more complicated story.

Christian villages often split between those who supported the revolt and those who supported the mandate. Sometimes villagers used the war between insurgents and the French to prosecute local feuds. In the final months of 1925 rebels called on and requested food from the Greek Catholic *mukhtâr* of the village of Ṣaydnâyâ. The *mukhtâr* protested that he could only feed ten and sent them to visit the mother superior of the Greek Orthodox convent that dominates Ṣaydnâyâ. She offered to feed them all and undertook a collection from the village so that any rebels who appeared could be fed once each week. Elderly villagers remember collecting and herding sheep for the weekly collection.[29] It seems likely that the collection was not totally voluntary and may have exacerbated divisions between Orthodox and Catholic villagers over the revolt. Many elderly Syrians have reported that Orthodox Christians were generally more supportive of the revolt and the nationalist program, while Catholic Christians were generally more supportive of the French government.

After the end of the revolt in Ṣaydnâyâ in 1928, and months after the mandate government reasserted control of the region, members of the Greek Catholic al-Aḥmar family killed a member of the Greek Orthodox al-Naddâf family. The families were two of the largest and most prominent in the village. A lengthy file found its way into the mandate archives in connection with the case, including arrest warrants, legal briefs, and requests for amnesty. In 1928 and 1929 Tawfîq and Ibrâhîm b. Ilyâs al-Aḥmar, Niqûlâ b. Buṭrus al-Aḥmar, and Mûsâ b. ʿAbduh al-Aḥmar were tried and sentenced to five years at hard labor for the revenge murder of an unspecified member of the Naddâf family. The court stated that the murder was in retaliation for an act of arson committed by the Naddâf family against Aḥmar family property during the revolt.[30]

Today elderly villagers remember the incident differently. Both families were large and rich; but while the Naddâf family was popular and well regarded, the Aḥmar family was disliked and resented for its wealth and arrogance. Members of the Naddâf family joined the rebellion and were active in the region. The Aḥmar family was aligned with the French and reported Naddâf rebel activities to the mandate authorities. The revolt was widely popular in Ṣaydnâyâ, and the Aḥmar family became increasingly unpopular for its position. During the revolt, a member of the Naddâf family killed at least one member of the Aḥmar family, reportedly in retaliation for collaboration with French agents. After the reassertion of mandate control over the region in 1928, the killing was avenged by an Aḥmar. A trial and sentencing of the Aḥmar family members took place.[31]

In 1930 an attorney for the Aḥmar family filed a request for amnesty for the Aḥmars still in prison. The attorney, Elias Namour, stated that during the revolt Ṣaydnâyâ had been isolated from government control. He claimed that during this time members of the Naddâf family, taking advantage of the disorder and in league with the insurgents, killed a member of the Aḥmar family. The lawyer contended that, although the revenge against the Naddâf family was the work of only one unspecified member of the Aḥmar family, the Naddâf family sought charges against fourteen Aḥmar family members. Meanwhile the original Naddâf assassin had supposedly emigrated to America.[32]

The court record is obviously fragmentary and incomplete. The court claimed that the original crime during the revolt was arson, while the lawyer and living memory claimed it was murder. The only views represented are those of the mandate government and those of the lawyer for one of the parties. Members of the Naddâf family, and the insurgents they were said to have joined, are silent in the written record. All of those concerned, including the lawyer, were Christians. The case illustrates vividly how villagers harnessed local concerns to the power shifts of resistance and the reassertion of mandate control. It is impossible to say whether members of the Naddâf family were enthusiastic nationalist insurgents or opportunistic criminals, to mention two apparent, but perhaps not actual, extremes. It is of course likely that members of the Naddâf family encompassed all the variations between these two extremes, as they lived in a changing local environment, just as their village rivals, the Aḥmar family, exploited power shifts with more or less conviction to adapt themselves to life in Ṣaydnâyâ under nominal insurgent or nominal French control.

Rebel leaders recognized that the revolt's success depended on Syria's villagers. Sulṭân al-Aṭrash and others among the leadership made efforts to calm fears and reassure terrified villagers that injustices brought in the name of the revolt would not be tolerated. Ramaḍân Shallâsh, to name one rebel leader, was eventually tried by his rebellious peers for victimizing villagers. His guilt or innocence remains obscure, but the actions of the insurgents underscore the fact that the meaning of patriotism and resistance was a source of contention. While the crimes of French forces were invariably worse, revolt leaders could neither afford to allow crimes in the name of the revolt to go unpunished nor impose much order and discipline on the insurgency. Every leader claimed to be a general commander, and patriotism and plunder often went together.

Villagers of Ghûṭa and Marj:

Greetings and God's blessings upon you.

You know from our written manifestos that our revolution is a national movement for a sacred cause: the liberation of our cherished homeland from the clutches of the enemy colonizer.

We have learned that some have not maintained proper behavior, and have come to your villages demanding money in the name of the revolution and under the pretext of our movement.

We want you to know that all rebels who have come into your homes to pillage or to demand money in the name of the revolution will be tried and severely punished.

We have charged our police officers, Salîm Bek al-Ḥalabî and Ḥusnî Bek Ṣakhr, with the execution of these orders. They will watch over security in the villages, and as you have requested, they will protect you from those who have abused you. They will see that they are punished.

We ask that you persevere in your conduct, which we note with great pride, and know that there is certain victory for the revolutionaries and for our country.

Sulṭân al-Aṭrash[33]

ELITE POLITICS AND MANDATE COUNTERINSURGENCY

European opinion was highly critical of the French bombardment of Damascus in late October. The French Senate recalled high commissioner General Sarrail on 30 October. While foreign observers criticized the shelling of Damascus, they were unaware of or unconcerned with the continuous bombardment of the surrounding countryside. As Philip Khoury notes, critics claimed that the French overreacted relative to the threat that the insurgents posed to the mandate. The same critics failed to question the right of the mandatory power to use such force.[34] The harshest foreign criticism of the bombardment appeared in the *Times* of London.[35] The *Times* article was damning and provoked diplomatic protest in Damascus and Paris. Despite the outcry, the article concentrated on damage to property and ancient monuments, with less regard for loss of life and no attention at all to the grievances of the insurgents. British consul Smart played a double game: he obviously gave the *Times* correspondent extensive information and access, while claiming in his reports that he urged moderation and restraint from "excessive indictments," sure to annoy the French and encourage rebellion.[36] European critics consistently pointed to the low level of rebel organization and coordination; though

French public sources echoed this contention, French intelligence and the documents of the rebels themselves tell a different story.

Sarrail entered retirement in Paris in disgrace and died shortly thereafter. The job of defending his role was left to his personal secretary, who penned a fierce rebuttal to Sarrail's right-wing critics. Sarrail's successor as high commissioner, Henry de Jouvenel, arrived in Beirut in early December. Jouvenel began issuing press statements before his arrival. He indicated his willingness to hold peace talks with Syrian nationalists, subject to certain conditions, and his willingness to consider amnesty of the rebels. In addition to peace talks, Jouvenel promised "war for those who wish war."[37] Jouvenel's statements provoked immediate response in Syria. Ḥasan al-Kharrâṭ's warning has been discussed above, but mandate intelligence recorded other, more equivocal responses as well.

Ṣubḥî Barakât, president of Syria's puppet government, quickly proclaimed his loyalty to the new high commissioner. In a daily report also matter-of-factly chronicling the aerial and artillery bombardment of several Syrian villages, including lists of those wounded and killed and houses destroyed, Ṣubhî Bek exclaimed: "My convictions are unshakable; all the French in Syria are my friends . ."[38] Even mandate authorities realized that such sycophancy lent credibility to the rebels; and in keeping with Jouvenel's new policy, intelligence officers went to some trouble to cultivate and determine the opinion of "moderate" nationalists among elite Syrians. A lengthy survey on elite opinion in the wake of Jouvenel's declarations made its way into the archives.

Mandate intelligence noted that elite Damascenes were generally unsympathetic to the rebellion. The young, particularly former and current law students, were an exception, however. Legal students, who were lumped among the "nationalistes extrémistes," included several young men from very prominent Damascene families. They were, according to the survey, "unable to contain their enthusiasm and were imbued with ideas of revolution and independence," which they considered part of a worldwide struggle against European colonialism.[39] They sent letters to newspapers and sympathetic political organization in Europe, and eventually several young lawyers joined the rebels in the Ghûṭa.[40]

The report listed notables, merchants, intellectuals, and landowners among the "moderate nationalists." Such people viewed the new high commissioner with reservations and noted that proclamations did not constitute promises, which, in any case, frequently had been broken in the past. The report claimed that "reasonable members of the nation, particularly big merchants and landowners of all religions, believed that if France responds to the voice of the population without first suppressing the insurgents, the insurrection would increase with disastrous consequences for the influence and prestige of France."[41] The landowning notables clearly realized that they would share the disastrous consequences if mandate officials saw fit to negotiate directly with the insurgent leadership. Intelligence officers noted that marauding armed peasants frightened Syrian landlords more than the French army frightened them. Jouvenel, unlike Sarrail, recognized the basic convergence of interests between France and Syrian notables in pacifying the countryside.

Jouvenel shifted mandate policy immediately. He first issued an offer of amnesty, applicable only to rank-and-file rebels and thus calculated to separate the Ḥawrân Druze from their leaders. The amnesty was declared at short notice and could not possibly have reached all rebels before its expiration on 6 January. Rebel leaders were informed that if they surrendered during the amnesty they would remain liable for imprisonment but not execution. One week before the expiration of the amnesty French airplanes dropped thousands of leaflets signed by Jouvenel all over Ḥawrân. "Why do you continue to fight?" the leaflet asked. It vaguely promised the Druze a new constitution, self-rule, and the right to elect leaders. "The continuation of your struggle is against your hopes and against the liberty that have you fought for!" The leaflet blamed Sulṭân al-Aṭrash and his unnamed foreign supporters for all the suffering visited on Ḥawrân but exclaimed: "Only France can give you wheat, running water, roads, and the national liberty you desire."[42] A French officer confided to the British consul general at Beirut that the amnesty was not actually intended to lead to a truce but to create a favorable impression among Europeans before the real offensive began.[43] The amnesty led neither leaders nor anonymous rebels to surrender to the mandate power.

By the third week in December Jouvenel had asked for and received the resignation of Ṣubḥî Barakât's government and had made plans for the selection of a new moderate nationalist government. To this end agents had cultivated Shaykh Tâj al-Dîn al-Ḥasanî (son of Shaykh Badr al-Dîn al-Ḥasani, Damascus' leading Islamic scholar) and asked if he would be willing to form a government. On 15 December Jouvenel allowed a meeting of nationalist politicians, not directly involved in the revolt, to discuss and submit peace terms. The participants included some prominent moderately pro-French notables, but they also included Luṭfî al-Ḥaffâr and Fâris al-Khûrî, who were former members of the People's Party. The council forwarded to Jouvenel the following demands:

1. A general amnesty.

2. Unification of the country to include the whole of the present state of Syria, the territory of the Alawites, and the districts added to the prewar Lebanon to form the "Grand Liban," including Beirut and the other coastal towns. The prewar Lebanon would be excluded from this unification. The capital of united Syria would be Damascus.

3. National Supremacy, by which is meant that the native government should have real authority and no longer be a figurehead; that the French advisors should be confined to an advisory role and should not as now constitute virtually the Executive.

4. The election of a Constituent Assembly to frame the constitution of the new Syrian State.

5. A limitation of the period of the French mandate, on the analogy of Iraq.[44]

The demands had changed little since the beginning of the revolt; and despite Jouvenel's seemingly more receptive attitude, they remained totally unacceptable to mandate authorities. Two weeks later Jouvenel's candidate for president of Syria, Shaykh Tâj al-Dîn al-Ḥasanî, submitted a list of nearly identical demands as a starting point for the assembly of a new government. His list was no more acceptable than it had been when submitted earlier, and the mandate government resolved to wait for reinforcements in order to suppress the uprising by overwhelming military force. Events forestalled the cosmetic cover of a native government. Syrians and French alike resigned themselves to a bleak forecast of war.

MILITARY SUPPRESSION AND MANDATE COUNTERINSURGENCY

Daily bombing from the air continued. Towns and villages from Mount Lebanon east to the Anti-Lebanon range and south to the border with British-ruled Palestine experienced destruction from the air. The 1925 revolt was the first time in history that civilian populations were subjected to daily systematic aerial bombardment. Homeless, ruined villagers made motivated insurgents. By late December scores of villages in the area around Damascus had been bombed. Aerial bombardment was punishment for the crime or suspicion of harboring rebels.

A random report reads: "The aerial bombardment of the village of Madaya [Maḍâyâ] was conducted on 15 December with the following results: 6 dead, 2 injured, 30 houses seriously damaged."[45] Pro-French Damascus newspapers listed thirty villages damaged or destroyed, and the Syrian-Palestinian Executive Committee claimed that forty additional villages were bombed and not listed.[46] The village of Maḍâyâ, for example, was in the mountains west of Damascus near Zabadânî. The mandate census lists it as a large village of over 1,000 inhabitants in the late 1930s.[47] The British consul, returning from Beirut, spoke with the *qâ'immaqâm* (district head) of Zabadânî two days after the bombardment. The *qâ'immaqâm* reported that he had resigned in protest over what he described as the pointless destruction of Maḍâyâ, which was in his district. He reported eight dead and many wounded and claimed that the village was innocent and had only been involuntarily occupied by rebels overnight.[48]

Such attacks provided strong arguments for insurgents and strong incentive for revenge. Maḍâyâ was on the Damascus-Beirut train line, and French reports claimed that its train station had come under attack a few days earlier. Maḍâyâ was in the normal area of operations of the Sa'îd 'Akâsh band. But the attack on the train station was reportedly the work of Jum'a Sawsaq along with 500 men.[49] The bands were able to concentrate their attention on the region west of Damascus because the areas north of the capital, stretching toward the area of al-Nabk, had been securely under rebel control since early November 1925.[50]

The 'Akâsh band, however, was reported in the Ghûṭa along with Ramaḍân Shallâsh and Ḥasan al-Kharrâṭ. The same intelligence report confirmed that "a number of the inhabitants of the Ghûṭa are joining the bands, so that their effectiveness increases day by day." Meanwhile unnamed "bandits" in the area of Blûdân, near Maḍâyâ, probably part of the Jum'a Sawsaq band, cut the telegraph lines and attacked an armored train and a detachment of gendarmes sent to guard the repair of the line. Jum'a's brother Aḥmad Sawsaq was still in the region of al-Nabk, their apparently more normal area of operation. He was reported to have joined with Khâlid al-Nafawrî and Tawfîq al-Ḥaydar for an attack on the train station at al-Quṣayr, just south of Ḥumṣ on the Damascus rail line.[51]

The French were unable to counter this type of warfare. People the intelligence officers described as bandits and outlaws seem to have had nearly superhuman powers of organization and coordination. The only response was aerial bombardment. After airplanes bombed the villages, tanks and troops followed. By then, of course, most rebels were long gone; but the villages were usually far from abandoned, and there was no quarter for those who did not leave. An account by Foreign Legion soldier Bennett Doty, who deserted soon after, describes the scene:

> We took part in a pleasant little punitive expedition on our second day here [al-Qadam, just outside Damascus]. There was a small village about five kilometers away, on the railroad, and some of its inhabitants lately had taken to the amusement of sniping at the military trains as they passed. Several had been killed and several more wounded. The *caïd* had been ordered to produce the guilty. He had answered in the usual dilatory oriental manner. There had not been any shooting. If there had, he did not know who had done it. And anyway, he did not know where they were hiding; he could not produce them.[52]

This would have been in mid-October 1925 and could refer to any one of several villages destroyed in that month.[53] Doty goes on to describe machine-gunning the inhabitants who refused to flee the village, looting everything present, and burning the remains to the ground. He recounts that Colonel Andréa ordered the summary execution of all prisoners and any Syrian found with a firearm.[54] This was the campaign in the eastern Ghûṭa of late October, centering on Malayḥa (discussed in Chapter 5).

The Legionnaires later marched into the Maydân, the center of resistance in Damascus. French forces alternated between ignoring the quarter of Maydân completely and sending armored patrols to destroy some houses at random and then immediately leaving. Doty describes destroying inhabited houses in the Maydân with close-range tank and artillery fire in order to clear a safe path for troop movement. This was the beginning of Andréa's operation to create the Damascus ring road, which he started late in 1925 and finished in February. It was a fortified security cordon isolating the city from its outlying districts and countryside. The cordon cut the Maydân in half. Andréa was promoted to general in late December 1925 and was usually credited with crushing the revolt.[55] Eventually the quarter was destroyed, and its inhabitants dispersed, by the long-term concentration of artillery and aerial bombardment.

Foreign Legion and French metropolitan troops were not accused of the worst atrocities. The most damning charges were leveled at locally raised troops from the various minorities, especially Armenian refugees, Circassians, and French colonial troops from North and East Africa. Damascus was full of homeless refugees from villages destroyed and pillaged by French forces, and all brought stories of plunder, destruction, and misery.

> During the recent expeditions in the Eastern Oasis [Ghûṭa] much plundering of villages and killing of villagers, not always guilty, have taken place. Natives state that purely French soldiers have not taken part in these acts of violence. The culprits are stated to be North African soldiers and more especially the irregulars under French command, who consist mainly of Circassians with Armenian and Kurdish elements. These irregulars are a byword for every kind of rapine and cruelty. The presence, in these irregular formations, of Christians who, to add to native resentment, are Armenians, refugees dependent on Arab hospitality, has aroused dangerous passions among the Moslems.

British consul Smart went on to add:

> The director of the Victoria hospital told me that he met a peasant acquaintance coming along the road with the usual pitiful accompaniment of a mule piled up with the greatest variety of household goods. The doctor asked his acquaintance why he had left his village. The man replied that he had been compelled to depart because Armenians were plundering his house.[56]

Mandate forces were criticized for fueling sectarian tensions and for widespread atrocities, but the policy of recruiting irregulars and using them for punitive missions is not difficult to understand. The colonial Civilizing Mission was based on protecting "Oriental Christians" from their less civilized neighbors. The indigenous Christians and refugees were envisioned as worthy and convenient couriers for the project of advancing "European civilization." But with a widespread nationalist rebellion that brought Muslims and at least some indigenous Christians together, French military officers turned to the refugee populations. The attraction of a monthly wage of seven gold pounds, the use of weapons, and the opportunity to brutalize others as they themselves had been brutalized must have been a powerful prospect for hungry refugees in Syria. To blame the atrocities on the irregular troops, recruited from the most miserable and rootless Syrians, as foreign observers like Smart did, however, misses the point. The irregulars surely acted with the knowledge and approval of their French paymasters, who had been sworn to uphold the interests and the well-being of the entire mandatory population.

In the short term these methods served only to increase resistance. Despite Andréa's optimism and the accolades of his superiors, the security cordon severing the Maydân from the city was not immediately successful. Smart reported that rebels stole building materials and barbed wire with impunity to use on their own barricades *inside* the city.[57] The bands remained active through January and continued to increase in size. Vast groups of rebels controlled all access to Damascus. Their numbers increased daily.

The ʿAkâsh band continually disrupted communications to the north, south, and east from Damascus. On the night of 11 December they cut phone and rail lines between Damascus and Beirut. They were apparently joined by Shakîb Wahâb from the Shûf, Nasîb ʿAryân from Ayha, and Muḥammad Sharaf along with three others from Jabal Druze. Workers with a military escort repaired the tracks during the day, but the next night the rebels did a more thorough job.

The following night the ʿAkâsh band tore up lengthy sections of track even closer to Damascus, near Dummar. At eleven o'clock that night the armored train derailed, and a freight train following it also derailed. "The band fired on the armored train from the surrounding peaks, injuring two train employees, one seriously. Traffic will be interrupted for several days . ."[58] On the same night of 12–13 January a passenger train near ʿAyn al-Fija was trapped by the disruption of the rail line and came under rebel fire. Its military escort engaged the rebels and supposedly managed to prevent them from capturing the munitions carried in the train, but the first relief expedition sent disappeared entirely and was reported probably captured. By 16 January the train had still not been relieved, but an armored train was expected to reach it that night.[59] It was unclear where the intelligence officer got his information, since the condition of the train was not reported until four days after it was attacked, and apparently it had been under siege and isolated by the insurgents since that time. The report stated with casual and almost surely inaccurate optimism that the passengers and the munitions were safe and untouched. The rail lines were finally reopened on the evening of 16 January, and no losses were reported on the trapped train.

Within a week the insurgents were massing outside Damascus for a renewed attack on the train lines, this time in even greater force. Reports from 22 January indicate 600–700 armed insurgents in the region of Dummar under the command of ʿAbd al-Qâdir Sukkar, in cooperation with the ʿAkâsh band. Meanwhile somewhere around 1,000 armed "Druze" and "bandits" in several groups were active in the other areas surrounding Damascus.[60] This pattern prevailed throughout January and into February. Rebel activity continued in Wâdî Baradâ, the Ghûṭa and Maydân, and north toward al-Nabk and in the Anti-Lebanon range. The insurgents controlled the initiative with impressive organization and coordination of tactics. They repeatedly targeted and destroyed the lines of transportation and communication from Damascus in all directions.[61] Intelligence reports reveal a desperate military situation, despite their bloodless language and determined avoidance of casualty figures.

The reports provide a clear negative imprint of the insurgent consciousness of the armed enemies of the mandate. They show that the rebels of the Damascus countryside were organized, coordinated, and focused on the strategic goal of expelling the French from the mandated territory by destroying the structures and rhetorical claims of mandatory rule. The power of the insurgents to disrupt every aspect of mandatory military rule seemed to awe French intelligence officers. British reports sketch clearly what the French reports only hint at: the rebels had the committed support of vast numbers of the Syrian population, both in the countryside and in the capital. People that the French identified as bandits and criminals were identified by their compatriots as national heroes.

DEBATING REBELLION

Who led the Great Syrian Revolt of 1925–1926? How did people who took part see their role in history? Insurgent documents record major meetings on several occasions to discuss and decide the direction and the strategic priorities of the revolt. Early in December 1925 insurgent leaders met at the house of Abî ʿAbdû al-Saqbânî, *mukhtâr* of the Ghûṭa village of Saqbâ.[62] This was approximately the same time as the multiple attacks of early December. The meeting brought together many of those named in French intelligence reports as well as others rarely named as fighters. Nasîb al-Bakrî was there; and his private papers, preserved in the Syrian Archives, name him as president of the rebel council.[63] He was joined by Muḥammad ʿIzz al-Dîn al-Ḥalabî, ʿAlî al-Aṭrash, and Zayd al-ʿÂmr (all Druze from the south), and Nazîh al-Muʾayyad al-ʿAẓm, ʿAbd al-Qâdir Sukkar, Saʿîd al-ʿÂṣ, Zakî al-Ḥalabî, Zakî al-Durûbî, and the council secretary Fâʾiq al-ʿAsalî (who were mostly from Damascus or Ḥamâh). Half of these men were former Ottoman army officers, and half were involved in the Ḥawrân grain trade.

Two main bands fighting in the Ghûṭa were represented at the conference. According to Saʿîd al-ʿÂṣ, the "Druze" band had become the strongest since he, ʿAlî al-Aṭrash, and Muḥammad ʿIzz al-Dîn al-Ḥalabî had come from the Jabal Druze, Nazîh al-Muʾayyad al-ʿAẓm had come from the Golan to join the band, and ʿAbd al-Qâdir Sukkar had come from the Maydân. The other principal band was the al-Shâghûr quarter band of Ḥasan al-Kharrâṭ. Nasîb al-Bakrî had major influence over Kharrâṭ's band. Saʿîd al-ʿÂṣ wrote that, as the Druze band eclipsed the al-Shâghûr force, Bakrî sought to extend his influence over it too.[64] There was clear tension between rebel leaders over responsibilities and leadership, and command structure was one of several matters under discussion, including operational regions and responsibilities, upcoming military operations, and, most notably, a debate and judgment against rebel leader Ramaḍân Shallâsh for "transgressing the objectives of the nationalist revolt."[65] The accusations against Shallâsh seemed to stem from his activities in Dûmâ (discussed earlier in this chapter).

The debate over Ramaḍân Shallâsh was apparently fractious. It is not entirely clear what he was accused of or why. Details of the Saqbâ meeting and debate appear in the papers of Nasîb al-Bakrî and the books of Munîr al-Rayyis and Saʿîd al-ʿÂṣ. Bakrî was a member of Damascus' landowning elite; Munîr al-Rayyis was a journalist and activist who participated in and chronicled all the Arab revolts against colonial rule. And Saʿîd al-ʿÂṣ, like Shallâsh, was a former Ottoman officer of modest background. Secret intelligence documents and letters suggest that Shallâsh had become a kind of Robin Hood figure of the insurgency. He combined nascent patriotism and nationalism with a mix of social justice, popular religious fervor, and class warfare that was deeply appealing to rural villagers and deeply threatening to Syrian elites. The three extant accounts of his trial differ widely. In their varied emphases, they provide a shadowy rendering of the tensions and conflicts of the revolt and interwar Arab society more generally. Such tensions included the struggle between traditional urban elites and new elites of modest rural and often military background, conflicts over the militancy and radicalism of nationalist politics, and the acceptable degree of popular participation in politics and revolt. Nasîb al-Bakrî attacked Shallâsh for levying revolt taxes. French intelligence documents show that these levies fell on urban elites and big landlords, rather than on Syria's peasants and small cultivators. Shallâsh and his call thus represented a threat to the material prerogatives of Syria's traditional landowners. Munîr al-Rayyis, the radical nationalist, defended Shallâsh and attacked Bakrî family retainer Ḥasan al-Kharrâṭ for vengefulness. Saʿîd al-ʿÂṣ attacked Bakrî and defended Shallâsh as an effective military leader. The former military officers clearly objected to the procedure against Shallâsh, but ultimately they stood aside and allowed Bakrî and Kharrâṭ to determine his fate.

Ramaḍân Shallâsh, bedouin chief and veteran of Hanânû's revolt and the battles of Ghûṭa and Damascus, was to be "expelled from the revolt and stripped of his office and insignia."[66] A graduate of the Ottoman war college, Shallâsh had served in the Ottoman army in Libya in 1912 and the Arab army during the First World War and was a schoolmate and friend of ʿAlî al-Aṭrash from the Ottoman school for sons of tribal chiefs.[67] Saʿîd al-ʿÂṣ claimed that Ramaḍân requested a meeting with Nasîb al-Bakrî and ʿAlî al-Aṭrash, and Nasîb used the opportunity to eliminate him from competition for leadership. Munîr al-Rayyis, who was also at Saqbâ but arrived after the trial, claimed that Ḥasan al-Kharrâṭ called the meeting expressly to seek revenge against Shallâsh and that their personal animosity was well known. Kharrâṭ accused Shallâsh of "impositions and ransoms and financial collections in the name of the revolt."[68]

Saʿîd al-ʿÂṣ, however, claimed that Nasîb al-Bakrî accused Shallâsh of demanding one thousand *ginayh* (Ottoman pounds) in gold from the people of Dûmâ; and Shaykh Ḥijâz, the co-leader of Kharrâṭ's band, accused him of molesting a woman in the village of Ḥamûra. Al-ʿÂṣ reported that he himself argued forcefully that the accusations were baseless and that they should refer the judgment to Sulṭân al-Aṭrash, the commander in chief of the revolt. In his memoir Saʿîd al-ʿÂṣ cursed Bakrî and charged him with harboring "secret hatreds and ambitions."[69] He condemned Kharrâṭ only by implication. Rayyis, by contrast, condemned Kharrâṭ and had harsh words for Bakrî and al-ʿÂṣ merely because they did not restrain Kharrâṭ and prevent the injustice to Shallâsh.

> When I heard what had happened to Ramaḍân Shallâsh, I admonished Saʿîd al-ʿÂṣ for keeping silent about the ridiculous trial. Kharrâṭ did it only for revenge, and I wondered how he managed it in the presence of al-ʿÂṣ and Muḥammad ʿIzz al-Dîn and Nasîb al-Bakrî and the others who had to approve the unjust procedures, which were neither logical nor legal. Al-ʿÂs explained that they had only agreed to summon Shallâsh in order to investigate the accusations against him.[70]

Saʿîd al-ʿÂṣ blamed Nasîb al-Bakrî for the injustice against Ramaḍân Shallâsh. He implied that Ḥasan al-Kharrâṭ, whom French troops killed two weeks later in an ambush in the Ghûṭa, was simply a tool of Bakrî's ambition.[71] Perhaps, writing soon after the death of Kharrâṭ, al-ʿÂṣ sought to avoid harsh criticism of a martyred hero of the revolt.[72] Still, quite apart from sparing Kharrâṭ from condemnation, Saʿîd al-ʿÂṣ identified Nasîb al-Bakrî as the undisputed power behind Kharrât and his band, and al-ʿÂṣ contested Bakrî's leadership at every turn. Almost alone among the revolt leadership, Bakrî hailed from an important landowning family and had received an elite, nonmilitary education. He had been involved in traditional politics and, unlike almost any of the others who took part in the revolt, was a part of Damascus' traditional landowning upper class. Bakrî has sometimes been portrayed as the preeminent leader of the revolt in the countryside of Damascus, but his traditional political and military leadership was clearly not without challenge.[73] Saʿîd al-ʿÂṣ accused Bakrî of cozying up to ʿAlî al-Aṭrash in an attempt to gain access to the Druze leadership and become "general leader, unhindered dictator, or *(ḥâkim bi-amrihî)* of the revolt."[74]

Nasîb al-Bakrî preserved a different version of events in his private papers. The judgment contained in his papers claimed that Shallâsh was guilty of extracting heavy fines for his own pocket from the villages of Madîʿa, al-Qasa, and Ḥirrân al-ʿAwâmîd in the eastern Ghûṭa. The report stated that the villagers had accused Ramaḍân and that he had admitted his misdeeds before the revolt's official tribunal. Accordingly, Shallâsh would be expelled from the ranks of the rebels. But his life would be spared and his freedom would be unhindered. The otherwise unspecified judgment was to be carried out by Ḥasan al-Kharrâṭ.[75]

No one had claimed Shallâsh was not an effective guerrilla leader. Intelligence documents suggest that his confusing mix of Islam, tribal honor, revenge against French Christians, nationalism, and class warfare was enormously popular in Syrian villages and neighborhoods. Shallâsh promised villagers that he represented a movement like that of Turkish nationalist Mustafa Kemal, that he would wage *jihâd* to restore the honor of the Arab nation, and that he fought for the greater glory of Islam. Further, he threatened the big pro-French landlords who dominated much of the countryside more effectively and more directly than did others among the revolt leadership.

Shallâsh and his methods provoked disapproval from some among his comrades. Yet it is surely notable that his staunchest critic and prosecutor, Nasîb al-Bakrî, hailed from a major landowning family. His defenders were former military officers of modest background. Among other things, Shallâsh was accused of stealing money from the people of Dûmâ; but his letters, collected by mandate intelligence, show that he did not seek one thousand pounds from the inhabitants of Dûmâ, as he was accused of doing, but two thousand pounds from the biggest landlord of the town, who was also an important pro-French politician and supporter of the mandate government.[76]

After the conclusion of the first night's meeting and the judgment against Ramaḍân Shallâsh, they argued over the direction of the revolt. Al-ʿÂṣ reported that he urged Bakrî to relinquish offices he was unable to fulfill. As a politician, his talents as a military leader were limited, and he always sought to rule by decree. He could not hope to supplant Muḥammad ʿIzz al-Dîn al-

Ḥalabî, who, as a former officer, understood military matters and was a son of the tribe (Druze) and comrade of ʿAlî. They also debated an upcoming attack on the Circassian village of Murj al-Sulṭân. Saʿîd al-ʿÂṣ argued against ʿAbd al-Qâdir Sukkar, who fervently wanted to teach the "treacherous collaborators" a lesson. Saʿîd al-ʿÂṣ reported that he argued against attacking a Circassian village because they would be playing into the hands of the French, who sought to exacerbate ethnic and sectarian divisions by utilizing Circassian and Armenian troops against the rebels.[77]

Both Saʿîd al-ʿÂṣ and Munîr al-Rayyis reserved their most damning condemnation for the sentence against Shallâsh. He had barely arrived the following day when Ḥasan al-Kharrâṭ and his band arrested him and removed his weapons, horse, and money. They placed him under guard and proceeded to divide the spoils. Al-ʿÂṣ claimed that this was all done while he himself was absent and in contradiction to what they had agreed upon. He later protested that they had to return Shallâsh's belongings, but they were unwilling to reconsider, apart from leaving him his horse. Shortly afterward the French bombed the area from the air, and the rebels fled. Saʿîd al-ʿÂṣ released Shallâsh, who mounted his horse and rode off alone. Shaykh Muḥammad al-Ḥijâz had taken his sword, and Ḥasan al-Kharrâṭ had taken his firearms. They divided his supposedly plundered gold among themselves.[78]

Munîr al-Rayyis reported events differently. In his account, Kharrâṭ's men seized Shallâsh on his orders and transported him to Saqbâ. When they arrived, Kharrâṭ gave orders to search his belongings. He took Shallâsh's documents and began reading them aloud. They found nine pounds of gold, which al-Rayyis claimed Shallâsh had borrowed while he and Nasîb al-Bakrî were guests of a Maydânî notable. Kharrâṭ seized his sword and dagger and tore from Shallâsh's jacket the medal given by Sharîf al-Ḥusayn, naming him "Bâshâ." Kharrâṭ put the medal on his own chest and proclaimed, "I deserve this more than you." Al-Rayyis added that Kharrâṭ appointed himself prosecutor and judge and that the others could not stop him, because everyone wanted to avoid trouble between the rebels. As mentioned by al-ʿÂṣ, soon afterward a French air raid on the village allowed Shallâsh to escape.[79]

The conference concluded with a list of resolutions recorded by Saʿîd al-ʿÂṣ. The first resolution stipulated that al-ʿÂṣ retained general leadership in battle. The second resolution summarized the order of communal battle leadership with respect to all decisions and listed Saʿîd al-ʿÂṣ, Nazîh al-Muʾayyad al-ʿAẓm, ʿAlî al-Aṭrash, Muḥammad ʿIzz al-Dîn al-Ḥalabî, and Abû ʿAbdû (ʿAbd al-Qâdir) Sukkar. The leaders supposedly allied with Nasîb al-Bakrî appear nowhere on the list. The resolution stressed an end to personalized leadership decisions. Sa'îd al-'Âṣ wrote that before Saqbâ they were each independent and sought to command alone; after Saqbâ they sought to command by communal decision and to coordinate their actions. He lamented that the affair of Ramaḍân Shallâsh showed the system did not work. They could attain unity on the battlefield; but unity in politics was far more difficult, and all their achievements could be squandered by personal rivalries.[80]

The Syrian revolt continued for eighteen months after these events. French intelligence reports recorded continual escalation of rebel pressure through winter and into the spring of 1926. Immediately after the meeting at Saqbâ, the "Druze" band led by Muḥammad 'Izz al-Dîn al-Ḥalabî moved toward Jabal Druze, though they returned to fight in the Ghûṭa later. Ḥasan al-Kharrâṭ was killed on 25 December 1925, but his band continued to fight. And Ramaḍân Shallâsh, in a move that surely vindicated his enemies, surrendered to French authorities and collaborated with them. He tried to convince some of his few remaining comrades to join him in fomenting revolt near Dayr al-Zûr with the help of his tribesmen. Agitation had increased in Aleppo and the northern regions, and Shallâsh proposed joining veteran guerrilla leader Ibrâhîm Hanânû, to spark revolt in the north. He and a few others left the region of al-Nabk, where they had been recruiting new fighters along with Sa'îd al-'Âṣ, Khâlid al-Nafawrî, Munîr al-Rayyis, and Jum'a Sawsaq, and headed toward Dayr al-Zûr. This was in mid-January, and the mountains were thick with snow. At al-Salimiyya, east of Ḥamâh, Shallâsh announced his intention to surrender to the French and sought mediation through a local notable. Two of his party remained with him, and two left. Rayyis wrote that Shallâsh kept the machine gun, and one of his party stole a rifle that belonged to one of the men who chose not to surrender. The two men who did not surrender, Jamîl al-'Alawanî and Ibrâhîm Ṣudqî, turned up later (exhausted and starving, with one horse and one rifle between them) to rejoin their comrades in the region of al-Nabk.[81]

The French counteroffensive finally came in the spring and summer of 1926. It drove the insurgents into Ḥawrân and the volcanic refuge of the Laja'a and by 1927 across the border into Transjordan and the new Saudi Kingdom. Ramaḍân Shallâsh, meanwhile, accepted a subsidy from the French government and French government scholarships for his sons.[82] He soon authored a letter to his former comrades urging them to surrender. Shallâsh defended his courage and his record as a fighter and maintained that his cooperation did not make him a collaborator or a traitor. He urged the insurgents to surrender to the new high commissioner, Henry de Jouvenel, claiming that he was fair

FIGURE 8. Ramaḍân Shallâsh surrendering to Henry de Jouvenel. Courtesy Archives du Ministère des Affaires Etrangères—Paris. Copyright Coll. Aujol.

and just and would accept the national demands without further violence.[83] This appeal had few takers. It must have been difficult for his former comrades to defend Shallâsh and criticize his attackers still among them, while they continued to fight and later went into exile as he returned to Dayr al-Zûr on a French subsidy.

Shallâsh's prosecutor, Nasîb al-Bakrî, also came out comparatively well from the revolt. Like many of the other leaders, he was forced into exile, but he was pardoned after less than a year, in March 1928. His family's estates, which the mandate authorities had bombed and confiscated, were also returned.[84] Hundreds of other insurgents such as Sulṭân al-Aṭrash, Muḥammad ʿIzz al-Dîn al-Ḥalabî, Nazîh al-Muʾayyad al-ʿAẓm, Fawzî al-Qâwuqjî, and Saʿîd al-Ḥaydar spent ten years in exile under sentence of death.[85] Saʿîd al-ʿÂṣ was killed fighting in Palestine in 1936 and never returned home. Most ordinary rebels simply returned to rebuild their ruined farms and villages. It is an enduring tribute to these ordinary rebels of the countryside of Damascus that—despite the bitter factional battles between their leaders and the brutal methods of the French forces—they fought and often defeated the mandate army day after day for more than a year. Fawzî al-Qâwuqjî, who resolutely refused to identify by name the rebel leaders he damned for their harm to the struggle, wrote:

> Events confirmed what I perceived and felt: the best among them were the ordinary class of people *[ṭabaqa al-shaʿb al-sâdhaja]*. All our calamities and defeats were due to the ambitions and rivalries of our leaders, who were concerned only with showing off and with their love of display. I saw that the true revolt against the imperialists should be based only on the ordinary and honest classes of the people.[86]

CHAPTER 7

Epilogue and Conclusions

EPILOGUE

The Great Syrian Revolt began with dramatic rebel victories, but it ended with the slow and inexorable reassertion of government control over the devastated countryside, district by district and village by village. Most of the hundreds of insurgents named and sentenced in absentia by government courts fled into exile. The truly anonymous rebel masses melted back into their ruined villages and urban quarters. With the exception of Nasîb al-Bakrî, none of the Damascene rebel leadership was allowed back into mandate Syria for years. Most of the traditional ruling classes of Damascus had never supported the revolt; and with the effective elimination of the revolt's militant leadership, the traditional elites were free to hammer out a working accommodation with the clear and now unchallenged rulers of Syria: the French government. Politics reverted to a new variation of an old pattern as Damascus' leading notable families supplied moderate nationalist politicians to rule under the auspices of, and in cooperation with, the imperial power. The revolt proved to the mandate power that it needed Syria's urban elites. Damascus' leading politicians and the mandate power were able to ignore the exiled insurgents and their uncompromising visions for more than a decade.[1] Militant popular resistance was dead.

In 1928 the National Bloc (al-Kutla al-Waṭaniyya) emerged as the leading political formation in mandate Syria. It stood in sharp contrast to the revolt and to the previous confrontational character of politics under the mandate. With the National Bloc was born the policy of "honorable cooperation," dissected so thoroughly by Philip Khoury. The mandate power finally had a group of Syrian elites with whom accommodation was possible. Unlike the leadership of the revolt and the diverse mass mobilization during the uprising, the ranks of the bloc were resolutely elitist and uniform. Its members were big urban landowners and the recipients of privileged civil education. Unlike the insurgent leadership, the National Bloc did not draw its members from the countryside or the military. With few exceptions, Damascene notable politicians who figured prominently in the bloc and interwar nationalist politics had played no role in the revolt of 1925. In class origin, educational background, occupation, and ideological pragmatism, the National Bloc leadership was distinct from the insurgent leadership. A comparison between the most frequently mentioned insurgent leaders and the bloc leaders indicates that they were virtually mutually exclusive. The one exception is Nasîb al-Bakrî. Among the rebels, he was also one of the very few graduates of the elite Damascus Academy, Maktab ʿAnbar, long considered a nursery for nationalist political leaders.[2]

The distinction between Ottoman civil education and military education is important and generally unacknowledged. While Maktab ʿAnbar was the civil secondary school, there was also a military secondary school in Damascus. One provided students for the Mülkiye in Istanbul, the other for the Harbiye. Military education was fully subsidized by the government and was widely seen as a path for upward mobility among those of modest means. Civil education was generally not subsidized and was a path to higher government position for sons of families that were already prominent. The majority of National Bloc leadership had attended Maktab ʿAnbar and more advanced Ottoman or foreign institutions of civil education. While the bloc leadership and the insurgent leadership were of the same generation, all born around the year 1890, their experiences were by no means comparable. The crushing of the rebellion and the exile of its leaders allowed the leaders of the bloc to emerge into prominence. The mandate power knowingly exacerbated the postrevolt class and factional split by selectively pardoning prominent exiles who could pass seamlessly into the ranks of the National Bloc. When the French authorities pardoned first Nasîb al-Bakrî and later Shukrî al-Quwwatlî and Jamîl Mardam Bek, they strengthened the National Bloc's claims to lead and further fragmented the rebel opposition to the mandate.

The exiled insurgents, however, did not willingly fade into irrelevance. Despite massive French offensives in the Ghûṭa and Ḥawrân in the spring of 1926, Muḥammad ʿIzz al-Dîn al-Ḥalabî and Sulṭân al-Aṭrash continued to lead raids on French positions until the early summer of 1927.[3] Fawzî al-Qâwuqjî and Saʿîd al-ʿÂṣ also remained active in the region north of Damascus until mid-1927. During 1926 and 1927 Druze rebels moved to the refugee camp at al-Azraq in northern Transjordan. Many had sent their families there during the revolt; but in the summer of 1927 British mandatory forces expelled the rebels, including Sulṭân al-Aṭrash and his family, to Wâdî al-Sirḥân in the new Arabian Sultanate of ʿAbd al-ʿAzîz al-Saʿûd (Ibn Saʿûd).[4] Others went to Haifa, Jaffa, and Jerusalem in Palestine, while still others went to Cairo. Military officers like Fawzî al-Qâwuqjî and Saʿîd al-ʿÂṣ worked their way to

Baghdad, where they offered their services to the government of King Fayṣal and helped organize and train his army.

In Jerusalem rebel supporters started a new newspaper to advance the viewpoints of the exiled insurgents. The first issues of the new paper, called *Jâmiʿat al-ʿarabiyya* (The Arab Federation), appeared in January 1927 under the editorial direction of Munîf al-Ḥayanî. The paper was intended to reach a readership inside mandatory Syria and to maintain the centrality of the rebel leadership's claims to speak for Syria.[5] Its outlook was both Druze and nationalist, and it had detailed coverage of the increasingly desperate battles of Ḥawrân and the volcanic badland refuge of al-Lajaʾa, where the rebels made their final stand.

Despite its Ḥawrân Druze focus, *Jâmiʿat al-ʿarabiyya* also had reports filed by Fawzî al-Qâwuqjî and Saʿîd al-ʿÂṣ from the region surrounding Damascus. And while it was primarily concerned with the coverage of what it called the nationalist struggle against imperialism, tyranny, and the atrocities of the colonial government in Syria, it covered other news as well. Its sixth issue, for example, contained an article about American intervention in Nicaragua, pointing out that Calvin Coolidge's American Republic, considered a paragon of anti-imperialist Great Power virtue by some, was also guilty of imperialist crimes.[6]

Jâmiʿat al-ʿarabiyya illustrates the final months of the uprising vividly and poignantly. The mostly anonymous writers of the paper protested desperately that the fight must continue and criticized such things as an article in the Cairo daily *al-Ahrâm* of 31 May 1927, claiming the revolt was finished. Two weeks later, on 23 June 1927, *Jâmiʿat al-ʿarabiyya* published a list of goals and demands under the headline "Future of Syria." By this time everyone knew that the future of Syria would be dictated by France; but the newspaper, and the rebels it represented, had no choice but to persist with now quixotic goals. The demands reflected the dwindling fortunes of the uprising and did not include a call for the evacuation of France from its mandates. They did call, however, for France's recognition of Syria's independence and France's support for Syria's entry into the League of Nations at the same time as Iraq, which had recently been agreed to by treaty as 1932. They further demanded Syrian unity, with the Druze region's incorporation into the state based on the "American pattern," by which the authors presumably meant some kind of federalism. The demands included unrestricted amnesty, although with negotiable exceptions. The final demand was open talks between Syria and Lebanon, with further union or incorporation to be decided by the respective populations and subject to vote.

These demands were modest by comparison with the fiery objectives of eighteen months earlier. At about the same time a number of former insurgents expressed the somewhat forlorn wish that all they wanted was an arrangement like that which Iraq had with Britain—a major rhetorical retreat from the vague but trenchant proclamations of the triumphant months of 1925. Still, exiled nationalists of the Syrian-Palestinian Congress, based in Cairo, had repeatedly put forward variations on these proposals since December 1925. The Mount Lebanon Druze aristocrat and international activist Amîr Shakîb Arslân had met with General Sarrail's successor, Henry de Jouvenel, in Paris in December 1925 to advance similar demands.[7] The insurgent leadership, particularly Sulṭân al-Aṭrash and Shahbandar, had been outraged by Amîr Shakîb's claim to speak for the rebellion and by the moderate proposals he advanced without their approval or consultation. There is no doubt that Shakîb Arslân—in his wish to occupy a central place in the revolt, albeit from the safety of Geneva—harmed the possibility for fruitful negotiations. Further negotiations took place between members of the Syrian-Palestinian Congress and Jouvenel in Cairo in the next month, reverting to an uncompromising position on the evacuation of French troops. When the insurgents themselves advanced demands eighteen months later in line with Arslân's original position (from a position infinitely weaker than that of December 1925), de Jouvenel's successor, Henri Ponsot, ignored them completely. He issued his first public proclamation a month later in July 1927. After ten months of silence, Ponsot's first public statement began with the words "France will not renounce its mandate."[8]

Meanwhile Ponsot had negotiated with the British to force the insurgent refugees as far from mandate Syria as possible. A series of articles in *Jâmiʿat al-ʿarabiyya* chronicled the progress of Franco-British negotiations on forcibly expelling the exiles and their families from al-Azraq. Finally, on 27 June 1927, the paper published a telegram from Sulṭân al-Aṭrash to the Offices of the New Syria Party of Detroit, Michigan, explaining that "the military powers have decided to evict all the families from al-Azraq and expel them from East Jordan [Transjordan]." The insurgents briefly returned over the border to Syria, where they engaged mandate forces again. The situation in Ḥawrân was impossible, however, and members of the exiled Syrian-Palestinian Congress, foremost probably Shukrî al-Quwwatlî, negotiated with Ibn Saʿûd to allow the rebels refuge in his new desert sultanate. Ibn Saʿûd had first become the sultan of Najd and then the king of Ḥijâz, usurping Sharîf al-Ḥusayn's title and territory. Sulṭân al-Aṭrash and the mostly Druze rebels with him moved their families to the desert oasis of Wâdî al-

Sirḥân, about 150 kilometers southeast of Amman, just across the new border near the village of al-Ḥadîtha. They would stay there until 1937, living in tents and surviving on handouts distributed by the Syrian-Palestinian Congress from donors in Syria and Lebanon and contributions from Arab immigrants in North and South America.[9]

Remote exile removed the insurgents from any role in mandate Syria's political life. Not only did the mandate power and Syria's newly ascendant nationalist elites ignore the former rebels, but the exiled nationalists of the Syrian-Palestinian Congress ignored them too. In the annual celebration of Syria's Independence and Martyrs Day on 8 March 1928 in Cairo, the congress commemorated the nation's martyrs in a public ceremony and in a published pamphlet but failed to include any living revolt fighters in the celebrations. The pamphlet included a list of prominent martyrs from the Great War, Maysalûn, and the Syrian Revolt; but with the exception of Tawfîq Hûlû al-Ḥaydar and Dr. Khâlid al-Khaṭîb, who had both spent most of the revolt in Palestine and Egypt, there were no insurgents present.[10]

The following year the exiled insurgents organized their own conference. In September 1929 Sulṭân al-Aṭrash and other refugees of Wâdî al-Sirḥân sent a large number of invitations to journalists, nationalists, and former insurgents in Syria and abroad. They sent the notice to newspapers in Syria, Egypt, and elsewhere and expected the meeting to be well attended and apparently inclusive.

To Our Syrian Brothers:

On 25 September, the insurgents of the desert held a meeting to study the present situation of the country. We have unanimously decided to request the publication of a general appeal to all Syrian parties to announce a great national assembly for the examination of the situation, and in preparation for important political changes in the country. In conformance with the desire of the insurgents, and in view of the realization of the wishes of the nation, we make this general appeal to all political parties and national groups that are intent on the victory of our cause. We ask that they attend the assembly, which will take place on 25 October 1929 at Wâdî al-Sirḥân. We are certain that the nation will not hesitate to respond to our invitation and to the important results this meeting will have for the advancement of our cause.

Wâdî al-Sirḥân, al-Ḥadîtha
Commander in Chief of the
Syrian Revolt
Sulṭân al-Aṭrash[11]

The reception in Damascus was disappointing. The two most prominent nationalist newspapers of the capital in the years after the revolt, *al-Sha'b* and *al-Qabas*, both refused to publish the notice on the spurious but unchallengeable grounds that their editors doubted its authenticity. French intelligence reported definitively that the invitation was genuine and in the same report documented the Damascene reaction in nationalist circles. Prominent nationalist politicians also publicly disparaged the authenticity of the notice; Riyâḍ al-Ṣulḥ, Beirut National Bloc delegate and future Lebanese prime minister, said that though he had received a personal appeal from Sulṭân al-Aṭrash he doubted the legitimate interests of the meeting and advised against the participation of the National Bloc.[12] He need not have worried. By 1929 the mandate government's heavy-handed censorship was no longer necessary, and Syria's nationalist elites had resolved to deal with the national movement's more unruly elements themselves. Ultimately they were able to silence dissent far more effectively than the mandate power had done alone.

The conference went on without representatives of the National Bloc and without representation or even acknowledgment by most of Syria's interwar elite. Its participants were predictable. Sulṭân al-Aṭrash organized and led the meeting; and a number of other former insurgents attended, many as representatives of some group or organization hastily formed to lend official weight to the proceedings. Dr. Khâlid al-Khaṭîb of the Syrian-Palestinian Congress sat as secretary and kept the minutes. ʿÂdil al-ʿAẓma, brother of Nabîh al-ʿAẓma and like his brother a former Ottoman army officer, also represented the Syrian-Palestinian Congress. ʿUthmân al-Sharâbâtî, the Damascene merchant at whose house a number of secret People's Party meetings had taken place prior to the arrests of August 1925, also attended as a delegate of the congress. Saʿîd al-ʿÂṣ was officially the delegate for a group called the National Charter (al-Mîthâq al-Waṭanî). ʿAbd al-Qâdir Sukkar, the Maydânî grain merchant and rebel band leader, represented the insurgents of the Ghûṭa. Muḥammad al-Ashmar, popular religious shaykh of the Maydân quarter, merchant, and rebel leader, represented the Damascus Council of Merchants. ʿUqla al-Quṭâmî, Greek Orthodox shaykh of the Jabal Ḥawrân village of al-Kharbâ, rebel leader, and lifelong friend of Sulṭân al-Aṭrash, was listed, along with several others, "among the insurgents of the desert."[13] Dr. Shahbandar helped organize and publicize the meeting from his base in Cairo, but he did not attend. In a letter intercepted by French intelligence a few days later, he declared his satisfaction with the conference's work and with his friend ʿUthmân al-Sharâbâtî's organizational efforts. He noted that the "insolent ones," by which the intelligence officer filing the report opined he meant members of the Istiqlâl Party, had wanted to exploit the conference for their benefit. He further noted that ʿÂdil al-ʿAẓma had communicated details of the proceedings to the editors of *al-Ahrâm*, who would publish them. In contrast to the newspapers in Syria, *al-Ahrâm* published a very brief notice of the conference. It was clearly of little importance to the editors, however, and they buried it halfway down the fifth page.[14]

Sulṭân al-Aṭrash opened the meeting with a brief but forceful speech. He outlined the postrevolt situation in Syria and refrained from dwelling on the past or pointing out the prominent nationalists or members of the nascent National Bloc who were conspicuous by their absence. He noted that Robert de Caix's declarations before the League of Nations explicitly enforced injustices against the Syrian people and strongly contradicted their rights and aspirations. He mentioned favorably that the new Labour government in Britain had acquiesced to the demands of Egypt and Iraq. His pro-British enthusiasm, perennially distressing to the French and perennially annoying to nationalist rivals, was apparently undiminished. He concluded with references to "foreign influences" and "factional rancor," which, he implied, diminished the efforts of some patriots but would not damage the present efforts. Their actions would serve as an "example for all national struggles."[15]

Tenaciously preserving the fiction of their relevance, the delegates discussed and agreed upon a series of resolutions. The published resolutions centered on a joint condemnation of both British and French mandatory policies in Syria and Palestine. They contrasted France's fine words as a beacon of liberty and civilization with its colonial policy in Algeria and Syria. They expressed the hope that Britain's new government would "exchange its old imperialist methods" and put its lofty talk into effect not only in Egypt and Iraq but especially in Palestine by revoking the Balfour Declaration. The conference condemned the decision of the World Zionist Congress at Zurich and acts of aggression committed by Jews against Arabs.

British intelligence reports of the conference listed some unpublished proposals in addition to the published resolutions. The unpublicized proposals had a distinct pan-Syrian character and included the institution of a general Arab committee to coordinate all political action in Palestine, Transjordan, and Syria under mandate, an effort to disseminate propaganda against the Balfour Declaration in Europe and America, and the total boycott of association with Jews in Palestine. They further proposed addressing petitions to the League of Nations demanding the unification of Palestine, Transjordan, and Syria under one—preferably British—mandate and the establishment of a Palestinian parliament of all citizens without regard to religion. Finally,

FIGURE 9. Desert conference, Wâdî al-Sirḥân, October 1929. Sulṭân al-Aṭrash is seated at the center. To his left are Muḥammad al-Ashmar and ʿAbd al-Qâdir Sukkar. To his right are an unidentified man and Saʿîd al-ʿÂṣ. Courtesy Markaz al-Wathâʾiq al-Târîkhiyya.

they proposed the division of Palestine into zones in which the Arab inhabitants would be organized militarily under the command of centrally designated leaders. French intelligence was evidently dismayed by the claim of support for an expanded mandate under British control. The French intelligence officer compiling the report offered three hypotheses to explain this. He first suggested inaccurate reporting, followed by "Anglo fantasy," and finally residual pro-British enthusiasm on the part of some Ḥawrân Druze.[16] And yet the idea of free and undivided Greater Syria lived on.

The published resolutions were more general and intended to be less controversial. The insurgents "reaffirmed their solemn pledge to fight for free Syria and to advance their legitimate demands." They "proclaimed to the whole world that all Syrians, from the different nationalist parties and political organizations, were united as one before this sacred pledge." They asserted their right to speak for all Syrians; while many ordinary Syrians may have agreed that the rebels had led the nation in resistance, no one—not Syria and certainly not the "whole world"—was able to hear their voices. Despite tireless efforts to disseminate their nationalist vision and their claims to lead, the conference and the resolutions it produced ended up as silent testimony among the innumerable files in the British and French mandate intelligence services' archives.[17]

CONCLUSIONS

The Great Syrian Revolt was the first episode in a contest that has defined much of modern Syrian history. Hanna Batatu, Patrick Seale, and many others have noted that the postindependence history of Syria and other Arab countries has been characterized by a struggle between old landed elites who took part in colonial rule and new classes of more modest origin. Men like Jamâl 'Abd al-Nâṣir, 'Abd al-Karîm Qâsim, Ḥâfiẓ al-Asad, and even Mustafa Kemal Atatürk emerged from the countryside or the provinces, benefited from state-subsidized military education, and ultimately transformed the power structures of their countries. They displaced old urban notable classes and the dominant families who had enjoyed political prominence since Ottoman times. The Syrian revolt demonstrates that this process of transformation began much earlier than has been argued before and that the structural conditions that led to the transformation lay not only in the changes of the mandate but in the social and economic changes of the last Ottoman decades and the experience of the First World War. Expansion of rural commerce in agriculture and the expansion of Ottoman education to include young men of comparatively modest provincial background brought social changes in the Ottoman successor states that are still unfolding.

The revolt was a popular political movement inspired in part by evolving and variable notions of national community. Its tactics of armed revolt were radical and constituted a decisive subaltern break with the traditional elite politics of Damascus. The revolt drew its leaders from the ranks of rural shaykhs, demobilized military officers, and village and quarter leaders and not from the great landowning notable families who sought before and especially after the uprising to become national leaders in a negotiated process with the French.

Wide popular participation in the revolt rested on two specific structural elements: relationships forged in the Ḥawrân grain trade and the prevalence of men in their mid- to late thirties who had shared subsidized Ottoman military education and the experience of the Great War. Druze migrants had settled the southern countryside in large numbers during the middle and late nineteenth century. They expelled or subjugated the local bedouin and came to dominate agriculture in both Jabal Ḥawrân and the surrounding plain.

With the aid of a rising class of merchant families from the Maydân quarter of Damascus, they developed the wide cultivation and export of Ḥawrânî grain. The relationships between Ḥawrân villages and Maydânî merchants began with long-term business contracts and evolved into social and political ties between the two regions. Just as the merchants were rarely from the great landowning families of Damascus, who usually had vast holdings in other parts of Syria, the village leaders were not great landlords or estate holders. These trade networks and relationships were precisely the conduits of transmission for rebellion and nationalist agitation.

The 1925 revolt began in the Druze grain-producing regions and soon shifted to the Maydân quarter of Damascus. Many of the revolt's leaders came from the Ḥawrân or from the Maydân and were connected by business or family to the grain trade. They were more militant in tactics and aims than the nationalist elite of Damascene notables, some of whom joined the uprising in order to escape imprisonment and to preserve their political credibility. Mandate authorities failed to comprehend the significance of these relationships and the interdependence and connections among regions, classes, and sectarian groups in Syria. They sought to govern mandate Syria along a series of ageless and essential divisions of sect, region, and class. This governing strategy was based on orientalist assumptions about religion, town, and countryside that informed the colonial imagination in North Africa, Egypt, and India, to name but a few places. These assumptions, quite apart from the self-justification at their core, contradicted historical processes that had increased connections between Syrians in the years before the mandate. Commercial and social relations that colonial functionaries—and many scholars since—believed separated rural people from one another and from urban populations actually served to bring them together. But commerce was not the only bond between the insurgents of 1925.

Ottoman secondary education had recently forged links between people of diverse class, regional, and sectarian origins. While there was an elite, tuition-based civil preparatory school in Damascus, readying students for high government civil employment, there was also a fully subsidized military secondary school. The Damascus Ottoman military secondary school has never been a subject of historical study; but its influence was wide, and it was once well known in Greater Syria. A large proportion of the Great Syrian Revolt's leaders received their schooling there.

When young men of modest background came from the countryside, it was usually the military school they entered, not the civil school (known locally as Maktab ʿAnbar). When they went on to further study, it was at the

Ottoman Imperial Military Academy, not the Ottoman Civil Service Academy or foreign universities. Over forty years ago Patrick Seale observed that the ascendance of rural military officers in Syria's postcolonial government was in part a result of the distaste of Damascus' ruling classes for the army. He wrote of the 1940s, but the pattern was established much earlier. When Damascus' landed elite sent their sons for higher education, the young men came back as lawyers, engineers, and scholars. When rural shaykhs, village leaders, and middling urban merchants sent their sons for higher education, they came back as graduates of the only schools their families could afford: state-subsidized military academies.

The revolt of 1925 owed much of its national character to the bonds among such former officers. There is no way to know what experiences they shared in Istanbul and on the battlefields of the Great War, because as exemplars of an emerging Syrian Arab nationalism they rarely wrote about their Ottoman experiences. Whether the Ottoman project of education and assimilation had served to bind these young men to the Ottoman state or to nascent ideas of Syrian nationalism or to both, at different times, there is no question that the experience served to bind them to one another and, in time, to ideas of an independent Syrian state that could be.

They were soldiers rather than theorists, and their chronicles and their actions display frustration with and trenchant criticism of the civilian nationalist elite of Damascus. They identified themselves as nationalists and patriots, but their nationalism was practical and unsystematic; they focused on expelling the French from Syria and sometimes mixed in popular Islamic religion, anti-Christian agitation, and even class warfare against urban landlords and notables. Men such as these, of modest background and representing an emerging social class fostered by military education, were able to communicate with and organize the resistance of ordinary urban and rural Syrians far better than the self-appointed nationalist elite of intellectuals and western-educated politicians. They shared a fragmentary ideology based on the geographical entity of independent Greater Syria and on shifting elements of regionalism, religion, and popular and rural Arab culture.

When former officers, shaykhs, and local leaders rode into a village or urban quarter to announce the coming of the revolt against the mandate power, much of the populace responded. In this book I have represented some of the possible range of this call and its popular response. I have argued that the Syrian revolt was a catalyst for the formation of popular notions of Syrian-Arab identity. These nationalisms, however, were always locally conditioned. People who had perhaps not thought much about being part of a larger, national community entered a struggle against a clearly but negatively defined enemy. When rebels and insurgents conceived notions of their "imagined community," the conception was theirs. They imagined it themselves in negative relation to the colonial occupier. In this process of imagining, they incorporated elements that made sense in terms of, and coexisted with, their existing ideas of self. Because new notions of identity were historically and culturally subjective, they differed from place to place, along with different local histories. Such notions of identity resist easy categorization and generalization. A central goal of this study has been to show that a collective national identity can exist without a unitary, elite-guided notion of what such membership means.

When people who had only one or more facet of identity in common faced an enemy that was clearly an "Other" (such as a colonial military power), a new facet could emerge or a preexisting facet might be pushed to the foreground, as a basis for collective action. When insurgents joined together to resist a colonial oppressor, for example, they did not hold identical conceptions of their national identity. The way one conceived or imagined the community obviously differed from person to person. But it was the common *notion* of membership that was important, not the common understanding of what membership meant. At moments of intense collective crisis, this notion of common membership could expand dramatically, almost overnight, and erase or subordinate differences between members of a single national community. The Syrian revolt of 1925 was such a moment of crisis. Despite its ultimate failure, the revolt had the lasting effect of permanently drawing disparate regions together under the idea of a Syrian-Arab nation. In spite of the determined efforts of the mandate power to divide Syrian society permanently, the revolt helped allow Syrians to imagine themselves a unified nation.

Connections born of Ottoman-era trade and education made such new notions of community possible. Just as the Syrian revolt of 1925 spread along grain-trade networks, the same Ḥawrân-Maydân commercial alliance had sustained the Arab Revolt during the Great War. These patterns continued long after the 1925 uprising was crushed and its participants relegated to exile and political irrelevance. Decades later, sons of Damascene grain merchants and Druze shaykhs became the first proponents and adherents of a radical new nationalist ideology that became Baʿthism in the 1940s. Both Ṣalâḥ al-Dîn al-Bîṭâr and Michel ʿAflaq were the sons of Maydân grain merchants with extensive business in Jabal Ḥawrân; and some of their first followers were young Druze, among whom was Manṣûr Sulṭân al-Aṭrash. The grain trade alliance and the Syrian revolt that it facilitated allowed a challenge not only to the French mandate but to the great landowning notables of Damascus who dominated Syrian politics until after independence. Just as their fathers had challenged the ruling elite of Damascus during the Great Revolt, young Baʿthist nationalists in the 1940s and 1950s sought to upend the postindependence political system, only to be displaced in the 1960s by another generation of young men of rural origin who had received fully subsidized military education. These connections and structures thus run through much of modern Syrian history.

Insurgents and their enemies understood the colossal stakes of the uprising. Rebel documents show a fear both of the destruction wrought by overwhelming French military force and of the efforts of Syrian elites to speak for the revolt and marginalize rebel sacrifices. The insurgency failed. Massive military force destroyed villages, farms, and neighborhoods, killed thousands, and drove many into lengthy exile. The military government of the French mandate, sworn to foster the development, rights, and interests of the population under mandate, used means of repression and mechanized warfare never before unleashed on civilians. The revolt forced French colonial authorities and Syrian elites to recognize their common interests in preserving civil order and a social system inherited from Ottoman times. It also helped to entrench the huge internal security apparatus that would become an enduring feature of mandate and postindependence government. For twenty years France would rule Syria in cooperation with moderate nationalists and urban elites of Damascus. Surviving rebels gradually returned to their devastated homes, their hopes dashed, the record of their struggles suppressed. And yet, in the archives of their enemies and in the memories that old insurgents passed on, an echo of their voice remained.

NOTES

CHAPTER 1. INTRODUCTION

1. League of Nations Permanent Mandates Commission, *Minutes of the Eighth Session*, Van Rees to Session (1926), pp. 125–126. Van Rees was a member of the commission investigating the revolt and charged with protecting the mandate population from the excesses and abuses of the mandatory power.

2. Excerpt from the widely disseminated "To Arms" proclamation and manifesto distributed in Damascus on 23 August 1925 and signed by Sulṭân al-Aṭrash. See Ministère des Affaires Etrangères, Archives Diplomatiques-Nantes (hereafter MAE-Nantes), carton 1704, *Bulletin de Renseignements* (BR) 155, 28 August 1925, and Chapter 4. It appeared in the archives of France, Britain, and the League of Nations as well as in newspapers in Cairo, Paris, and London.

3. Ḥannâ Abî Râshid, *Jabal al-durûz* (1961 ed.), pp. 180–181. He reproduced the letters. See Chapter 2, note 25, for a full discussion of this work.

4. I compiled the story of the "First Revolt of Sulṭân al-Aṭrash" from a number of sources, including several interviews with his son Manṣûr Sulṭân al-Aṭrash between 1999 and 2002 and many interviews in Jabal Ḥawrân. See also Abî Râshid, *Jabal al-durûz;* Salâma ʿUbayd, *al-Thawra al-sûriyya al-kubrâ: 1925–1927 ʿalâ ḍauʾ wathâʾiq lam tunshar,* pp. 92–95; Elizabeth Pauline MacCallum, *The Nationalist Crusade in Syria,* pp. 108–109; and Kais M. Firro, *A History of the Druzes,* pp. 266–267.

5. Albert Hourani, "Ottoman Reform and the Politics of Notables," in William R. Polk and Richard L. Chambers, eds., *Beginnings of Modernization in the Middle East: The Nineteenth Century,* p. 47.

6. Philip S. Khoury, *Syria and the French Mandate: The Politics of Arab Nationalism, 1920–1945.*

7. Linda Schatkowski Schilcher, *Families in Politics: Damascene Factions and Estates of the 18th and 19th Centuries.*

8. Rashid Khalidi and James L. Gelvin have made recent ground-breaking contributions to understanding popular politics. See Khalidi's *Palestinian Identity: The Construction of Modern National Consciousness* and his "Ottomanism and Arabism in Syria before 1914: A Reassessment," in Rashid Khalidi, Lisa Anderson, et al., eds., *The Origins of Arab Nationalism,* pp. 50–69. See Gelvin's *Divided Loyalties: Nation-*

alism and Mass Politics in Syria at the Close of Empire for Damascus between 1918 and 1920.

9. Beshara Doumani, *Rediscovering Palestine: Merchants and Peasants in Jabal Nablus, 1700–1900,* p. 157. See also Marion Farouk Sluglett and Peter Sluglett, "The Application of the 1858 Land Code in Greater Syria: Some Preliminary Observations," in Tarif Khalidi, ed., *Land Tenure and Social Transformation in the Middle East.*

10. See Norman N. Lewis, *Nomads and Settlers in Syria and Jordan, 1800–1980.*

11. Najib Elias Saliba, "Wilayat Suriyya 1876–1909," pp. 195–197; Selim Deringil, *The Well-Protected Domains: Ideology and the Legitimation of Power in the Ottoman Empire, 1876–1909,* pp. 99–100.

12. This is clear from a random survey of Syrian newspapers during the mandate. The Damascus daily *al-Muqtabas,* for example, had a weekly column entitled "News from Istanbul" as well as features like "Who Is Mustafa Kemal?" In April and May 1926 *al-Muqtabas* ran an eight-part serialized front-page feature titled "Mudhakkirât Musṭafâ Kamâl."

13. Linda Schatkowski Schilcher has laid the groundwork for considering the urban-rural linkages between Damascus and Ḥawrân in a series of articles. See, for example, "The Grain Economy of Late Ottoman Syria and the Issue of Large-Scale Commercialization," in Çağlar Keydar and Faruk Tabak, eds., *Landholding and Commercial Agriculture in the Middle East,* pp. 173–195.

14. See the Private Papers collection of all three politicians in the Markaz al-Wathâ'iq al-Târîkhiyya (MWT), Damascus (Center for Historical Documents).

15. Jacques Weulersse, *Paysans de Syrie et du Proche-Orient.* He argued that all Syria, and by extension the Arab East, was dominated by large estates and feudal exploitation. See Haim Gerber, *The Social Origins of the Modern Middle East,* pp. 95–101, for a concise critique.

16. The following are the best and most representative of their generation: Adham al-Jundî, *Târîkh al-thawrât al-sûriyya fî ʿahd al-intidâb al-fransî;* Munîr al-Rayyis, *al-Kitâb al-dhahabî lil-thawrât al-waṭaniyya fî al-mashriq al-ʿarabî: al-thawra al-sûriyya al-kubrâ;* Ẓâfir al-Qâsimî, *Wathâ'iq jadîda ʿan al-thawra al-sûriyya al-kubrâ;* Dhûqân Qarqûṭ, *Taṭawwur al-ḥaraka al-waṭaniyya fî sûriyya, 1920–1939;* Muḥî al-Dîn al-Safarjalânî, *Târîkh al-thawra al-sûriyya;* and Salâma ʿUbayd, *al-Thawra al-sûriyya al-kubrâ: 1925–1927 ʿalâ ḍau' wathâ'iq lam tunshar.*

17. Robert Blecher, "When Television Is Mandatory: Syrian Television Drama in the 1990s," in Nadine Méouchy, ed., *France, Syrie et Liban: Les ambiguïtés et les dynamiques de la relation mandataire,* pp. 169–180.

18. Ẓâfir al-Qâsimî, *Wathâ'iq jadîda ʿan al-thawra al-sûriyya al-kubrâ,* pp. 103–109. Qâsimî, a prominent Damascene Muslim jurist and intellectual, describes Sulṭân al-Aṭrash in glowing terms as a nationalist hero and partner with Dr. ʿAbd al-Raḥman Shahbandar. When Sulṭân al-Aṭrash died in 1982, it was claimed that more

people came to his funeral than to any other in Syrian history. He remains a potent symbol in southern Syria inside and outside the Druze community. Birgit Schaebler has discussed some of these issues. See her "Coming to Terms with Failed Revolutions: Historiography in Syria, Germany, and France," *Middle Eastern Studies* 35, no. 1 (January 1999): 17–44. And for a classic review of Arab-Ottoman historiography generally, see Rifaat Ali Abou-El-Haj, "The Social Uses of the Past: Recent Arab Historiography of Ottoman Rule," *IJMES* 14 (1982): 185–201.

19. Ḥasan Amîn al-Biʿaynî, *Durûz sûriyya wa lubnân fî ʿahd al-intidâb al-fransî, 1920–1943*, *Jabal al-ʿarab ṣafaḥât min târîkh al-muwaḥḥidîn al-durûz (1685–1927)*, and *Sulṭân Bâshâ al-Aṭrash: Masîra qâi'd fî târîkh umma.*

20. See Kamal Salibi, *A House of Many Mansions: The History of Lebanon Reconsidered.*

21. Firro, *A History of the Druzes.* Birgit Schaebler's work also falls in this category. See Birgit Schäbler, *Aufstände im Drusenbergland: Ethnizität und Integration einer Ländlichen Gesellschaft Syriens vom Osmanischen Reich bis zur Staatlichen Unabhängigkeit, 1850–1949.*

22. Books along this line are, of course, numerous. I mention only a few of the most important here: Général Charles Joseph Andréa, *La révolte druze et l'insurrection de Damas;* Capitaine Gabriel Carbillet, *Au Djébel Druse, choses vues et vécues;* and Paul Coblentz, *Le silence de Sarrail.* Andréa crushed the revolt, Carbillet was the French governor of the Jabal Druze, and Coblentz was the personal secretary and posthumous apologist for High Commissioner Sarrail, who was relieved of his post for his handling of the revolt.

23. Khoury, *Syria and the French Mandate,* and his "A Reinterpretation of the Origins and Aims of the Great Syrian Revolt, 1925–1927," in *Arab Civilization: Challenges and Responses: Studies in Honor of Constantine K. Zurayk,* pp. 241–271; Hanna Batatu, *Syria's Peasantry, the Descendants of Its Lesser Rural Notables, and Their Politics.* Lenka Bokova's *La confrontation franco-syrienne à l'époque du mandat, 1925–1927* is likewise an important work on the revolt. She covers the elite politics of the revolt, both French and Syrian, from a Marxist perspective.

24. Just as he broke new ground for the history of the mandate, Khoury has since led a rethinking of the universal claims of Syria's interwar nationalist movement. See "The Paradoxical in Arab Nationalism: Interwar Syria Revisited," in James Jankowski and Israel Gershoni, eds., *Rethinking Nationalism in the Arab Middle East,* pp. 273–287.

25. See Philip S. Khoury, *Urban Notables and Arab Nationalism: The Politics of Damascus, 1860–1920.*

26. See Gelvin's *Divided Loyalties;* and Hasan Kayalı, *Arabs and Young Turks: Ottomanism, Arabism, and Islamism in the Ottoman Empire, 1908–1918.* Another former student of Khoury's, Eugene Rogan, has published a valuable study of the Ottoman frontier region that became Jordan. See *Frontiers of the State in the Late*

Ottoman Empire: Transjordan, 1850–1921. He focuses on rural integration in the final years of the Ottoman Empire and is thus not primarily concerned with the rise of nationalism.

27. Rashid Khalidi is a rare exception on both counts. His book *Palestinian Identity* considers the bases of popular nationalism in the countryside. And his earlier articles stressed the emergence of nationalism among new classes of non-elites. See his "Ottomanism and Arabism in Syria before 1914: A Reassessment," in Rashid Khalidi, Lisa Anderson, et al., eds., *The Origins of Arab Nationalism,* pp. 50–69.

28. Khoury, *Syria and the French Mandate,* p. 12.

29. See Batatu, *Syria's Peasantry,* pp. 254–255, on Asad's sympathy for and identification with Syria's farmers.

30. E. J. Hobsbawm, *Nations and Nationalism since 1780: Programme, Myth, Reality,* pp. 8–10. Elsewhere he distinguishes between the rise of imagined, national communities and the decline of *real* communities, by which he presumably means more traditional communities, p. 46 (original emphasis). I am following here the arguments of Partha Chatterjee in *Nationalist Thought and the Colonial World: A Derivative Discourse?* (pp. 19–22).

31. Partha Chatterjee, *The Nation and Its Fragments: Colonial and Postcolonial Histories,* p. 5.

32. Frantz Fanon, *The Wretched of the Earth.*

33. See Benedict Anderson, *Imagined Communities: Reflections on the Origin and Spread of Nationalism,* revised ed. (London: Verso, 1991); and, for an incisive critique, Chatterjee, *Nationalist Thought and the Colonial World,* pp. 19–22, and *The Nation and Its Fragments,* pp. 3–5.

34. Rashid Khalidi discusses overlapping identities in *Palestinian Identity,* p. 153. The crystallization of national identity in moments of collective crisis is also central to Gelvin's argument in *Divided Loyalties,* p. 12.

35. Two recently published books dealing with modern Syria have profitably utilized the Archives Diplomatiques at Nantes. See Elizabeth Thompson, *Colonial Citizens: Republican Rights, Paternal Privilege, and Gender in French Syria and Lebanon;* and Gelvin, *Divided Loyalties.* The singular example of the use of police and intelligence records is Hanna Batatu, *The Old Social Classes and the Revolutionary Movements of Iraq: A Study of Iraq's Old Landed and Commercial Classes and of Its Communists, Baʿthists, and Free Officers.* Martin Thomas has recently published a useful exploration of the French mandate intelligence service: "French Intelligence-Gathering in the Syrian Mandate, 1920–40," *Middle Eastern Studies* 38, no. 2 (2002): 1–35.

36. Ranajit Guha, *Elementary Aspects of Peasant Insurgency in Colonial India,* pp. 15–16.

37. It is thanks to the generous help of people like Dr. Ḥasan al-Biʿaynî, Dr. Fandî Abû Fakhr, Shaykh Muḥammad Ṭarabayh, Mr. Ziyad Abû Shaqra, and especially

Mr. Ṭalâl Kamâl Rizq that I gained access to such sources. Songs and poems are an important source in rural Syria. See Shiblî al-Aṭrash, *Dîwân Shiblî al-Aṭrash;* Ḥasan al-Qaysî Naṣr, *Qabsât min turâth al-sha'bî: ma'ârik wa qaṣâ'id;* 'Alî 'Ubayd, *'Alî 'Ubayd rubâbat al-thawra: qaṣâ'id shurûqiyya waṭaniyya;* and 'Aṭâ Allâh al-Zâqût, *Aḍwâ' 'alâ al-thawra al-sûriyya al-kubrâ.*

38. See, for example, Ḥannâ Abî Râshid, *Ḥawrân al-dâmiyya,* and *Jabal al-durûz;* Muḥammad Sa'îd al-'Âṣ, *Ṣafaḥat min al-ayyâm al-ḥamrâ';* Hilâl Bek 'Izz al-Dîn al-Ḥalabî, "Mudhakkirât Hilâl Bek 'Izz al-Dîn al-Ḥalabî"; Fahmî al-Maḥâyrî, *al-Mudhakkirât 'an al-thawra al-sûriyya;* 'Abdallâh Najjâr, *Banû ma'rûf fî jabal ḥawrân;* Niqûlâws al-Qâḍî, *Arba'ûn 'âman fî ḥawrân wa jabal al-durûz;* 'Alî Sayf al-Dîn al-Qinṭâr, "'Alâ hâmish al-thawra"; 'Alî Sayf al-Dîn al-Qinṭâr, "Murâsalât sir-riyya 'an thawrat Sulṭân al-Aṭrash"; Fawzî al-Qâwuqjî, *al-Mudhakkirât: 1914–32;* 'Alî 'Ubayd, *'Alî 'Ubayd rubâbat al-thawra: qaṣâ'id shurûqiyya waṭaniyya;* and 'Alî 'Ubayd, "Mudhakkirât 'Alî 'Ubayd."

39. A mostly complete collection of *al-Muqtabas* is in the Asad Library in Damascus and the French Institute, also in Damascus. *Lisân al-ḥâl* from Beirut is in the AUB Jafet Library. *Alif bâ'* and a few others are represented in spotty collections in the Asad Library. The smaller-circulation Damascus dailies are often known only from French mandate press reports. *L'Echo de Paris* and *L'Humanité* are in the French National Library in Paris. *Al-Ahrâm* and *Filasṭîn* are in the University of Chicago Regenstein Library.

CHAPTER 2. THE ḤAWRÂN FRONTIER

1. Jabal (Mount) Ḥawrân is the traditional geographical name for this series of high, though gently sloping, mountains. During the nineteenth century it became known for its predominantly Druze inhabitants and was called Jabal al-Durûz (Druze Mountain). Postindependence efforts to deemphasize symbols of sectarian difference dictated the change to an earlier name, Jabal al-'Arab (Arab Mountain), originally so named for the seminomadic tribes who lived there before the mid-nineteenth century. I have opted to utilize the traditional geographical name.

2. Some of these events have been described in other places. See Khoury, *Syria and the French Mandate,* p. 151; Firro, *A History of the Druzes,* p. 285; and 'Ubayd, *al-Thawra al-sûriyya al-kubrâ,* pp. 124–125.

3. Kais Firro, alone among historians of Druze society, points out that the feudalism of Jabal Ḥawrân differed from European feudalism; see *A History of the Druzes,* p. 212.

4. On the reasons for continued migration, see ibid., pp. 155–164. Lewis, drawing on many sources, estimates that the population of Jabal Ḥawrân nearly tripled in the decade of the 1860s; see *Nomads and Settlers in Syria and Jordan,* p. 94. The wars and the postwar settlements in nineteenth-century Mount Lebanon have been the topic of several fine books. See Engin Deniz Akarlı, *The Long Peace: Ottoman Leba-*

non, 1861–1920; Caesar E. Farah, *The Politics of Interventionism in Ottoman Lebanon, 1830–1861* (London: I. B. Tauris, 2000); Leila Tarazi Fawaz, *An Occasion for War: Civil Conflict in Lebanon and Damascus in 1860* (Berkeley: University of California Press, 1994); and Ussama Makdisi, *The Culture of Sectarianism: Community, History, and Violence in Nineteenth-Century Ottoman Lebanon.*

5. A rich and growing literature on the institution of *mushâ'* now exists. See, for example, Ya'akov Firestone, "The Land-Equalizing Musha' Village: A Reassessment," in Gad G. Gilbar, ed., *Ottoman Palestine, 1800–1914: Studies in Economic and Social History;* and Martha Mundy, "Qada' 'Ajlun in the Late Nineteenth Century: Interpreting a Region from the Ottoman Land Registers," *Levant* 28 (1996): 77–95, and "Village Land and Individual Title: Musha' and Ottoman Land Registration in the 'Ajlun District," in Eugene L. Rogan and Tariq Tell, eds., *Village, Steppe and State: The Social Origins of Modern Jordan,* pp. 58–79. The latest contribution focuses on Jabal Ḥawrân: see Birgit Schaebler, "Practicing Mushâ': Common Lands and the Common Good in Southern Syria under the Ottomans and the French," in Roger Owen, ed., *New Perspectives on Property and Land in the Middle East,* pp. 241–307. My thanks to Birgit Schaebler for providing advance proofs of her article.

6. This section draws on many sources. See, for example, the classic study of rural Syria, Lewis, *Nomads and Settlers in Syria and Jordan;* and 'Abdallâh Ḥannâ, *al-'Ammiyya wa al-intifâḍât al-falâḥiyya (1850–1918) fî jabal ḥawrân,* pp. 303–308. 'Abdallâh Ḥannâ is the foremost historian of rural Syria. See also Fandî Abû Fakhr, *Târîkh liwâ' ḥawrân al-ijtimâ'î: al-suwaydâ'- dar'â- al-qunayṭra- 'ajlûn, 1840–1918;* and al-Bi'aynî, *Jabal al-'arab ṣafaḥât min târîkh al-muwaḥḥidîn al-durûz,* pp. 55–71.

7. The relevant statistics seem to originate from a report commissioned by the Syrian government and completed in 1947. See Republic of Syria (Sir Alexander Gibb & Partners, Consulting Engineers), *The Economic Development of Syria,* p. 20, Table 10. They have been reproduced many times, though usually without citing the source. See Bureau des Documentations Syriennes et Arabes, *Etudes sur l'agriculture syrienne* (Damascus, 1955), p. 24; and Haim Gerber, *The Social Origins of the Modern Middle East,* p. 96 and Table 6.1, p. 97, adapted from Doreen Warriner, *Land Reform and Development in the Middle East,* p. 83. Also 'Abdallâh Ḥannâ, *al-Qaḍiyya al-zirâ'iyya wa al-ḥarakât al-fallâḥiyya fî sûriyya wa lubnân (1820–1920),* vol. 2, pp. 44–48. They are impossible to authenticate, since I have found no mention of the original source or survey method. Still, they are certainly illustrative of general trends. Warriner stated that the first Syrian cadastral survey was begun in 1923. My research to date indicates that it was probably never finished. See Jacques Weulersse, *Paysans de Syrie et du Proche-Orient,* pp. 189–190.

8. Descriptions of abandoned villages and endless fallow fields are legion and figure in all travelers' accounts until the 1860s.

9. I have drawn on the work of Linda Schatkowski Schilcher for the importance of the grain trade. See "The Grain Economy of Late Ottoman Syria and the Issue

of Large-Scale Commercialization," pp. 173–195, "The Hauran Conflicts of the 1860's: A Chapter in the Rural History of Modern Syria," IJMES 13 (1981): 159–179, and "The Great Depression (1873–1896) and the Rise of Syrian Arab Nationalism," *New Perspectives on Turkey* 5–6 (Suraiya Faroqhi, guest editor) (Fall 1991): 167–189.

10. Firro describes the rise of Ismâʿîl best: *A History of the Druzes,* p. 188.

11. Muḥammad Saʿîd al-Qâsimî, *Qâmûs al-ṣinâʿât al-shâmiyya,* p. 55. Grain dealers were called *bâʾika* (plural *buwâykî*) in Damascus.

12. "Mudhakkirât Sulṭân," serialized in *Bayrût al-masâʾ* 97–120 (1975–1976), part 98, p. 25. The importance of these relationships did not end with the Great Revolt of 1925. Sulṭân al-Aṭrash's son Manṣûr al-Aṭrash married the daughter of his father's Christian Maydânî grain merchant, Yûsuf al-Shûwayrî, who had a house in their village. Yûsuf ʿAflaq, grain merchant and father of Baʿth Party founder Michel ʿAflaq, also had a house in the village of al-Qrayâ. Ṣalâḥ al-Dîn al-Bîṭâr, the other founder of the party, was also the son of a Maydânî grain merchant who dealt with Jabal Ḥawrân. Manṣûr al-Aṭrash joined the Baʿth Party as a student at AUB. See Batatu, *Syria's Peasantry,* pp. 134 and 142. Manṣûr al-Aṭrash followed the party leaders to advanced study in Paris.

13. Ministère des Affaires Etrangères, Archives Diplomatiques-Nantes (MAE-Nantes), carton 984, "hauran," "Requête des habitants des villages," 20 March 1930. Beshara Doumani has best described the capitalist integration of the hinterland of Nâblus at approximately the same time. He argues convincingly that the emerging rural middle class worked hand in hand with urban merchants to exploit poorer peasants. While the behavior of Druze shaykhs in the plain of Ḥawrân is consistent with his argument, their Jabal co-religionists resisted exploitation more effectively. See *Rediscovering Palestine,* pp. 162–173.

14. Abû Fakhr, *Târîkh liwâʾ ḥawrân al-ijtimâʿî,* p. 90. Al-Khâlidî's service began in 1893. The job of the governor was always difficult. Some formed bonds, however, that would reemerge later. The Damascene Ghazzî family was deeply involved in the revolt of 1925. Rashid Khalidi suggests that the appointment of Yûsuf Ḍiyâʾ as *qâʾimmaqâm* of Jabal Ḥawrân was punishment for criticism of Sultan Abdülhamid's repressive policies. He characterizes Yûsuf Ḍiyâʾ as an "Arabist, in the sense of a cultural nationalist." It is intriguing to contemplate what influence the ideas of Yûsuf Ḍiyâʾ may have had on the Druze shaykhs he lived among. He was evidently the most widely accepted outside governor of Jabal Ḥawrân. See *Palestinian Identity,* p. 85.

15. Firro, *A History of the Druzes,* pp. 231–233.

16. The events of 1910 have been recounted elsewhere. See, for example, al-Aṭrash, "Mudhakkirât Sulṭân," part 97, p. 36; Firro, *A History of the Druzes,* pp. 243–244. See also the works of Engin Deniz Akarlı, *Some Ottoman Documents on Jordan: Ottoman Criteria for the Choice of an Administrative Center in the Light of Documents on Hauran, 1909–1910;* and Samir M. Seikaly, "Pacification of the Hawran (1910):

The View from Within." I thank the authors for kindly giving me copies of these articles. Fandî Abû Fakhr has a copy of the death warrant for Dhûqân al-Aṭrash and some other shaykhs, signed by the grand vizier. Reproduced in his *Târîkh liwâ' ḥawrân al-ijtimâ'î,* Document 13, p. 344.

17. The classic treatment, now a historical document in its own right, is Marc Bloch, *La société féodale: La formation des liens de dépendance* (Paris: A. Michel, 1939). Another relevant text, still influential, is Weulersse, *Paysans de Syrie et du Proche-Orient.* He argues that all Syria, and by extension the Arab East, was dominated by large estates and feudal exploitation. See Gerber, *The Social Origins of the Modern Middle East,* pp. 95–101, for a concise critique.

18. Engin Deniz Akarlı, "Abdülḥamîd II's Attempt to Integrate Arabs into the Ottoman System," in David Kushner, ed., *Palestine in the Late Ottoman Period: Political, Social, and Economic Transformation,* pp. 74–89. He notes the separate existence of military high schools in Damascus and Baghdad (p. 78).

19. John Presland, *Deedes Bey: A Study of Sir Wyndham Deedes, 1883–1923* (London: Macmillan, 1942), p. 87. Quoted in Selim Deringil, *The Well-Protected Domains: Ideology and the Legitimation of Power in the Ottoman Empire, 1876–1909,* p. 101. This notion of discipline and enticement is a commonplace in most examples of imperial rule. See Timothy Mitchell, *Colonising Egypt,* p. 95.

20. See the work of Stefan Weber, "Images of Imagined Worlds: Self-Image and Worldview in Late Ottoman Wall Paintings of Damascus," in Jens Hanssen, Thomas Philipp, and Stefan Weber, eds., *The Empire in the City: Arab Provincial Capitals in the Late Ottoman Empire.* He demonstrates vividly that nineteenth-century Damascene domestic architecture and decoration reflects deep identification with the symbols of the Ottoman state.

21. Khoury, *Syria and the French Mandate,* pp. 255–257 and 410–411. By my count, seven out of the twelve listed from the Damascus National Bloc leadership graduated from Maktab 'Anbar. Only one of the twelve, Aḥmad al-Laḥḥâm, attended the military school, in both Damascus and Istanbul. Among them, only he and Nasîb al-Bakrî were directly involved in the revolt of 1925.

22. I have found few references to the Damascus Military School. It is known from oral sources in Damascus, the World War I German cadastral surveys of Damascus, and passing mentions in memoirs, biographical dictionaries, and the Ottoman *Sâlnâme* (yearbook) for Syria. There was a military primary school, al-Madrasa al-Rushdiyya al-'Askariyya, and a secondary school, Maktab al-I'dâdiyya al-'Askariyya (*Sâlnâme,* 1315/1897–1898, p. 154; *Sâlnâme,* 1316/1898–1899, p. 160; *Sâlnâme,* 1317/1899–1900, p. 161). It was open by 1897, and probably before. Aḥmad al-Laḥḥâm, who was born in 1883, is the oldest pupil that I have noticed. See Jûrj Fâris, *Man huwa fî sûriyya, 1949,* p. 389. Like most others, Aḥmad al-Laḥḥâm went on to the Imperial Military School in Istanbul. Other graduates with central roles in the Great Revolt, all of whom were born within a few years of 1890, include

Sa'îd al-'Âṣ, Zakî al-Durûbî, Muḥammad 'Izz al-Dîn al-Ḥalabî, Zakî al-Ḥalabî, Yaḥyâ al-Ḥayâtî, Maẓhar al-Sibâ'î, and Fawzî al-Qâwuqjî. Ramaḍân Shallâsh from Dayr al-Zûr and 'Alî al-Aṭrash from Suwaydâ' went from the Tribal School to the Mekteb-i Harbiye, while most of the others went from the Damascus Military School to the Harbiye. For Sa'îd al-'Âṣ, see Muḥammad Sa'îd al-'Âṣ, *al-Tajârib al-ḥarbiyya fî ḥarûb al-thawra al-sûriyya,* pp. 11–12. For Zakî al-Durûbî, see al-Jundî, *Târîkh al-thawrât al-sûriyya,* p. 507. For Muḥammad 'Izz al-Dîn, see Fâris, *Man huwa fî sûriyya,* pp. 129–130. For Zakî al-Ḥalabî, see al-'Âṣ, *Ṣafaḥat,* pp. 44–45. For Fawzî al-Qâwuqjî, see al-Jundî, *Târîkh al-thawrât al-sûriyya,* p. 557. And for Ramaḍân Shallâsh, see al-'Âṣ, *Ṣafaḥat,* p. 109. For other examples and a fuller discussion of this emerging class, see Rashid Khalidi, "Society and Ideology in Late Ottoman Syria: Class, Education, Profession and Confession," in John P. Spagnolo, ed., *Problems of the Middle East in Historical Perspective: Essays in Honour of Albert Hourani,* p. 118. He makes the point that radicalized provincial military officers of humble background would yet have their part to play in Syrian history, as they did in Turkey, Iraq, and Egypt. Their entry into national politics in Syria would have to wait for another generation. My thanks to Stefan Weber for references to the military schools.

23. Patrick Seale, *The Struggle for Syria: A Study of Post-War Arab Politics, 1945–1958,* p. 37. The notion of military education as a means of advancement for the ambitious poor still exists in Damascene oral history. Obviously, it existed elsewhere in the former Ottoman realms as well, since the number of village and provincial boys who made good in the army includes Atatürk and Jamâl 'Abd al-Nâṣir.

24. See Eugene L. Rogan, "Aşiret Mektebi: Abdülhamid II's School for Tribes (1892–1907)," IJMES 28 (1996): 83–107. His article is the best treatment of this strange and interesting institution.

25. Ibid., Table 1, p. 88, and Table 4, p. 101. In the first table he includes a certain Druze Fahd, with no family name or father listed. In the fourth table he mentions Fatḥ b. Farḥân al-Aṭrash, who I think is the same person, with two first names due to scribal error. Fahd b. Farḥân al-Aṭrash is pictured in Ḥannâ Abî Râshid's *Jabal al-durûz* (1961 edition, which has identical text but different pagination). Ḥannâ Abî Râshid's two books, *Jabal al-durûz* and *Ḥawrân al-dâmiyya,* are the most valuable primary source documents extant for the local history of Ḥawrân in the early twentieth century. The two 1961 editions have sequential pagination. *Jabal al-durûz* was translated by the French Service des Renseignements in its entirety and is in the French archives, MAE-Nantes, carton 551, "djebel *[sic]* druze." Published in Cairo, it was banned in Syria during the mandate. Abî Râshid helpfully states that the dapper gent shown graduated from the Tribal School in Istanbul and is now the *qâ'immaqâm* of Ṣarkhad *[sic]*—probably Ṣalkhad (*Jabal al-durûz,* p. 120).

26. al-'Âṣ, *Ṣafaḥat',* p. 107; Rogan, "Aşiret Mektebi," p. 88, Table 1. Shallâsh is listed in the first graduating class, and a certain 'Alî from Suwaydâ' is also listed

without further information. The dates match, and al-ʿÂṣ documents that this was probably ʿAlî b. Fâris b. Ibrâhîm al-Aṭrash, brother of Tawfîq, who was assistant chief of police in 1925, and not ʿAlî, the brother of Sulṭân, who was born in 1895. I thank Manṣûr Sulṭân al-Aṭrash for clarification.

27. Fâris, *Man huwa fî sûriyya,* pp. 129–130.

28. The autonomy agreement is controversial. Abî Râshid reproduced it in his *Jabal al-durûz,* pp. 128–129. But Sulṭân al-Aṭrash claimed in his memoirs that it did not exist. See also Firro, *A History of the Druzes,* pp. 250–251.

29. Al-Aṭrash, "Mudhakkirât Sulṭân," part 98, p. 36. He listed Shahbandar, Nasîb al-Bakrî, Aḥmad Mudrî, Rafîq al-Tamîmî, Shaykh Saʿad al-Bânî, ʿAbd al-Laṭîf al-ʿAsalî, Zakî al-Durûbî, ʿIzz al-Dîn al-Tanawkhî, Nazîh al-Muʾayyad al-ʿAẓm, Taḥsîn Qadrî, Khalîl al-Sukâkînî, Rustum Ḥaydar, and Khalîl Ṣaydaḥ, among many others. Khoury was first to outline the ties between Damascus and Jabal Ḥawrân during the revolt: *Syria and the French Mandate,* p. 165. Wartime Sharîfian patronage was limited to grain sales and guns in the Jabal, but postwar patronage was more expansive and benefited many Damascene participants in the revolt of 1925, particularly members of the Bakrî family. See Gelvin, *Divided Loyalties,* p. 58.

30. Abî Râshid, *Jabal al-durûz,* pp. 126–127. Biographical information on Fawzî and Nasîb al-Bakrî is in Fâris, *Man huwa fî sûriyya,* pp. 67–68. See also Schilcher, *Families in Politics,* p. 156.

31. George Antonius, *The Arab Awakening: The Story of the Arab National Movement,* pp. 149–153; Gelvin, *Divided Loyalties,* pp. 57–58.

32. According to Ramez Tomeh's extraordinary survey of Damascus landowners compiled from land reform expropriation records in 1958 and 1963, only one member of the Bakrî family had enough land even to qualify for expropriation. See Ramez George Tomeh, "Landownership and Political Power in Damascus: 1858–1958," Table 27, Raʾifah al-Bakrî, 29.654 hectares of irrigated and unirrigated land in west Ghûṭa. When one considers that some of the famous families of Damascus had tens of thousands of hectares expropriated, the Bakrîs seem very modest by comparison. It bears mention that *waqfiyya* and urban property were not reported or expropriated. Since the Bakrîs were urban landlords in al-Shâghûr, their material wealth is difficult to assess accurately. Suffice it to say, however, that scores of Damascene families were richer.

33. Linda Schatkowski Schilcher, "The Famine of 1915–1918 in Greater Syria," in John P. Spagnolo, ed., *Problems of the Middle East in Historical Perspective: Essays in Honour of Albert Hourani.* See also Najwa al-Qattan, "Safarbarlik: Collective Memory and Identity," unpublished paper delivered at the Syrian Land Conference, Erlangen, Germany, June 2000.

34. In what might be considered a typical complaint of a front-line officer, Otto Viktor Karl Liman von Sanders, commander-in-chief of the Arab front, wrote in his memoirs that Istanbul not only seemed uninterested in reinforcing his forces but

actively sought to divert troops and equipment to other fronts. The unmistakable implication is that Enver, anyway, sought to reinforce the more "Turkish" regions. See Otto Viktor Karl Liman von Sanders, *Five Years in Turkey*, p. 254 for officer re-postings, pp. 257–259 for resupply problems, and p. 265 for British propaganda. See Hasan Kayalı's *Arabs and Young Turks: Ottomanism, Arabism, and Islamism in the Ottoman Empire, 1908–1918*, for a more nuanced view of Ottoman wartime policy.

35. Schilcher, "The Famine of 1915–1918 in Greater Syria," p. 246.

36. Al-Aṭrash, "Mudhakkirât Sulṭân," part 98, p. 35; Liman von Sanders, *Five Years in Turkey*, p. 262. He reproduced an intelligence report dated 19 August 1918, from a Dr. Brode. "For about two months an organized caravan traffic has existed from Akaba across the Huarun, the Druse mountains *[sic]*. Sugar, coffee, and cotton goods are imported, and apricot paste is exported, together with great quantities of grain from the Hauran." Elsewhere Liman von Sanders wrote: "Had the money been available, all requirements of the Army Group, and large additional supplies, could have been purchased from the Arabs. As the money was not forthcoming, a large part of the harvest of the Arabian grain lands and thousands of camel loads from Hauran, inhabited by Druses, went to the British, who paid in gold" (p. 236).

37. Abî Râshid, *Jabal al-durûz*, pp. 131–133. Qarqûṭ also reproduces the letters, without attribution, in his *Taṭawwur al-ḥaraka al-waṭaniyya fî sûriyya*, pp. 264–266.

38. Gelvin's *Divided Loyalties* covers this period in detail.

39. Batatu, *The Old Social Classes and the Revolutionary Movements of Iraq*, pp. 319–320; Khoury, *Urban Notables and Arab Nationalism*, pp. 79–81.

CHAPTER 3. MOBILIZING THE MOUNTAIN

1. See Gelvin's *Divided Loyalties*, pp. 111–113, 296–297, for popular nationalism and the quarter-based mobilization of Damascus. Gelvin makes it clear that the Damascus-based committee of national defense and the popular committees of Fayṣal's short reign formed the nucleus of Damascus Great Revolt fighters in 1925.

2. Khoury, *Syria and the French Mandate*, pp. 99–108. Al-Jundî, *Târîkh al-thawrât al-sûriyya*, covers all the revolts and rebels in encyclopedic fashion.

3. Khoury, *Syria and the French Mandate*, pp. 58–60.

4. See the following for more comprehensive views of the origins and aims of the mandate: Khoury, *Syria and the French Mandate*, pp. 55–62; Edmund Burke III, "A Comparative View of French Native Policy in Morocco and Syria, 1912–1925," *Middle Eastern Studies* 9 (May 1973): 175–186; Thompson, *Colonial Citizens*.

5. The document has been well circulated. See the English translation in Foreign Office (FO) 371/4310, 13028/214, enclosure, 23 June 1925. The original agreement was dated 4 March 1921 (Abî Râshid, *Jabal al-durûz*, pp. 168–171; 'Ubayd, *al-Thawra al-sûriyya al-kubrâ*, p. 87). My thanks to Dr. Ḥasan Amîn al-Bi'aynî for a copy of the original agreement. Abî Râshid's reproduction matches exactly. Bi'aynî has also reproduced it in his *Jabal al-'arab*, pp. 288–290.

6. Capitaine Gabriel Carbillet, *Au Djébel Druse, choses vues et vécues.* This book has recently been translated into Arabic by Nabîl Abû Ṣaʿb. See *Mudhakkirât al-kâbitan kârbiyyih fî jabal al-ʿarab* (Suwaydâʾ, 1999).

7. Abî Râshid, *Jabal al-durûz,* pp. 221–222; ʿUbayd, *al-Thawra al-sûriyya al-kubrâ,* p. 116; Paul Coblentz, *The Silence of Sarrail,* trans. Arthur Chambers, p. 223 (Coblentz was Sarrail's secretary and posthumous apologist); Firro, *A History of the Druzes,* p. 277.

8. Abî Râshid, *Jabal al-durûz,* p. 252. Abî Râshid reproduced the petition and a full list of signatories, which included Amîr Ḥamad al-Aṭrash, Nasîb Bek al-Aṭrash, ʿAbd al-Ghaffâr Bâshâ al-Aṭrash, Mitʿib Bek al-Aṭrash, Faḍl Allâh Bâshâ al-Aṭrash, Najim Bâshâ ʿIzz al-Dîn [Ḥalabî], Hilâl Bek ʿIzz al-Dîn [Ḥalabî], Quf-ṭân Bek ʿAzzâm, Nasîb Bek Naṣâr, Saʿîd Bek Abû ʿAssâf, Ḥamad Bek ʿAzzâm, Dâwud Bek Abû ʿAssâf, Ḥamûd Bek Naṣr, Jâd Allâh Bek Salâm, Asʿad Bek Murshid, Khalîl Bek Kaywân, ʿUmâr Bek al-Ḥanâwî, Firḥân Bek Abû Râs, Shabîb Bek Qinṭâr, Muḥammad Bek Abû ʿAsalî, Ḥamûd Bek Jurbûʿ, Burjis Bek al-Aṭrash, Sulaymân Bek al-Aṭrash, Ṣayâḥ Bek al-Aṭrash, Ḥusayn Bey al-Ḥunaydî, Fawâz Bek al-Ḥalabî, ʿAbdallâh Bek Najjâr, Ḥasan Bek al-Laḥḥâm, and the author, al-Ustâdh Ḥannâ Abî Râshid. The titles listed are significant. Amîr Ḥamad received his title of "Amîr" through the community's choice of him to succeed Amîr Salîm, whose title was bestowed by Amîr Fayṣal; see *al-Muqtabas,* 11 October 1923. Those men denoted "Bâshâ" were mostly so titled by the Ottoman government, which had a policy of bestowing honors and titles to gain loyalty. "Bek" means little more than "Mister" in this context—an honorific for a local leader. Sulṭân al-Aṭrash claimed that Sharîf al-Ḥusayn also granted him the title of "Amîr," but he refused it. Sulṭân al-Aṭrash received two Ottoman medals and the title "Bâshâ" from the Ottoman state in 1917. See Fâris, *Man huwa fî sûriyya,* pp. 31–32. The Damascus press also reported the delegation and its aims of union with the state of Syria. See MAE-Nantes, carton 892, "Journal Syrienne al-Ahrar," 27 May 1925.

9. Abî Râshid, *Jabal al-durûz,* p. 252. See also Firro, *A History of the Druzes,* p. 280.

10. Hilâl Bek ʿIzz al-Dîn al-Ḥalabî, "Mudhakkirât, 1925–1927," p. 28.

11. Abî Râshid, *Jabal al-durûz,* p. 265.

12. For Ḥusayn Murshid Riḍwân, see Fâris, *Man huwa fî sûriyya,* pp. 178–179.

13. Abî Râshid, *Jabal al-durûz,* pp. 266–267; al-Aṭrash, "Mudhakkirât Sulṭân," part 103, p. 35. Abî Râshid was an eyewitness and a professional journalist. His account is extraordinarily valuable and rich with detailed information and accurately reproduced documents. Firro mentions that Abî Râshid apparently had access to French intelligence documents in 1925, since his translations match the French originals exactly: *A History of the Druzes,* p. 285 and note 23. Nevertheless, Abî Râshid provides assured numerical figures for demonstrators and fighters in the multiple hundreds, while other accounts mention crowds, bands, and groups, and he

consistently attributes the vilest motives and actions to all French personnel except Raynaud, while the Druze are portrayed as more patient and peace-loving than in any chronicle before or since. Ḥannâ Abî Râshid was not a Druze but a Maronite Christian and journalist who lived in the Jabal.

14. Abî Râshid, *Jabal al-durûz,* p. 267.

15. Ibid. (p. 257 in the 1925 edition, which has only has a photo and short biography on Fâris). Fâris al-Aṭrash later fled to Darʿâ under the protection of the French garrison there to escape retribution for his pro-French politics (Andréa, *La révolte druze et l'insurrection de Damas,* p. 57). Fâris al-Aṭrash, seemingly alone among the Druze shaykhs, never joined the uprising and continued to support the mandate government during the revolt. See the Damascus daily *al-Muqtabas,* 12 January 1926, for a front-page article on Fâris al-Aṭrash and his politics.

16. ʿUbayd, *al-Thawra al-sûriyya al-kubrâ,* p. 120. Damascus British consul W. A. Smart's report, probably drawing on French oral sources, substantially agrees with this account, adding that Maurel was injured by stones and sticks. Foreign Office (FO) 371/4310, 13028/217, Smart to Chamberlain, 10 July 1925.

17. Firro, *A History of the Druzes,* pp. 282–283.

18. Abî Râshid, *Jabal al-durûz,* pp. 270–271.

19. FO 371/4310, 13028/217, 10 July 1925, Smart to Chamberlain.

20. Abî Râshid, *Jabal al-durûz,* pp. 271–272. See also Narcisse Bouron, *Les Druzes: Histoire du Liban et de la montagne haouranaise,* pp. 237–238; ʿUbayd, *al-Thawra al-sûriyya al-kubrâ,* p. 121.

21. Firro, *A History of the Druzes,* pp. 283–284.

22. ʿUbayd, *al-Thawra al-sûriyya al-kubrâ,* p. 121.

23. Ministère des Affaires Etrangères (MAE), *Syrie-Liban 1918–1929,* vol. 240, "Les causes de la révolution Druze," p. 174. Cited in Firro, *A History of the Druzes,* p. 284.

24. Henri de Kerillis, "Les scandales Sarrail: La navrante vérité sur le soulèvement des Djebel Druses," *L'Echo de Paris,* 8 August 1925. Sarrail was the object of a long series of vitriolic attacks in the French right-wing press. The Right was not alone in attacking Sarrail, however; see *L'Humanité,* the French Communist Party paper, for more comprehensive critiques of colonial policy generally.

25. Jan Karl Tanenbaum, *General Maurice Sarrail, 1856–1929: The French Army and Left-Wing Politics,* p. 202. It is well established that Raynaud wanted Carbillet's job and probably encouraged agitation against Carbillet and in favor of his own permanent appointment. It is also clear that Sarrail knew this.

26. See the Damascus newspapers *al-Muqtabas,* 17 July 1925, and *Alif Bâʾ,* 14 July 1925; Firro, *A History of the Druzes,* p. 284.

27. MAE-Nantes, carton 551, personal letter from Martin to Dentz, Suwaydâʾ, 17 July 1925. Dentz was his successor as chief of the Service des Renseignements and later Vichy high commissioner in 1941. On the same day Martin sent an offi-

cial letter to the high commissioner's delegate in Damascus, warning of imminent revolt. Reproduced in Henri de Kerillis, "Le Capitaine Raynaud: Gouverneur par intérim des Druses prévient vainement Sarrail," *L'Echo de Paris*, 30 September 1925.

28. Coblentz, *The Silence of Sarrail*, pp. 227–228. See also *Journal Officiel, Débats Sénat*, 17 December 1925, p. 1735; and Abî Râshid, *Jabal al-durûz*, p. 286.

29. Coblentz, *The Silence of Sarrail*, p. 228. See the Damascus newspapers *al-Muqtabas*, 17 July 1925, and *Alif Bâ'*, 14 July 1925. *Muqtabas*, the nationalist paper published by Muḥammad Kurd ʿAlî, reported that they had been exiled for requesting the replacement of Carbillet.

30. Coblentz, *The Silence of Sarrail*, p. 229.

31. ʿUbayd, *al-Thawra al-sûriyya al-kubrâ*, p. 124.

32. FO 371/4313, 13028/218, Smart to Chamberlain, 15 July 1925. Another account from Damascus, critical of Sarrail, is Alice Poulleau, *A Damas sous les bombes: Journal d'une Française pendant la révolte syrienne, 1924–1926*, p. 43. It was difficult even for apologists of mandate rule to explain these tactics, but some managed; see Andréa, *La révolte druze et l'insurrection de Damas*, pp. 51–52. See Bouron, *Les Druzes*, p. 237, for a slightly more critical, and more detailed, account.

33. ʿUbayd, *al-Thawra al-sûriyya al-kubrâ*, pp. 125–126.

34. Ibid. p. 125. ʿUbayd translated a colloquial song into standard Arabic. I based my translation on the standard text. His father, ʿAlî ʿUbayd, was there. See Fâris, *Man huwa fî sûriyya*, p. 281. I record my thanks to Lor Wood for help with poetry translation. Several privately published collections of poems and songs connected to the revolt exist and show the importance of this literary form in rural life—especially during uprisings. See al-Qaysî Naṣr, *Qabsât min turâth al-shaʿbî;* al-Zâqût, *Aḍwâ' ʿalâ al-thawra al-sûriyya al-kubrâ;* and ʿUbayd, *ʿAlî ʿUbayd rubâbat al-thawra.*

35. MAE-Nantes, carton 551, No. 3.617/E.D., "Renseignements sur la révolte druse," p. 9, French translation; Bouron, *Les Druzes*, p. 238.

36. See Bouron, *Les Druzes*, p. 239. ʿUbayd has offered a less ideological interpretation: *al-Thawra al-sûriyya al-kubrâ*, p. 125. Bouron's text matches exactly a secret French report prepared by Captain Desideri of the Service des Renseignements, Jabal Druze, in 1927. The intelligence report is lacking some of Bouron's colonial mission advocacy but is clearly the principal source for his account, and some sections are reproduced word for word. See MAE-Nantes, carton 551, No. 3.617/E.D., "Renseignements sur la révolte druse," Desideri to Catroux, 18 October 1927, p. 10. For ʿAlî Muṣṭafâ al-Aṭrash, see Fâris, *Man huwa fî sûriyya*, p. 33; and Abî Râshid, *Jabal al-durûz*, p. 239; MAE-Nantes, carton 924, "Bayân maktab al-lajna al-markaziyya al-isʿâf aṭfâl al-ṣaḥrâ' fî Bayrût, 1935."

37. MAE-Nantes, carton 551, No. 3.617/E.D., p. 10; Bouron, *Les Druzes*, p. 239; and ʿUbayd, *al-Thawra al-sûriyya al-kubrâ*, p. 125.

38. ʿUbayd, *al-Thawra al-sûriyya al-kubrâ*, p. 126. These men would have been members of the al-Slûṭ tribe of the Laja'a and Jabal. They had long-term commer-

cial ties with the Druze based on pasture agreements and the supply of camel transport for Ḥawrânî wheat to Damascus.

39. ʿUbayd, *al-Thawra al-sûriyya al-kubrâ,* p. 126; Firro, *A History of the Druzes,* p. 286.

40. ʿUbayd, citing an interview with one of the Druze gendarmes who was there, claimed that the Normand column numbered nearly 300 and carried a number of automatic weapons. Among the column were a few French officers, no more than 30 mounted troops, and about 10 Druze foot soldiers, who were locally called "partisan" *(al-bârtîzân),* with the remainder Tunisian colonial troops (*al-Thawra al-sûriyya al-kubrâ,* p. 125). Bouron claimed "une Compagnie d'Infanterie, et deux pelotons de Spahis Tunisiens," or probably between 150 and 250 men (*Les Druzes,* p. 241).

41. Bouron mentions nothing about emissaries to Normand or negotiations but repeats a line from the intelligence report: "une fantasia guerrière se développa . . . Soltan tenait son monde" (*Les Druzes,* p. 240); and MAE-Nantes, carton 551, No. 3.617/E.D., p. 12. Andréa and the report offer a variation on the emissary story. They claim that the chief of the village of al-Kafr was a "friend of France" and alerted Normand that an attack was imminent, but Normand preferred to keep to his orders (*La révolte druze et l'insurrection de Damas,* pp. 52 and 12). The French accounts are marked by a persistent, and persistently successful, search for "friends of France"; compare note 32 above. See also FO 371/4310, 13028/235, Smart to Chamberlain, 6 August 1925. Smart claimed, based on the stories of two Christians from al-Kharbâ, the village of Christian rebel leader ʿUqla al-Quṭâmî, that the shaykh of al-Kafr, Asʿad Murshid, insisted on providing food for the soldiers; while they were eating, the rebels attacked. Whether this is accurate or not, it is no surprise that treachery by a "friend of France" did not find its way into the French or Arab histories.

42. The numbers are a source of contention and vary widely. Munîr al-Rayyis, a Damascene journalist who was not there but knew most of the leaders and was involved in later battles, wrote that the number of rebels (both on foot and mounted) was less than 250. He provides the most detailed account of the survivors, wounded, and dead among the mandate forces and claims that 8 escaped, 65 were wounded and left behind, and 111 were killed. He also emphasizes the superior arms of the French, including light and heavy machine guns and grenades *(qâdhifât al-qanâbil).* See his *al-Kitâb al-dhahabî lil-thawrât al-waṭaniyya fî al-mashriq al-ʿarabî,* p. 165. Bouron, by contrast, claims that about 1,000 Druze attacked one company of foot soldiers and two squads of Tunisian cavalry, or approximately 150–250 men and officers, and that they killed 120 Druze (*Les Druzes,* pp. 240–241); ʿUbayd, *al-Thawra al-sûriyya al-kubrâ,* p. 129; Andréa, *La révolte druze et l'insurrection de Damas,* p. 53. The right-wing Paris newspaper *L'Echo de Paris,* with unusually good military and Foreign Ministry sources, later claimed that 103 men and 4 officers were killed. Their numbers match al-Rayyis closely. See *L'Echo de Paris,* 2 September 1925.

43. Al-Rayyis, *al-Kitâb al-dhahabî,* p. 167.

44. 'Ubayd, *al-Thawra al-sûriyya al-kubrâ,* p. 129; Firro, *A History of the Druzes,* p. 286.

45. FO 371/4310, 13028/225, Smart to Chamberlain, 25 July 1925.

46. Ibid.

47. Guha, *Elementary Aspects of Peasant Insurgency,* p. 251. He wrote: "One would perhaps be quite justified in saying that rumour is both a *universal* and *necessary* carrier of insurgency in any pre-industrial, pre-literate society" (original emphasis). While mandate Syria was hardly "pre-literate," it was pre-mass literacy, and a press blackout meant that literacy did not matter much. Obviously, rumor still functions today as the news source that authoritarian governments and military occupiers cannot control.

48. Enclosure in FO 37/4310, 13028/225, 25 July 1925. A careful review of the French Diplomatic Archives Mandate and Great Revolt files in Nantes failed to turn up any of these pro-mandate testimonials from this period. Many later petitions exist, usually requesting government compensation for losses due to pillage or bombardment, from both rebels and colonial forces. See MAE-Nantes, carton 2389, "insurrection druze."

49. See Fâris, *Man huwa fî sûriyya,* p. 357. In 1925 the mandate census found that the *qaḍâ'* (district) of Suwaydâ' contained 30 villages, 14,740 Druze, 2,386 Greek Orthodox, 380 Greek Catholics, 192 Muslims, 16 Maronites, 26 Armenians, and 10 Jews. MAE-Nantes, carton 2381, "Djebel Druze—situation générale."

50. Carbillet himself seems to have been the origin of this story. See MAE-Nantes, carton 892, No. 4571, Carbillet to délégué du haut-commissaire, 5 November 1923. 'Uqla al-Quṭâmî was imprisoned by the mandate authority in April 1925. MAE-Nantes, carton 406, "*SECRET* historique des négociations entreprises avec les druzes," 8 September 1925.

51. Both the rebels and foreign observers argued that inciting sectarian conflict was part of mandate policy for fighting the revolt. See U.S. Department of State, *Papers Relating to the Foreign Relations of the United States,* 1925, Beirut Consul Knabenshue to Secretary of State, 16 November 1925, vol. 2 (Washington, D.C., 1940), p. 123. No less an observer than George Antonius noted this policy. See *The Arab Awakening,* p. 378.

52. Letter from Ḥamad and Sulṭân al-Aṭrash to the Greek Orthodox Patriarch, MAE-Nantes, carton 1704, BR 155, 28 August 1925, French translation.

53. FO 371/4310, 13028/225, Smart to Chamberlain, 25 July 1925, 13028/226, 27 July 1925, and 13028/229, 29 July 1925. See Lewis, *Nomads and Settlers in Syria and Jordan,* p. 94; and FO 371/4310, 13028/225, Smart to Chamberlain, 25 July 1925. French demographic figures concur.

54. FO 371/4310, 13028/229, Smart to Chamberlain, 29 July 1925.

55. MacCallum, *The Nationalist Crusade in Syria,* pp. 112–113. Cited in Khoury, *Syria and the French Mandate,* p. 157.

56. FO 371/4310, 13028/236, Smart to Chamberlain, 5 August 1925, and FO 371/4310, 13028/240, Satow to Chamberlain, 7 August 1925. Major Aujac's unit fitness report is reproduced in Henry Kerillis, "Le crime: Sarrail envoie au massacre le colonne Michaud," *L'Echo de Paris,* 5 October 1925. Coblentz, Sarrail's secretary, whose account was a direct response to Kerillis' attacks on Sarrail, grudgingly vouched for the authenticity of this document, in *The Silence of Sarrail,* p. 235. MacCallum, *The Nationalist Crusade in Syria,* p. 119, ʿUbayd, *al-Thawra al-sûriyya al-kubrâ,* pp. 130–137; Abî Râshid, *Jabal al-durûz,* p. 240; Bennett J. Doty, *The Legion of the Damned: The Adventures of Bennett J. Doty in the French Foreign Legion as Told by Himself,* pp. 167–169. Henry Kerillis reported authoritatively that the French lost 600 men and 40 officers killed, 420 wounded, 10 cannons (including two 75 mm and two 105 mm), 40 machine guns, 25,000 artillery rounds, and 1 million rounds of small arms ammunition. See *L'Echo de Paris,* 2 September 1925. The insurgents later went to some trouble to find former Ottoman artillery officers to operate their spoils (see Chapter 4).

CHAPTER 4. MOBILIZING THE CITY

1. Reproduced in MAE-Nantes, carton 1704, BR 140 Damas, 3 August 1925, French translation.

2. Poulleau, *A Damas sous les bombes,* p. 54; FO 371/4310, 13028/246, 25 August 1925; MAE-Nantes, carton 1704, BR 140, 3 August 1925, "Sultan Atrache et la Transjordanies (autorités anglaises)."

3. FO 371/4310, 13028/245, Smart to Chamberlain, 21 August 1925.

4. MAE-Nantes, carton 1704, BR 142, 6 August 1925.

5. MAE-Nantes, carton 1704, BR 149, 17 August 1925. See MAE-Nantes, carton 1593, "tracts divers," for full coverage of the trial. The boys were tried and condemned to death on 4 December 1925. Their sentences were later commuted to two- to three-year prison terms.

6. FO 371/4310, 13028/245, Smart to Chamberlain, 21 August 1925, and dispatch 13028/246, 25 August 1925.

7. "The Revolt in Jabal Druse, Sharp Fighting, Reported French Reverse," *Times* (London), 7 August 1925; Henry Kerillis, "Le crime: Sarrail envoie au massacre le colonne Michaud," *L'Echo de Paris,* 5 October 1925.

8. Tanenbaum, *General Maurice Sarrail,* p. 204, especially note 88; MacCallum, *The Nationalist Crusade in Syria,* pp. 126–127; ʿAbd al-Raḥman al-Shahbandar, *al-Thawra al-sûriyya al-waṭaniyya: mudhakkirât al-duktûr ʿAbd al-Raḥman al-Shahbandar,* p. 31.

9. Gelvin concentrated on those opposed to Fayṣal between 1918 and 1920. Not all 1925 revolt participants were supporters of Fayṣal, of course, but many among the Druze and the Damascenes were. See *Divided Loyalties.*

10. Khoury, *Syria and the French Mandate,* p. 144.

11. Shahbandar, *Mudhakkirât wa khuṭab,* pp. 145–151. Speech for the opening ceremony of Ḥizb al-Shaʿb, 5 June 1925. Summarized in Hisham A. Nashabi, "The Political Parties in Syria, 1918–1939," pp. 95–96. Nashabi makes it clear that the party encompassed a wide range of opinion from accommodation to total rejection of the mandate.

12. Khoury, *Syria and the French Mandate,* p. 123.

13. Meetings took place at Shahbandar's house and at the house of Damascene merchants and journalists, including ʿUthmân al-Sharâbâtî in Ṣâliḥiyya: al-Rayyis, *al-Kitâb al-dhahabî,* p. 191. For Sharâbâtî, see Fâris, *Man huwa fî sûriyya,* p. 228.

14. Shahbandar, *al-Thawra al-sûriyya,* p. 12. For *al-Fayḥâʾ,* see Nadine Méouchy, "Les formes de conscience politique et communautaire au Liban et en Syrie à l'époque du mandat français, 1920–1939," Appendix 4.

15. Shahbandar, al-*Thawra al-sûriyya,* p. 13. Saʿîd Ḥaydar also recounted meetings before the revolt; see Nashabi, "The Political Parties in Syria," p. 98.

16. ʿAbdallâh Ḥannâ is the exception. See his *ʿAbd al-Raḥman al-Shahbandar (1879–1940): ʿAlam nahḍawî wa rajal al-waṭaniyya wa al-taḥtarur al-fikrî* (Damascus, 1989), pp. 57–58; Sulṭân al-Aṭrash, "Mudhakirrât Sulṭân," part 98, p. 36; Abî Râshid, *Ḥawrân al-dâmiyya,* pp. 408–409. *Ḥawrân al-dâmiyya* is the sequel to his *Jabal al-durûz.* The 1961 editions have sequential pagination and are cited here. While there are extant 1925 editions of *Jabal al-durûz,* the 1926 edition of *Ḥawrân al-dâmiyya* is very rare, and I have never seen a copy. The French were aware of these contacts too. See Andréa, *La révolte druze et l'insurrection de Damas,* p. 78.

17. Abî Râshid, *Jabal al-durûz,* p. 252. See Chapter 3, note 8 above, for a full list of signatories. See also al-Aṭrash, "Mudhakkirât Sulṭân," part 100, p. 35. The delegation and its aims of union with the state of Syria were also reported in the Damascus press. See MAE-Nantes, carton 892, "Journal Syrienne *al-Ahrar,*" 27 May 1925.

18. Abî Râshid, *Jabal al-durûz,* p. 257; Firro, *A History of the Druzes,* p. 282.

19. Abî Râshid, *Ḥawrân al-dâmiyya,* p. 408.

20. Shahbandar quoted in ibid., p. 409.

21. Ẓâfir al-Qâsimî, *Wathâʾiq jadîda ʿan al-thawra al-sûriyya al-kubrâ,* pp. 198–199.

22. MAE-Nantes, carton 1704, BR 145, 11 August 1925. For Luṭfî al-Ḥaffâr, see Fâris, *Man huwa fî sûriyya,* p. 118.

23. Khoury, *Syria and the French Mandate,* p. 147. By mid-October 1925 the mandate government had shut down Ḥizb al-Waḥda al-Sûriyya too, since even the puppet party was becoming too independent. Of course, with the People's Party outlawed, there was no need for a loyal opposition. See FO 371/4310, 13028/275, Smart to Chamberlain, 12 October 1925.

24. MAE-Nantes, carton 1704, BR 139, 1 August 1925.

25. MAE-Nantes, carton 1704, BR 141, 5 August 1925.

26. MAE-Nantes, carton 1704, BR 142, 6 August 1925; MAE Nantes, carton 1704, BR 237, 1 December 1925, p. 5.

27. His cousin Munîr al-Rayyis covered the arrests; see his *al-Kitâb al-dhahabî*, p. 190.

28. Firro, *A History of the Druzes*, pp. 288–289.

29. MAE-Nantes, carton, 406, "*SECRET* historique des négociations entreprises avec les druzes," 8 September 1925, p. 4. Raynaud wrote a full report on the negotiations, including peace conditions of both sides and correspondence. The Druze delegation was Sulaymân al-Aṭrash, Hâyl ʿÂmr, Muḥammad ʿIzz al-Dîn al-Ḥalabî, Faḍl Allâh Bâshâ Hinaydî, and Sulaymân Naṣṣâr.

30. "*SECRET* historique des négociations entreprises avec les druzes," p. 4.

31. Ibid., Annexe II, "Demandes du peuple Druze." Abî Râshid, *Ḥawrân al-dâmiyya*, pp. 418–419.

32. Ibid., p. 7.

33. Ibid., p. 9. Abî Râshid mentions him too; see *Jabal al-durûz*, p. 295. The French kept track of him later as well. He was probably named Weisil. See MAE-Nantes, carton 1704, BR 160, 9 September 1925.

34. "*SECRET* historique des négociations entreprises avec les druzes," pp. 9 and 11.

35. MAE-Nantes, carton 1704, BR 152, 21 August 1925, "Rassemblements aux points d'eau."

36. Shahbandar, *al-Thawra al-sûriyya*, pp. 32–34; ʿUbayd, *al-Thawra al-sûriyya al-kubrâ*, p. 139; Nashabi, "The Political Parties in Syria," p. 102. Munîr al-Rayyis expressed his exasperation with some Damascene nationalists who were not members of the People's Party. He reported talking with his cousin Najîb al-Rayyis: "I was angry with the Syrian nationalists who were not working . . . to spread the revolt, and turn the revolt in the Jabal from a local Druze uprising into a complete nationalist revolution, directed to the independence of Syria—not merely to exchange one governor for another" (*al-Kitâb al-dhahabî*, p. 186).

37. Al-Jundî, *Târîkh al-thawrât al-sûriyya*. See p. 507 for Tawfîq al-Ḥalabî (1887–1926), p. 478 for Zakî al-Durûbî (1888–1939). Sulṭân al-Aṭrash mentioned that both fled the Ottoman government and stayed in Jabal Ḥawrân during the war. See "Mudhakkirât Sulṭân," part 98, p. 36.

38. Abî Râshid, *Ḥawrân al-dâmiyya*, pp. 408–409; al-Aṭrash, "Mudhakkirât Sulṭân," part 98, p. 36. He claimed to have been in continuous contact with Damascene nationalists since 1918.

39. ʿUbayd, *al-Thawra al-sûriyya al-kubrâ*, p. 139 (original exclamation point).

40. FO 371/4310, 13028/250, Smart to Chamberlain, 29 August 1925.

41. MAE-Nantes, carton 1585. Bell to Secretariat of the High Commissioner for Iraq, 3 November 1925, "*SECRET:* The Syrian Situation and Its Bearings on ʿIraq," p. 6. She had returned from a short visit during which she spoke with Service des Renseignements head Dentz and various Syrian nationalists.

42. FO 371/4310, 13028/329, Smart to Chamberlain, 9 November 1925.

43. MAE-Nantes, carton 1704, BR 152, 21 August 1925, "mouvements des rebelles."

44. "*SECRET* historique des négociations entreprises avec les druzes," Annexe VI, 23 August 1925, letter from Sulṭân al-Aṭrash to Captain Raynaud. Coblentz claimed that Raynaud eventually admitted that Sulṭân al-Aṭrash had duped him: *The Silence of Sarrail,* p. 223.

45. FO 371/4310, 13028/231, Consul-General Beirut to Chamberlain, telegraph, 12 August 1925: "Following from liaison officer for Air Ministry: 'French are taking no further offensive action against Druses for at least ten days'"; and dispatch 13028/234, telegraph, 17 August 1925: "'French still endeavouring to settle Druse trouble amicably. Rebels yesterday handed over one French officer prisoner and fifty-three men. Rebels no longer firing at French aeroplanes.'"

46. Fâris, *Man huwa fî sûriyya,* p. 129; MAE-Nantes, carton 406, "Armée Française du Levant, Commandement des troupes de la région de Damas, *SECRET:* Listes des chefs de Djebel Druze," 24 December 1925. Hâyl ʿÂmr is listed there and in Fâris, *Man huwa fî sûriyya,* pp. 272–273.

47. FO 371/4310, 13028/250, Smart to Chamberlain, 29 August 1925; MAE-Nantes, carton 1704, BR 153, 26 August 1925. Some French sources claimed the rebels numbered as many as 15,000. See Tanenbaum, *General Maurice Sarrail,* p. 204.

48. MAE-Nantes, carton 1704, BR 153, 26 August 1925; FO 371/4310, 13028/250, Smart to Chamberlain, 29 August 1925. For panic in Damascus, see Poulleau, *A Damas sous les bombes,* p. 55.

49. MAE-Nantes, carton 1704, BR 155, 28 August 1925; printed without the final paragraph. It turns up in a number of places and was probably first published in the Cairo newspapers in late August 1925. It was published in translation in the Paris newspaper of the Communist Party, *L'Humanité,* on 9 September 1925. It appears in slightly abridged form in the League of Nations archives, Permanent Mandates Commission, minutes of the Eighth Session, Appendix 12, pp. 191–192, in English translation with the final paragraph; and the FO archives, FO 371/5273, vol. 10851, Damascus to FO, 25 August 1925. Supposedly it made its way into newspapers in North and South America, though I have not seen these examples. It has appeared, sometimes considerably abridged, in many histories of the revolt in Arabic. See al-Qaysî Naṣr, *Qabsât min turâth al-shaʿbî,* p. 120; and al-Biʿaynî, *Jabal al-ʿarab,* Appendix 34, pp. 436–437.

50. MAE-Nantes, carton 1704, BR 157, 31 August 1925. Although Samî al-Sarrâj appears rarely in Great Revolt sources, he had been around and causing problems for the French for some time. He participated in Hanânû's revolt and organized resistance to the French occupation of Aleppo. See al-Jundî, *Târîkh al-thawrât al-sûriyya,* p. 262; Gelvin, *Divided Loyalties,* pp. 59, 84, 134, and 218. Gelvin gives Sarrâj credit for introducing rhetorical militancy to the political discourse in the waning days of Fayṣal's government.

51. MAE-Nantes, carton 1704, BR 154, 27 August 1925. A band of bedouin at-

tacked and robbed a three-wagon French caravan carrying Oriental carpets on the road to Beirut. Considering that the carpets were probably made by bedouin, it is a particularly concrete example of reclaiming the symbolic patrimony.

52. MAE-Nantes, carton 1704, BR 154, 27 August 1925.

53. Lewis, *Nomads and Settlers in Syria and Jordan*, p. 203.

54. MAE-Nantes, carton 1704, BR 154, 27 August 1925, French translation. It begins with a call to God to protect them and give them victory. It is signed: "Sayah Ben Ali, Nemr Abu Oukl, Mechane El Jeneiki, Jarou Ben Sarta, Meragh El Kaakaa *[sic]*, ainsi que tous les Rouallahs vous saluent."

55. MAE-Nantes, BR 163, 8 September 1925.

56. Al-Rayyis, *al-Kitâb al-dhahabî*, pp. 190–191; FO 371/4310, 13028/251, Smart to Chamberlain, 29 August 1925; Nashabi, "The Political Parties in Syria," p. 103.

57. MAE-Nantes, carton 1704, BR 157, 31 August 1925; "L'extension de la révolte," *L'Echo de Paris*, 12 September 1925.

58. This was the location of the massive demonstrations of April 1922 over the earlier arrests of Shahbandar and other nationalist leaders. See Khoury, *Syria and the French Mandate*, pp. 123–124. It has remained a focal point of public protest in Damascus. The first Asad government opened a square in front of the mosque for crowd control during the Islamist rebellion of the early 1980s.

59. MAE-Nantes, BR 156, 29 August 1925; FO 371/4310, 13028/251, 29 August 1925. See Poulleau, *A Damas sous les bombes*, pp. 58–59. She wrote that some of the good ladies of the al-Ṣâliḥiyya neighborhood spoke at the demonstration for liberty and called on France to make good on its claims of liberalism and enlightenment. In the following days, Shahbandar's wife organized women's protest marches in Damascus.

CHAPTER 5. THE SPREAD OF REBELLION

1. MAE-Nantes, carton 1704, BR 159, 2 September 1925, "Attitude de Mme. Shahbandar." This report came from the testimony of a Mme. Adîb Affandî ʿArab ʿUqla, who passed it on to the intelligence service.

2. MAE-Nantes, carton 1704, BR 161, 4 September 1925, and BR 162, 5 September 25.

3. MAE-Nantes, carton 1704, BR 164, 9 September 1925. The meeting of 7 September brought together thirty-seven women at the house of Mme. ʿUthmân al-Sharâbâtî. The conversations at the women's meetings were far more inflammatory than the conversations at the men's meetings recorded in intelligence reports before the arrests. The women discussed the valor of the fighters in the countryside, the readiness for patriotic martyrdom, and the work of bringing the rebellion to all of the country. It bears mention that women's discussion groups remain an important aspect of Syrian urban culture.

4. MAE-Nantes, carton 1704, BR 159, 2 September 1925, French translation of a

tract from al-Qunayṭra. At the same time another tract signed by Sulṭân al-Aṭrash appeared in Damascus.

5. MAE-Nantes, carton 1704, BR 160, 3 September 1925.

6. MacCallum, *The Nationalist Crusade in Syria,* p. 126. French agents were accused of raising Christian Assyrian refugees in Iraq for use as shock troops in Syria. Secret British report from Henry Dobbs, The Residency, Baghdad, to Colonial Secretary, 15 September 1926, in MAE-Nantes, carton 1585, "M Documents" [Mosul]. He reported that recruiters were signing up to twenty people per day to fight in Syria.

7. Most of the informants for French intelligence in Ḥawrân seem to have been Muslim shaykhs who took part in insurgent meetings. There is no doubt that these men, with clear fears of both Druze and mandate depredations, were playing their traditional roles and working to make the most of their historically weak position vis-à-vis the state and the Druze. See, for example, MAE-Nantes, carton 1704, BR 169, 16 September 1925, report of occasional agent Ḥaj Mûsâ [al-Hânî], shaykh of Buṣrâ al-Shâm. Dr. Fandî Abû Fakhr has documents in his possession dating from as far back as the 1850s signed by Ismâ'îl al-Aṭrash among other Druze shaykhs, and including a few Ḥawrânî shaykhs, that show clearly the historical roots of this tension. One peace treaty reads in part: "A session took place between the shaykhs to deal with problems between them and the Ḥawranî . . . There will be no sanctuary *[al-waṣîy al-dakhîl]* in cases of kidnapping of brides . . . We have common elements in that we are all the same before God . . . Our worries and their worries are one, and our interests and their interests are one . . . We affirm that no Druze shaykh has the right to remove any Ḥawrânî shaykh from his village, or to assign a shaykh, because the Ḥawrânîs know their own business . . ." This was witnessed by seventeen Druze shaykhs and two Ḥawrânî shaykhs. Even before the massive Druze migrations of the 1860s, it speaks volumes about the balance of power in Ḥawrân. Reproduced in Abû Fakhr, *Târîkh liwâ' ḥawrân al-ijtimâ'î,* pp. 222–223.

8. MAE-Nantes, carton 1704, BR 160, 3 September 1925, French translation of a "tract widespread in Beirut." Also found in MAE-Nantes, carton 1593, "tracts divers."

9. MAE-Nantes, carton 1893, "tracts divers," numerous copies. Final Service des Renseignements report, No. 2304, D.D. 2, 8 September 1925. Notices appeared in Ḥamâh about that time too. The Ḥamâh tract struck a different tone than those of Damascus and mixed Muslim religious language with calls to support the cause of independence and the brothers of the Jabal Druze (MAE-Nantes, carton 1704, BR 162, 5 September 1925, French translation).

10. MAE-Nantes, carton 1593, "tracts divers," Beirut, 9 September 1925, French translation.

11. MAE-Nantes, carton 1704, BR 159, 2 September 1925.

12. Damascenes and others present included Jamîl Mardam Bek, Nasîb, Fawzî,

and As'ad al-Bakrî, Zakî Zaybak, Shaykh [Muḥammad] Abû 'Abdu al-Ḥijâz from Maydân with thirty horsemen, Shahbandar, Ḥasan al-Ḥakîm, Ḥasan Aghâ al-Kurdî with five horsemen, Salîm al-Khatib (a Druze from Jaramânâ), Salîm 'Ubayd (a Druze from Jaramânâ), and Yaḥyâ al-Ḥayâtî, along with five other unnamed former officers (MAE-Nantes, carton 1704, BR 163, 8 September 1925). The source was Damascus Security, submitted by "très sérieux notable du Midan." He would have been a paid spy. It bears emphasis that the story of discord between the Druze and Damascenes and of Hashemite and Anglo intrigue was precisely what the French wanted to hear.

13. MAE-Nantes, carton 1704, BR 163, 8 September 1925. The Service des Renseignements later intercepted a letter from Rikâbî to his brother Aḥmad in Damascus, in which he stated with studied obliqueness that Aḥmad should not believe the lies against him in the (pro-mandate) press in Damascus and that he and Amîr 'Abdallâh agreed that they (the French, the rebels, or both?) could not disrupt the country (MAE-Nantes, carton 1704, BR 176, 24 September 1925, French translation).

14. Qarqûṭ reproduced the letters describing punishment for informers in his *Taṭawwur al-ḥarakat al-waṭaniyya fî sûriyya,* p. 270, 2 February 1926. For Ḥusnî Ṣakhr, see Fâris, *Man huwa fî sûriyya,* p. 255.

15. MAE-Nantes, carton 1704, BR 166, 12 September 1925, reported a cannon positioned near Suwaydâ' citadel; BR 167, 14 September, gave exact positions. Zakî al-Durûbî, who had been an Ottoman and Sharîfian artillery officer, went back and forth between Ḥawrân and Damascus at this time. See Chapter 4 and al-Jundî, *Târîkh al-thawrât al-sûriyya,* p. 478, for Zakî al-Durûbî.

16. FO 371/4310, 13028/ 258, Smart to Chamberlain, 18 September 1925.

17. MAE-Nantes, carton 1704, BR 169, 16 September 1926.

18. FO 371/4310, 13028/256, Satow to Chamberlain, 8 September 1925. "The recall of General Michaud and his replacement by General Gamelin is considered to be a severe blow to General Sarrail. It appears to be correct that the change was made without consulting the High Commissioner, who has persisted in regarding General Michaud as an officer of merit" (Coblentz, *The Silence of Sarrail,* p. 237).

19. MAE-Nantes, carton 1704, BR 169, 16 September 1925, report of occasional agent Ḥaj Mûsâ [al-Hânî, shaykh of Buṣrâ al-Shâm].

20. MAE-Nantes, carton 924, "rebelles réfugiés," "Djebel Druze," No. 221, 7 January 1925.

21. John Henry Harvey, *With the Foreign Legion in Syria,* p. 157.

22. Doty, *The Legion of the Damned,* p. 119. See Harvey, *With the Foreign Legion in Syria.*

23. Harvey recounts pillaging and burning a village and murdering the inhabitants for refusing to pay taxes. See *With the Foreign Legion in Syria,* p. 159.

24. MAE-Nantes, carton 2389, "Exposé de la situation des sinistrés de Djébel Druze," n.d. (approximately September 1925), in original French. See also Niqûlâws

al-Qâḍî, *Arba'ûn 'âman fî ḥawrân wa jabal al-durûz.* Qarqûṭ reproduced the letters describing punishment for informers in his *Taṭawwur al-ḥarakat al-waṭaniyya fî sûriyya,* p. 280. For Ḥusnî Ṣakhr, see Fâris, *Man huwa fî sûriyya,* p. 255.

25. Doty, *The Legion of the Damned,* p. 115; 'Ubayd, *al-Thawra al-sûriyya al-kubrâ,* p. 143.

26. 'Ubayd, *al-Thawra al-sûriyya al-kubrâ,* pp. 144–145.

27. Andréa, *La révolte druze et l'insurrection de Damas,* p. 61; MAE-Nantes, carton 1704, BR 171, 18 September 1925. The Service des Renseignements reported more than 2,000 Druze rebels in the attack. The next day's intelligence report reported both 1,500 and 5,000 rebels in the attack, in alternating parts of the bulletin. A contemporary reader, probably the Damascus delegate to the High Commission, M. Aubourd, pointed out the discrepancy in hand notations (BR 172, 19 September 1925).

28. Doty, *The Legion of the Damned,* pp. 119–120. Harvey mentions a French officer who went into a frenzy and murdered several shackled "Druze" prisoners with his pistol and saber (*With the Foreign Legion in Syria,* pp. 165–166).

29. See MAE-Nantes, carton 894, Service des Renseignements, No. 3000, 7 July 1926; and "armée, police, légion syrienne." See also Francis A. Waterhouse, *'Twixt Hell and Allah* (London: Sampson Low, 1933). This book purports to be a Foreign Legionnaire's account of the revolt of 1925. Unlike the other two, it is a fictional fake.

30. FO 371/4310, 13028/261, Smart to Chamberlain, 29 September 1925; Andréa, *La révolte druze et l'insurrection de Damas,* p. 65.

31. MAE-Nantes, carton 1704, BR 183, 3 October 1925, "demande de soumission," letters of submission enclosed. They were principally members of the 'Âmr, Ḥunaydî, and Naṣr families.

32. "Soueïda est délivrée," *L'Echo de Paris,* 25 September 1925.

33. See MAE-Nantes, carton 1704, BR 164, 9 September 1925, "O Syrian People, Why are you resigned to remain in darkness? Awake from your slumber . . . [signed] the party of [female] revolutionaries," French translation. By this time it was clear that Damascenes would have to lead themselves out of the metaphorical darkness of mandate rule. With a few exceptions, their nationalist leaders were already outside the country, trying to raise financial and military help.

34. The "compact minorities" are generally held to be the rural heterodox sects in Syria, including the Druze, the 'Alawîs, and the Ismâ'îlîs. Anthropologists and others have viewed them as insular and uninterested in larger political issues. It is usually argued that their defining characteristic is an effort to stay aloof from outside conflict and only ally themselves with outsiders when absolutely necessary.

35. MAE-Nantes, carton 1704, BR 182, 2 October 1925, "rapport d'informateur."

36. Fawzî al-Qâwuqjî, *Mudhakkirât Fawzî al-Qâwuqjî,* ed. Khayriyya Qâsimiyya, pp. 15–20; also al-Jundî, *Târîkh al-thawrât al-sûriyya,* pp. 553–554. While Qâwuqjî's contention that the Unionist coup fostered Turkish linguistic domina-

tion is familiar, other evidence suggests that the situation in parts of the imperial bureaucracy was more complicated. For example, I spent two years reading the late Ottoman cadastral and land tax records of the *muḥâfaẓa* of Damascus at the General Directorate for the Administration of Immovable Property in Damascus. In these bureaucratic records, the language on the printed form and of the assessor's notations *changed* from Turkish to Arabic about two years after the revolution.

37. al-Qâwuqjî, *Mudhakkirât,* p. 102. His friends and fellow officers in Ḥamâh included Saʿîd Tarmânînî, ʿAbd al-Salâm al-Farjî, Muḥammad ʿAlî and Ṭâhir al-Dâghastânî, and ʿAbd al-Qâdir Maysir. Munîr al-Rayyis makes clear that, apart from patriotic reasons, Qâwuqjî had powerful personal grievances against his French masters in Ḥamâh. They were racists and treated him with persistent disrespect. See *al-Kitâb al-dhahabî,* p. 206.

38. al-Qâwuqjî, *Mudhakkirât,* p. 104. He first published his memoirs with the help of Dr. Khayriyya Qâsimiyya in 1975. The earlier writing is in the introduction to al-ʿÂṣ, *Ṣafaḥat,* p. 9. See also Abî Râshid, *Ḥawrân al-dâmiyya,* "al-Qâwuqjî yaṣifu thawra ḥamâh," pp. 479–482.

39. al-Rayyis, *al-Kitâb al-dhahabî,* p. 207.

40. al-Qâwuqjî, *Mudhakkirât,* p. 107. He apparently knew something of the spy network and how many insurgent letters and notices were ending up in French hands. Al-Jundî recounts the same story; see *Târîkh al-thawrât al-sûriyya,* p. 201.

41. For Sibâʿî, see al-Jundî, *Târîkh al-thawrât al-sûriyya,* p. 324. For Rayyis, see Fâris, *Man huwa fî sûriyya,* p. 178; also al-Rayyis, *al-Kitâb al-dhahabî,* and the same title with the following subtitles: *Thawra filisṭîn ʿâm 1936* and *Ḥarb al-ʿirâq ʿâm 1941* (Beirut, 1976 and 1978, respectively).

42. Introduction to al-ʿÂṣ, *Ṣafaḥat,* p. 10. The plan to plunder the banks and government offices does not appear in Qâwuqjî's later memoirs.

43. MAE-Nantes, carton 1704, BR 183, 3 October 1925. "Muslim public opinion in Ḥamâh continues to manifest sympathy for the Druze. The campaign of the hostile nationalist party had incontestably won the terrain." See Qâwuqjî's introduction to al-ʿÂṣ, *Ṣafaḥat;* and ʿAbd al-Raḥman Shahbandar's various publications, including *Mudhakkirât wa khuṭub* and *al-Qaḍâyâ al-ijtimâʿiyya al-kubrâ fî al-ʿâlam al-ʿarabî.*

44. MAE-Nantes, carton 1704, BR 184, 5 October 1925.

45. For late Ottoman Ḥamâh and the estates of these families, see Dick Douwes, *The Ottomans in Syria: A History of Justice and Oppression.*

46. Qâwuqjî refused to name these people apart from identifying them as members of the Barâzî family; introduction to al-ʿÂṣ, *Ṣafaḥat,* p. 10.

47. MAE-Nantes, carton 1704, BR 185, 6 October 1925, 15h.30. Two companies of troops totaled no more than 250 second-line troops. Despite the self-congratulatory tone of the dispatch of that evening, they could never have regained Ḥamâh without significant additional reinforcements. "Une détente marquée a été observée à Hama après l'arrivée des 2 Compagnies de renfort de RAYAK et de ALEP. La fusillade a cessé dans la ville."

48. Introduction to al-ʿÂṣ, *Ṣafaḥat*, p. 15. Lenka Bokova makes a similar argument in her fine book *La confrontation franco-syrienne à l'époque du mandat, 1925–27*, p. 205.

49. Bukova, *La confrontation franco-syrienne à l'époque du mandat*, p. 205.

50. MAE-Nantes, carton 1704, BR 189, 10 October 1925, "Opinion publique de Damas."

51. FO 371/4310, 13028/268, 10 October 1925. British consul Smart quoted Soule from a personal conversation a few evenings before. Soule was the officer who, after approval from Sarrail and Gamelin, gave the order to shell Damascus. Additional evidence indicates that the military command sought an excuse to bomb the capital. See Poulleau, *A Damas sous les bombes*, p. 81.

52. al-ʿÂṣ, *Ṣafaḥat*, pp. 35–36. He stresses that one of the officers managed to kill a rebel but that the rebels did not avenge the death because the officer was a prisoner: "To kill a prisoner is a shameful thing to the Arabs" (al-Rayyis, *al-Kitâb al-dhahabî*, pp. 288–289; FO 371/4310, 13028/266, Smart to Chamberlain, 10 October 1925). A less colorful, and less amused, version appears in MAE-Nantes, carton 1704, BR 188, 9 October 1925. See also the report of one of the captured officers: MAE-Nantes, carton 1704, BR 213, 7 November 1925, "Déclaration de Rafic Bey al-Azm, Capitaine de Gendarmerie à Damas, capturé 5/10/25 à Meiha par les bandits."

53. FO 371/4310, 13028/266, Smart to Chamberlain, 10 October 1925.

54. al-ʿÂṣ, *Ṣafaḥat*, p. 31. Munîr al-Rayyis echoed some of these criticisms of Kharrâṭ, though he never made the Bakrî-Kharrâṭ link. See *Kitâb al-dhahabî*, pp. 371–372, for example.

55. MAE-Nantes, carton 1704, BR 191, 13 October 1925, "La Bande Akkache opérant sur la route Damas-Beyrouth." By the middle of October 1925, Saʿîd ʿAkâsh already had been sentenced to fifteen years in prison. It soon became a death sentence; but he was never caught, though he was murdered—probably as revenge for his actions during the revolt—in the center of Damascus in 1941.

56. See ʿAdnân al-ʿAṭṭâr, *Thawrat al-ḥuriyya fî al-minṭiqa al-sâdisa bi-dimasq 1925–1926 wâdî baradâ wa al-muhâjirîn wa al-ṣâliḥiyya*. This is a privately published book by the grandson of Saʿîd ʿAkâsh. The centrality of Dummar as homeland is clear. The writer also had a display memorializing his grandfather and relatives in the 1925 revolt at the Damascus National Document Festival (Maʿriḍ al-Tawthîq al-Qawmî) in 1999. In 2000 his display was absent, and employees informed me that it had not been included because it was not a good example of the nationalist struggle. It is worth mentioning that this kind of book is only available today through the efforts of relatives. The grandson of Saʿîd al-ʿÂṣ is responsible for the republication of his memoir, *Ṣafaḥat min al-ayyâm al-ḥamrâ'*, first published in 1935. Al-ʿÂṣ, in uneasy contrast, has stronger but equally troubling nationalist credentials from the perspective of the current Syrian government. Anṭûn Saʿâda, leader of the militantly secular Greater Syria party, the Syrian Social Nationalist Party (al-Ḥizb al-Sûrî al-Qawmî al-Ijtimâʿî), considered Saʿîd al-ʿÂṣ the first posthumous

nationalist saint of the party. This party has been outlawed in Syria for forty years, and these books are banned there. See Anṭûn Saʿâda's introduction, "Dhikrâ al-rafîq Saʿîd al-ʿÂṣ," in al-ʿÂṣ, *al-Tajârib al-ḥarbiyya*. This was published under party auspices from unpublished manuscripts. Saʿîd al-ʿÂṣ was killed fighting the British and Zionists in Palestine in 1936.

57. The boy's name was Bashîr al-Hunaydî, from al-Malayḥa. See al-ʿÂṣ, *Ṣafaḥat*, p. 35. Al-ʿÂṣ is strangely silent on the atrocities committed by French troops. He calls the operation in the Ghûṭa a success for the rebels, which from a purely military standpoint perhaps it was. Doubtless, as he points out, the operations swelled the rebel ranks, if only because the French had destroyed the homes and livelihoods of so many peasants (p. 38).

58. MAE-Nantes, carton 1704, BR 191, 13 October 1925; FO 371/4310, 13028/28, Smart to Chamberlain, 15 October 1925; Poulleau, *A Damas sous les bombes*, p. 76. Poulleau describes in horrifying detail the spectacle of the dead in Marja Square, as all the high civilian and military officials of the mandate government in Damascus observed.

59. "Un splendide tableau de chasse," quoted in Poulleau, *A Damas sous les bombes*, pp. 80–81; "Parade of Corpses," *Times* (London), 27 October 1925.

60. Fakhrî al-Kharrâṭ quoted them as declaring on behalf of Jaramânâ: "We have to avenge the death of our women violated and murdered by the troops [text cut out] women soaked in their own blood. If these crimes remain unpunished, farewell to the honor of the Banî Maʿrûf" (MAE-Nantes, carton 1704, BR 200, 23 October 1925).

61. The Service des Renseignements compiled a minute-by-minute record of the uprising and bombardment of Damascus. See MAE-Nantes, carton 1704, BR 196, BR 197, BR 198, BR 199, 19, 20, 21, and 22 October 1925, for the events between 18 and 21 October 1925.

62. MAE-Nantes, carton 1704, BR 200, 23 October 1925, "Déclarations du nommé Fakhri Ben Hassan Kharat."

63. FO 371/4310, 13028/303, Smart to Chamberlain, 25 October 1925. French officials claimed doggedly that the bombardment was the only thing that had prevented a general massacre of Christians and foreigners. See FO 371/4310, 13028/305, Mayers to Chamberlain, 30 October 1925, U.S. Department of State, *Papers Relating to the Foreign Relations of the United States*, 1925, Knabenshue to Secretary of State, 19 October 1925, vol. 2, p. 108.

64. FO 371/4310, 13028/303, Smart to Chamberlain, 25 October 1925; "Damascus Riots, the Full Story, City Shelled for 48 Hours, Famous Places Destroyed," *Times*, 27 October 1925. French authorities evidently claimed that the bombardment was less intensive than it was. Most sources indicate the shelling began about 5 P.M., Sunday, 18 October, but the otherwise exhaustive French minute-by-minute chronology places the beginning almost exactly twenty-four hours later. It seems that the French sought to create evidence for the claim that the first day of bombardment

began with the widely reported blank shells, for the obvious reason of deflecting criticism of French barbarity. The report listed only those times when confirmed live ammunition was used. British consul Smart disputed this and wrote: "In various European press reports it is stated that on Sunday, the 18th of October, only blank shells were fired at the town of Damascus, and that the bombardment of live shells only began on Monday the 19th of October. A very palpable proof of the inaccuracy of this statement is a large fragment of a shell now in my possession, which fell into a drawing-room of the Irish Presbyterian School at 6 P.M. Sunday the 18th of October, i.e., less than half an hour after the beginning of the bombardment" (FO 371/4310, 13028/317, Smart to Chamberlain, 7 November 1925). See MAE-Nantes, carton 1704, BR 197, 20 October 1925, "19/10/25 16h.10: Un officier revenant de la citadelle signale le bombardement [text cut] partie de Souk est en feu. Résultat du bombardement, très effectif. Le bombardement continue méthodiquement."

65. Khoury, *Syria and the French Mandate,* p. 178. The commercial heart of Damascus between the Sûq al-Ḥamîdiyya and Sûq Ṭawîl (Straight Street) was utterly destroyed; and when it was rebuilt even the streets were redrawn. It stands out in the old city of today by its gridlike streets and modern buildings and retains the name it gained in 1925: al-Ḥarîqa (Great Fire).

66. Approximately $10 million in 2005. Damages to Damascus were estimated at twenty times this amount, $200 million. For weights and exchanges, see Sevket Pamuk, "Money in the Ottoman Empire, 1326–1914," in Suraiya Faroqhi et al., eds., *An Economic and Social History of the Ottoman Empire, Volume Two, 1600–1914* (Cambridge: Cambridge University Press, 1994), p. 972. My rough conversion is based on admittedly variable gold values.

67. MAE-Nantes, carton 1704, BR 198, 21 October 1925.

68. Fâris, *Man huwa fî sûriyya,* p. 92; Schilcher, *Families in Politics,* p. 215; Tomeh, "Landownership and Political Power in Damascus," Appendix Table A-11. At the time of land expropriation in 1958, they owned 5,261 hectares of agricultural land, mostly in the *muḥâfaẓa* of Ḥawrân and the *minṭaqa* of Darʿâ. By 1958 they had been selling off land for decades in Palestine but also in Syria.

69. Gelvin, *Divided Loyalties,* pp. 26–27; FO 371/4310, 13028/235, SECRET, Smart to Chamberlain, 9 November 1925. This report is some of the strongest evidence available that the British were intriguing against France or at least entertaining the fancy of those who were intriguing against France's mandate.

70. See MAE-Nantes, carton 1704, BR 200, 23 October 1925, "Déclarations du nommé Fakhri Ben Hassan Kharrat."

71. Al-ʿÂṣ, *Ṣafaḥat,* pp. 38–41; MacCallum, *The Nationalist Crusade in Syria,* p. 139. Khoury, examining some of the same sources, comes to similar conclusions but gives Nasîb al-Bakrî more credit for acting decisively: *Syria and the French Mandate,* pp. 176 and 180.

72. For the Mahâynî family, see al-Jundî, *Târîkh al-thawrât al-sûriyya,* pp. 475–

477; Fâris, *Man huwa fî sûriyya,* pp. 431–432; and Schilcher, *Families in Politics,* pp. 150–151. Tomeh demonstrated that the Mahâynî family owned no significant agricultural land at mid-century. See his "Landownership and Political Power in Damascus," Tables A-1 through A-27.

CHAPTER 6. THE POLITICS OF REBELLION

1. FO 371/4310, 13128/193, Damascus Consul Smart to Foreign Minister Chamberlain, 28 January 1926.

2. FO 371/4310, 13028/330, Smart to Chamberlain, 10 November 1925; MAE-Nantes, BR 211, 5 November 1925; also al-Jundî, *Târîkh al-thawrât al-sûriyya,* p. 205. ʿAbd al-Qâdir Sukkar and Ṣubḥî al-Mahâynî were both grain merchants and both later joined the insurgents in the Ghûṭa. Members of both families had long been involved in popular nationalist agitation in their quarter of Maydân. These families had been involved in the Ḥawrân and Jabal Ḥawrân grain trade since the mid-nineteenth century. See Gelvin, *Divided Loyalties.*

3. MAE-Nantes, carton 1704, BR 241, 5 December 1925, SR Damas, gendarmerie locale.

4. Gelvin, *Divided Loyalties,* pp. 111–112, 116.

5. al-Jundî, *Târîkh al-thawrât al-sûriyya,* pp. 536–537.

6. MAE-Nantes, carton 1704, BR 241, 5 December 1925, French translation. I have generally translated these letters from French translation except when Arabic originals were available. I list some details here. For *waṭan,* the French is usually rendered *patrie,* which I have rendered as homeland. For *mujâhid,* the French is either *combattant* or *mujâhid;* I have retained the Arabic. For *thâ'ir,* the French is usually *révolutionnaire;* I have used insurgent or rebel. Syrian contemporaries usually called the revolt the Thawra Sûriyya al-Waṭaniyya or Syrian Patriotic Revolution.

7. MAE-Nantes, carton 1704, BR 243, 7 December 1925, annexe 1, French translation.

8. MAE-Nantes, carton 1704, BR 243, 7 December 1925, annexe 3, French translation.

9. Ted Swedenburg, *Memories of Revolt: The 1936–1939 Rebellion and the Palestinian National Past,* pp. 30–31.

10. MAE-Nantes, carton 1704, BR 243, 7 December 1925, pp. 4–7.

11. MAE-Nantes, carton 1704, BR 210, 4 November 1925. It was ironic that intelligence officers could describe people with such obviously wide appeal as no more than bandits and common criminals, usually in the same report.

12. MAE-Nantes, carton 1704, BR 213, 7 November 1925. This report was confirmed by interviews with elderly Christian villagers, including Wadîʿ al-Maʿrî, 87-year-old former *mukhtâr* (headman) of Ṣaydnâyâ, 10 August 2002. His father was *mukhtâr* during 1925.

13. MAE-Nantes, carton 1704, BR 241, 5 December 1925, annexe 1, French translation.

14. Fâris, *Man huwa fî sûriyya,* p. 248.

15. MAE-Nantes, carton 1704, BR 241, 5 December 1925, annexe 1, French translation.

16. Rogan, "Aşiret Mektebi," Table 1, p. 89; al-ʿÂṣ, *Ṣafaḥat,* p. 109; Abî Râshid, *Jabal al-durûz,* pp. 299–300.

17. MAE-Nantes, carton 1704, BR 200, 23 October 1925, "Déclarations du nommé Fakhri Ben Hassan Kharat." The Damascus daily press reported his public execution in January 1926 along with those of several other men. See "Maḥalliyya: muḥâkama Fakhrî al-Kharrâṭ," *al-Muqtabas,* 29 January 1926.

18. MAE-Nantes, carton 1704, BR 243, 7 December 1925, French translation.

19. MAE-Nantes, carton 1593, "tracts divers," 4 February 1926, "Lettre de menace adressée par HASSAN KHARRAT à AMINE MAMLOUK, Grec orthodoxe," French translation. For Kharrâṭ's death, see al-Jundî, *Târîkh al-thawrât al-sûriyya,* p. 358. It is unclear why this letter took a month to find its way to the mandate authorities. On 9 December 1925 Kharrâṭ wrote a letter to the newspaper *al-Aḥrâr* preserved in the same intelligence file. In the letter he condemned mandate rule generally and the new high commissioner, Henry de Jouvenel, specifically. He concluded by proclaiming that the revolt had nothing to do with sectarianism and everything to do with patriotism and the complete independence of Syria *(hadhihi al-thawra hiya thawra al-waṭaniyya wa laysa ṭâ'ifiyya).*

20. al-ʿÂṣ, *Ṣafaḥat,* p. 107; see Poulleau, *A Damas sous les bombes,* p. 130.

21. al-ʿAṭṭâr, *Thawrat al-ḥuriyya fî al-minṭiqa al-sâdisa bi-dimasq,* p. 130; al-Jundî, *Târîkh al-thawrât al-sûriyya:* for the ʿAkash brothers, see p. 387; for Abû ʿUmar Dibû Aghâ, see pp. 396–397. For lists of the condemned and charges, see MAE-Nantes, carton 405, "Sûreté Générale, No. 340/S.D.," 5 May 1937.

22. Service Historique de l'Armée de Terre (SHAT) 4H65/D1, BR 8, 8 December 1925, "Région de Nebek-Homs." For rebel numbers, see SHAT 4H65/D1, BR 14, 22 December 1925, "Région de Homs." See also al-Safarjalânî, *Târîkh al-thawra al-sûriyya,* p. 227. He describes a much more limited range for each band and, like most Arabic secondary sources, ignores Ramaḍân Shallâsh and Saʿîd ʿAkâsh altogether. British diplomatic reports indicate much smaller rebel numbers but, unlike French reports, mention wide popular support for the rebels. See, for example, FO 371/4310, 13128/193, Smart to Chamberlain, 28 January 1926. The British consul probably did not have intelligence sources in the countryside and likely relied upon casual conversations with French officers.

23. Khoury, *Syria and the French Mandate,* pp. 144–145. See Nashabi, "The Political Parties in Syria," pp. 101–102. For Khâlid al-Nafawrî and others, see al-Rayyis, *al-Kitâb al-dhahabî,* p. 407.

24. SHAT 4H65/D1, BR 19, 2 January, 1926, "Région de Homs-Nebek."

25. The following accounts, already cited, make this clear: Doty, *The Legion of the Damned;* Harvey, *With the Foreign Legion in Syria;* Poulleau, *A Damas sous les bombes.*

26. MAE-Nantes, carton 1704, BR 211, 5 November 1925.

27. FO 371/4310, 13028/334, Consul General Mayers to Chamberlain, 15 November 1925; and FO 371/4310, 13028/340, Mayers to Chamberlain, 22 November 1925.

28. U.S. Department of State, *Papers Relating to the Foreign Relations of the United States,* 1925, Telegram 890d.00/259, Consul Knabenshue to Secretary of State, 16 November 1925, vol. 2, p. 124.

29. Story based on interviews with former *mukhtâr* Wadîʿ al-Maʿrî (born 1915), son of the *mukhtâr* in 1925 (Jamîl al-Maʿrî), and al-Ḥâja Kâtrîn Abî Ḥaydar, immediate successor of al-Ḥaja Kraytînâ Bâz (mother superior in 1925), 10 August 2002.

30. MAE-Nantes, carton 404, "Amnistie," "l'affaire de Sednaya." The file is thirty-three pages long and contains mostly documents pertaining to the apparently successful request for amnesty on the part of the Aḥmar family. There are no documents relating to the Naddâf family or relating directly to the original events during the revolt.

31. Based on numerous interviews in Ṣaydnâyâ, summer 2002. See note 29 above.

32. MAE-Nantes, carton 404, Etude de M. Elias Namour, Avocat, Beyrouth, "Affaire AHMAR, Syrie: la demande de grâce dont le dossier a été communiqué au Secrétaire Générale par la Délégation à Damas."

33. MAE-Nantes, carton 1704, BR 244, 8 December 1925, French translation.

34. Khoury, *Syria and the French Mandate,* pp. 179–180. See, for example, William Scheifley, "Syria's Rebellion against French Rule," *Current History* (New York) (January 1926): 485–490. He attributed the revolt to agitation by the French Left. Apparently Syrians lacked the political consciousness even to articulate their own grievances.

35. FO 371/4310, 13028/269, Telegram, Smart to Chamberlain, 21 October, 1925; and "Damascus Riots: The Full Story, City Shelled for 48 Hours, Famous Places Destroyed," *Times,* 27 October 1925.

36. *Times,* 27 October 1925. The correspondent was named Merton (FO 371/4310, 13028/303, Smart to Chamberlain, 25 October 1925).

37. Jouvel quoted in Khoury, *Syria and the French Mandate,* p. 183.

38. MAE-Nantes, carton 1704, BR 237, 1 December 1925.

39. MAE-Nantes, carton 1704, BR 238, 2 December 1925.

40. MAE-Nantes, carton 1704, BR 244, 8 December 1925.

41. MAE-Nantes, carton 1704, BR 238, 2 December 1926.

42. FO 371/4310, 13128/182, 4 January 1926, French translation included in dispatch, Smart to Chamberlain.

43. FO 371/4310, 13128/18, 17 January 1926, Mayers to Chamberlain.

44. BR 252, 16 December 1925; FO 371/4310, 13128/176, 28 December 1925, Smart to Chamberlain.

45. SHAT 4H65/D1 BR 10, 17 December 1925, "Région Ouest de Damas." See also *Alif Bâʾ,* 17 December 1925.

46. Cited in Qarqûṭ, *Taṭawwur al-ḥarakat al-waṭaniyya fî sûriyya,* pp. 268–269.

47. Service Géographique des Forces Françaises du Levant, *Syrie: Répertoire alphabétique des noms des lieux habités* (Beirut, 1945), p. 117.

48. FO 371/4310, 13028/358, Smart to Chamberlain, 18 December 1925.

49. SHAT 4H65/D1 BR 7, 12 December 1925, "Région Ouest de Damas." It was probably more like 50–100 men.

50. FO 371/4310, 13128/194, Smart to Chamberlain, 31 January 1926.

51. SHAT 4H65/ D1 BR 7, 12 December 1925, "Région Ouest de Damas." As my discussion of rebel sources shows, Ramaḍân Shallâsh could not have been with Kharrâṭ and the ʿAkâsh at this time.

52. Doty, *The Legion of the Damned,* pp. 172–175.

53. *Alif Bâʾ,* 28 October 1925, listing of villages in the Damascus countryside destroyed or damaged. *Alif Bâʾ* was subsidized by the French.

54. FO 371/4310, 13028/281, Smart to Chamberlain, 15 October 1925. Smart reported that the prisoners, including a British Indian subject, were shot after French troops brought them to Damascus. He added that the troops openly sold their plundered loot in Damascus.

55. Doty, *The Legion of the Damned,* pp. 120 and 185. General Andréa did not mention these events in his memoirs: see *La révolte druze et l'insurrection de Damas.* For the ring road, see pp. 85–86. The ring road still exists and, shorn of its barbed wire, is now elevated. Perhaps coincidentally, it remains unpopular among Maydânîs.

56. FO 371/4310, 13128/179, Smart to Chamberlain, 30 December 1925.

57. See FO 371/4310, 13128/204, Smart to Chamberlain, 15 February 1926.

58. SHAT 4H65/D2 BR 27, 12 and 13 January 1926, "Région de Damas." See also FO 371/4310, 13128/191, Smart to Chamberlain, 19 January 1926. The reports agree in general; but Smart condemned the authorities for not acting before the attack, and he gave the insurgents more credit for tactical skill. He added that—after relieving the trapped train—troops pillaged and burned two nearby villages, Ashrafiyya and Judayda, surely driving the male villagers into the arms of the rebels.

59. SHAT 4H65/D2 BR 30, 16 January 1926, "Région de Damas."

60. SHAT 4H65/D2 BR 34, 22 January 1926, "Région Nord-Ouest de Damas." These numbers are almost certainly exaggerated.

61. British reports confirm that even with 10,000 troops in Damascus the French did not control any part of the surrounding countryside and were unable to prevent attacks inside the capital. See FO 371/4310, 13128/194, Smart to Chamberlain, 31 January 1926.

62. al-ʿÂṣ, *Ṣafaḥat,* p. 109. This was probably the second meeting at Saqbâ. The first was on or around 26 November 1925 (p. 61).

63. Nasîb al-Bakrî papers, "al-Ḥukm ʿalâ aḥad qâdâʾ al-thawra: Ramaḍân Shallâsh," MWT, Damascus.

64. Al-ʿÂṣ, *Ṣafaḥat,* p.107.

65. Bakrî papers, "al-Ḥukm." The list of matters for discussion is from al-ʿÂṣ, *Ṣafaḥat,* p. 107. The judgment against Ramaḍân is the only item preserved in the Bakrî papers from the Saqbâ meeting. Unsurprisingly, he makes no mention of the apparently fractious debate over his leadership or its conclusion. A number of participants in the conference are mentioned by al-ʿÂṣ but not mentioned by Bakrî.

66. Bakrî papers, "al-Ḥukm." The legalistic language is unique to Bakrî's record. The judgment purports to be decision number 91 of the Leadership Council of the Nationalist Revolt in Ghûṭa and the Region of Damascus. It is also dated ten days after the date that al-ʿÂṣ and Rayyis give: 26–27 Jumâdâ al-aûlâ 1344 (14–15 December 1925) as opposed to 5 December 1925. Conversion from Akram al-ʿUlabî, *al-Taqwîm dirâsa lil-taqwîm wa al-tawqît wa al-târîkh* (Beirut, 1991), p. 337.

67. Al-ʿÂṣ, *Ṣafaḥat,* p. 109. See Rogan, "Aşiret Mektebi," p. 88, Table 1. Shallâsh is listed in the first graduating class, and a certain ʿAlî from Suwaydâʾ is also listed without further information. This is almost certainly ʿAlî Fâris al-Aṭrash.

68. Al-Rayyis, *al-Kitâb al-dhahabî,* p. 371.

69. Al-ʿÂṣ, *Ṣafaḥat,* p. 109.

70. Al-Rayyis, *al-Kitâb al-dhahabî,* p. 371.

71. Ibid., p. 398. See al-Jundî, *Târîkh al thawrât al-sûriyya,* p. 357, for the death of Kharrâṭ.

72. Saʿîd al-ʿÂṣ was killed fighting in Palestine in 1936. His memoir was first published in 1935 and is thus as close as possible to a contemporary account. Munîr al-Rayyis, by contrast, published his book in 1969, though it seems it was probably recorded at least in part at the time of the revolt. Nasîb al-Bakrî died in 1966, three years before the publication of al-Rayyis' memoir.

73. For example, see Khoury, *Syria and the French Mandate,* pp. 161–162.

74. Al-ʿÂṣ, *Ṣafaḥat,* p. 107 (original parentheses). Bakrî's record of the deliberations about Shallâsh does not mention the presence of the ʿAkâsh brothers or Ḥasan al-Kharrâṭ. Al-ʿÂṣ claimed these men were present and fully under Bakrî's control.

75. Bakrî papers, "al-Ḥukm." Even if these accusations were true, they would probably not have warranted a trial. The account of al-ʿÂṣ and the earlier sections of this chapter indicate clearly that nearly everyone was engaged in some pillaging and levying of "revolt taxes."

76. For Shallâsh's letters, see MAE-Nantes, carton 1704, BR 211, 5 November 1925, and BR 241, 5 December 1925, annexe 1, French translation.

77. Al-ʿÂṣ, *Ṣafaḥat,* p. 111.

78. Ibid., pp. 113–114.

79. Al-Rayyis, *al-Kitâb al-dhahabî,* pp. 371–372.

80. Al-ʿÂṣ, *Ṣafaḥat,* p. 112.

81. Al-Rayyis, *al-Kitâb al-dhahabî,* p. 407.

82. Ibid., p. 371.

83. MAE-Nantes, carton 1593, "tract divers," "Appel de Ramadan Challache," 2 February 1926.

84. Khoury, *Syria and the French Mandate,* p. 332.

85. See Nasîb al-Bakrî papers, Ministry of Justice Decree No. 1817 (MWT, No. 115), 20 February 1928, for a list of the condemned.

86. al-Qâwuqjî, *Mudhakkirât Fawzî al-Qâwuqjî,* p. 147.

CHAPTER 7. EPILOGUE AND CONCLUSIONS

1. Several sources provide lists of the condemned. The Damascus newspaper *al-Muqtabas* had nearly daily lists of those tried and sentenced in absentia between 1925 and 1927. Markaz al-Wathâ'iq al-Târîkhiyya (MWT) in Damascus has uncataloged revolt court records. See also MAE-Nantes, cartons 405 and 406, "amnistiés-condamnés," and MWT Nasîb al-Bakrî papers, Ministry of Justice decree No. 1817, 20 February 1928.

2. For the National Bloc leadership, see Khoury, *Syria and the French Mandate,* Table 10-2, pp. 254–257. While the leadership included men who were peripherally involved, like Jamîl Mardam Bek and Shukrî al-Quwwatlî, and Fakhrî al-Bârûdî, who was in jail during the revolt, their names are nearly absent from the mandate intelligence records and insurgent sources. All were graduates of Maktab 'Anbar. See Reeva Simon, "The Education of an Iraqi Ottoman Army Officer," in Khalidi, Anderson, et al., eds., *The Origins of Arab Nationalism,* pp. 153–154.

3. 'Ubayd, *al-Thawra al-sûriyya al-kubrâ,* pp. 205–206; Firro, *A History of the Druzes,* p. 298.

4. MacCallum, *The Nationalist Crusade in Syria,* p. 171.

5. *Jâmi'at al-'arabiyya* published twice weekly and printed its first issue on 19 January 1927 in Jerusalem. Munîf al-Ḥayanî was probably a pseudonym. I base my argument that it was intended for dissemination within Syria on the fact that I know of no library collection that has the newspaper, but I know of several people in Syria (mostly in Suwaydâ', but also in Damascus) who have full original editions in their private libraries. I thank Dr. Fandî Abû Fakhr for his unfailing generosity in allowing me to copy his collection.

6. "Al-jumhûriyya al-amrîkiyya al-kubrâ musta'amara ayḍan!!" (exclamation in original), *Jâmi'at al-'arabiyya,* 7 January 1926.

7. League of Nations Permanent Mandates Commission, *Minutes of the Eleventh Session,* Annex 5, Report by M. Freire d'Andrade (Geneva, 1927), p. 195. The League of Nations testimony and petitions make clear that the Syrian-Palestinian Congress, and Amîr Shakîb in particular, had no unified negotiating strategy. Philip S. Khoury, "Factionalism among Syrian Nationalists during the French Mandate," IJMES 13 (1981): 441–469, and *Syria and the French Mandate,* pp. 231–233; also William L. Cleveland, *Islam against the West: Shakib Arslan and the Campaign for Islamic Nationalism,* pp. 54–58. Cleveland discusses the Arslân-Shahbandar dispute in detail.

8. League of Nations Permanent Mandates Commission, *Minutes of the Eleventh Session,* Annex 5, Report by M. Freire d'Andrade: "The fifteenth petition shows us that the petitioners have reduced their claims, and that, after having asked for the withdrawal of the mandate and almost complete independence for Syria, they would be prepared, though with reluctance, to *[sic]* the conclusion of a treaty like that of Iraq" (p. 197) (MacCallum, *The Nationalist Crusade in Syria,* Appendix III, "The Ponsot Declaration of July 26, 1927," pp. 273–277).

9. The political and financial battles between rival nationalist factions are best treated in Khoury's "Factionalism among Syrian Nationalists during the French Mandate." He concentrates on the rivalries between the Syrian-Palestinian Congress and the Istiqlâl Party. I suspect, however, that the situation was perhaps even more confused, since certain individuals—ʿÂdil al-ʿAẓma and Shukrî al-Quwwatlî, for example—were apparently members of both organizations. Khoury makes it clear that the rebellion suffered by being in between rival politicians during and after the revolt.

10. Al-Mu'tamar al-sûrî wa al-filisṭînî bi-miṣr, *Dhikrâ al-istiqlâl wa al-shuhadâ'* (commemorative pamphlet, Cairo, 1928).

11. MAE-Nantes, carton 409, "Congrès Syrienne," annex to BR 198, 10 October 1929, French translation.

12. MAE-Nantes, carton 409, "Congrès Syrienne," "Renseignements sur le congrès de l'Ouadi Sirhan," 28 October 1929. For the two newspapers, see Méouchy, "Les formes de conscience politique et communautaire au Liban et en Syrie," Appendix 4. *Al-Shaʿb* was founded in 1927 under the patronage of Jamîl Mardam Bek and was closely affiliated with the National Bloc. *Al-Qabas* was founded in 1928 and was the successor to the famous nationalist paper *al-Muqtabas.* It was more radical than *al-Shaʿb* and was published by ʿÂdil Kurd ʿAlî and Najîb and Munîr al-Rayyis.

13. MAE-Nantes, carton 409, "Congrès Syrienne," "mu'tamar al-ṣaḥrâ'," program in original Arabic and French translation.

14. "Mu'tamar al-Nabk wa khulâṣa qarâratihi," *al-Ahrâm,* 29 October 1929; MAE-Nantes, carton 409, "Congrès Syrienne," No. 207, "Extraits d'une lettre adressée par le Docteur CHABANDAR du Caire, le 28/10/29 à TAYSSIR ZEBIAN à Damas," French translation. The letter was addressed and signed pseudonymously.

15. MAE-Nantes, carton 409, "Congrès Syrienne," "mu'tamar al-ṣaḥrâ'."

16. MAE-Nantes, carton 409, Officier de liaison Jérusalem, BR 37, "La conférence au camp de SOLTAN el ATRACHE," 12 November 1929, French translation compiled from British Air Intelligence.

17. MAE-Nantes, carton 409, "Congrès Syrienne," "mu'tamar al-ṣaḥrâ'." See also carton 409, Officier de liaison Jérusalem, BR 37, "La conférence au camp de SOLTAN el ATRACHE," 12 November 1929.

BIBLIOGRAPHY

Unpublished and Archival Sources

Private and Family Archives

Abû Fakhr, Fandî. Private Document Archive. Suwaydâ', Syria.
al-Bi'aynî, Ḥasan Amîn. Private Document Archive. Al-Shûf, Lebanon.
Ṭarabayh, Muḥammad. Private Document Archive. Suwaydâ', Syria.

Public and Government Archives

GREAT BRITAIN

Public Record Office. Archives of the Foreign Office.

LEBANON, AMERICAN UNIVERSITY OF BEIRUT JAFET LIBRARY

'Izz al-Dîn al-Ḥalabî, Hilâl Bek. "Mudhakkirât Hilâl Bek 'Izz al-Dîn al-Ḥalabî." Unpublished MS, n.p., n.d.
al-Qâsimî, Zâfir. "Oral History Interview Transcripts." AUB Oral History Project. Beirut, n.d. (ca. 1970).
al-Qinṭâr, 'Alî Sayf al-Dîn. "'Alâ hâmish al-thawra." Unpublished MS, n.p., n.d.
———. "Murâsalât sirriyya 'an thawrat Sulṭân al-Aṭrash." Unpublished MS and correspondence collection, n.p., n.d.
Syrian-American Society. "Memorandum to President Coolidge, Members of Congress, and the Secretary of State on the Application of the Mandates System of the League of Nations by France in Syria." New York, n.d. (ca. 1926).
'Ubayd, 'Alî. "Mudhakkirât 'Alî 'Ubayd." Unpublished MS, n.p., n.d.

FRANCE

Bibliothèque Nationale. Periodical collection. Paris.
Ministère de la Défense, Service Historique de l'Armée Terre. Armée du Levant, 1920–1927. Vincennes.
Ministère des Affaires Etrangères, Archives Diplomatiques. Mandat Syrie-Beyrouth, Cabinet Politique, 1920–1936. Nantes.

SYRIAN ARAB REPUBLIC

Archive of the Central Bureau of Statistics. Damascus.
Asad Library. Periodical collection. Damascus.
Institut Français d'Etudes Arabes. Damascus.
Markaz al-Wathâ'iq al-Târîkhiyya (Center for Historical Documents). Ottoman and French Mandate Mixed Court Records. Damascus.
———. Private Papers of Nationalist Leaders (Qism al-Khâṣ). Damascus.
Ministry of Agriculture. General Directorate for the Administration of Immovable Property, Ottoman and French Mandate Land Registers for the Governorate of Damascus (1890s–1930s). Damascus.
Ẓahiriyya Library. Damascus.

Published Primary Sources

ʿAbdallâh, Malik. *Mudhakkirât.* Amman, 1977.
Abî Râshid, Ḥannâ. *Ḥawrân al-dâmiyya.* Cairo, 1926; rpt. Beirut, 1961.
———. *Jabal al-durûz.* Cairo, 1925; rpt. Beirut, 1961.
Abû al-Ḥusan, Saʿîd. *Nirân ʿalâ al-qamam.* Damascus, 1994.
al-Ahrâm. Cairo daily newspaper. Various dates.
Alif bâ'. Damascus daily newspaper. Various dates.
Amîn, Saʿîd. *al-Thawra al-ʿarabiyya al-kubrâ.* 3 vols. Cairo, 1933.
Andréa, Général Charles Joseph. *La révolte druze et l'insurrection de Damas, 1925–1926.* Paris, 1937.
al-ʿÂṣ, (Muḥammad) Saʿîd. *Ṣafaḥat min al-ayyâm al-ḥamrâ': mudhakkirât al-qâ'id Saʿîd al-ʿÂṣ 1889–1936.* Jerusalem, 1935; rpt. Beirut, 1988.
———. *al-Tajârib al-ḥarbiyya fî ḥarûb al-thawra al-sûriyya.* Beirut, 1990.
al-Aṭrash, Shiblî. *Dîwân Shiblî al-Aṭrash.* Damascus, 1969.
Aṭrash, Sulṭân. "Mudhakkirât Sulṭân." A dictated memoir, serialized in *Bayrût al-masâ'* 97–120 (1975–1976).
Bordeaux, Henry. *Dans la montagne des Druzes.* Paris, 1926.
Bowring, John. *Report on the Commercial Statistics of Syria.* London, 1840.
Burckhardt, John Lewis. *Travels in Syria and the Holy Land.* London: J. Murray, 1822.
Carbillet, Capitaine Gabriel. *Au Djébel Druse, choses vues et vécues.* Paris, 1929.
Coblentz, Paul. *Le silence de Sarrail.* Paris, 1930.
———. *The Silence of Sarrail.* Trans. Arthur Chambers. London: Hutchinson & Co. Ltd., 1930.
Current History. New York. Various dates.
Doty, Bennett J. *The Legion of the Damned: The Adventures of Bennett J. Doty in the French Foreign Legion as Told by Himself.* New York: Century Co., 1928.
L'Echo de Paris. Paris newspaper. Various dates.

Ewing, William. *Arab and Druze at Home: A Record of Travel and Intercourse with the Peoples East of the Jordan*. London, 1907.
al-Fata al-'Arab. Damascus newspaper. Various dates.
Filisṭîn. Jaffa newspaper. Various dates.
"France in the Jabal Druze." *Cornhill Magazine* 65 (November 1928).
"The French Occupation of Syria." *Nation,* 13 January 1926.
Goodrich-Freer, A. M. *Arabs in Tent & Town*. London: Seeley, Service & Co., 1924.
Great Britain. Parliamentary Papers, Near Eastern Trade Reports. Various dates.
al-Ḥakîm, Ḥasan. *al-Wathâ'iq al-târîkhiyya al-muta'alliqa bil-qaḍiyya al-sûriyya fî al-'ahdayn al-'arabî al-fayṣalî wa al-intidâbî al-fransî, 1915–1946*. Beirut, 1974.
al-Ḥanbali, Shâkir. *Mûjaz fî aḥkâm al-arâḍi wa al-amwâl al-ghayr manqûla*. Damascus, 1928.
Harvey, John Henry. *With the Foreign Legion in Syria*. London, 1928.
L'Humanité. Paris. Various dates.
Jâm'iat al-'arabiyya. Jerusalem. Issues 1–69, 1927.
League of Nations Permanent Mandates Commission. *Minutes*. Geneva. Various dates.
Liman von Sanders, Otto Viktor Karl. *Five Years in Turkey,* Translated by Karl Reichmann. Baltimore: Williams & Wilkins Co., 1928.
Lisân al-ḥâl. Beirut daily newspaper. Various dates.
al-Maḥâyrî, Fahmî. *al-Mudhakkirât 'an al-thawra al-sûriyya*. Damascus, n.d.
Mallûḥî, 'Adnân. *Min ayyâm al-thawra al-sûriyya wa al-ma'ârik al-istiqlâl wa al-jalâ' ilâ al-ḥurûb wa al-ahdâth al-kubrâ al-'arabiyya wa al-'âlamiyya*. Damascus, 2001.
Ministère des Affaires Etrangères. *Rapport à la Société des Nations sur la situation de la Syrie et du Liban, 1925, 1926, 1927* (Annual Report). Paris, 1926–1928.
al-Muqtabas. Damascus daily paper. Various dates.
Musa, Suleimen (Mûsâ, Sulaymân). *al-Murâsalât al-târîkhiyya, 1914–18*. Vol. 1. Amman, 1973.
al-Muwayyad al-'Aẓm, Nazîh. Private Papers (Qism al-Khâṣ), Markaz al-Wathâ'iq al-Târîkhiyya. Damascus, Syria, including serialized memoir in *Majalat al-shurṭa wa al-amn al-'âm,* nos. 1–24 (1952–1954), Damascus. At issue no. 17 *Majalat al-shurṭa* changed its name to *Ṣawt sûriyya*.
Najjâr, 'Abdallâh. *Banû ma'rûf fî jabal ḥawrân*. Damascus, 1934.
Office Arabe de Presse et de Documentation. *Recueil des statistiques syriennes comparées (1928–1968)*.
Poulleau, Alice. *A Damas sous les bombes: Journal d'une Française pendant la révolte syrienne, 1924–1926*. Paris, 1926.
al-Qâḍî, Niqûlâws. *Arba'ûn 'âman fî ḥawrân wa jabal al-durûz*. Beirut, 1927.
al-Qâsimî, Muḥammad Sa'îd. *Qâmûs al-ṣinâ'ât al-shâmiyya*. Rpt. Damascus, 1988.

al-Qâwuqjî, Fawzî. *Mudhakkirât Fawzî al-Qâwuqjî*. Ed. Khayriyya Qâsimiyya. Rpt. of both volumes of the 1975 edition. Damascus, 1995.

al-Rayyis, Munîr. *al-Kitâb al-dhahabî lil-thawrât al-waṭaniyya fî al-mashriq al-ʿarabî: al-thawra al-sûriyya al-kubrâ*. Beirut, 1969.

Republic of Syria (Sir Alexander Gibb & Partners, Consulting Engineers). *The Economic Development of Syria*. Report commissioned by the Ministry of Public Works and Communications, Republic of Syria. London, 1947.

al-Safâʾ. Beirut. Various dates.

al-Shaʿb. Damascus. Various dates.

al-Shahbandar, ʿAbd al-Raḥman. *Mudhakkirât wa khuṭub*. Damascus: Syrian Ministry of Culture, 1993.

———. *al-Qaḍâyâ al-ijtimâʿiyya al-kubrâ fî al-ʿâlam al-ʿarabî*. Rpt. of 1932 ed. Damascus: Syrian Ministry of Culture, 1993.

———. *al-Thawra al-sûriyya al-waṭaniyya: mudhakkirât al-duktûr ʿAbd al-Raḥman al-Shahbandar*. Rpt. of 1933 ed. Damascus: Syrian Ministry of Culture, 1993.

Stark, Freya. *Letters from Syria*. London: J. Murray, 1942.

Syrian Arab Republic, Directorate of Statistics. *al-Taqsîmât al-idâriyya fî al-jumhûriyya al-ʿarabiyya al-sûriyya*. Damascus, 1952.

Times (London). Various dates.

ʿUbayd, ʿAlî. *ʿAlî ʿUbayd rubâbat al-thawra: qaṣâʾid shurûqiyya waṭaniyya*. N.p., n.d.

al-ʿUmrân. Damascus newspaper. Various dates.

U.S. Department of State. *Papers Relating to the Foreign Relations of the United States*. Washington, D.C.: Government Printing Office. Various dates.

Published and Unpublished Secondary Sources

Abû Fakhr, Fandî. *Târîkh liwâʾ ḥawrân al-ijtimâʿî: al-suwaydâʾ- darʿâ- al-qunayṭra- ʿajlûn, 1840–1918*. Ph.D. dissertation, Damascus University, 1999. Privately published.

Abu-Husayn, Abdul-Rahim. "The 'Lebanon Schools' (1853–1873): A Local Venture in Rural Education." In Thomas Philipp and Birgit Schaebler, eds., *The Syrian Land: Processes of Integration and Fragmentation: Bilâd al-Shâm from the 18th to the 20th Century*. Stuttgart: F. Steiner, 1998.

Abu-Izzedin, Nejla M. *The Druzes: A New Study of Their History, Faith, and Society*. Leiden: E. J. Brill, 1984.

Akarlı, Engin Deniz. "Abdülhamid II's Attempt to Integrate Arabs into the Ottoman System." In David Kushner, ed., *Palestine in the Late Ottoman Period: Political, Social, and Economic Transformation*. Jerusalem: Yad Izhak Ben-Zvi, and Leiden: distributed by E. J. Brill, 1986.

———. *The Long Peace: Ottoman Lebanon, 1861–1920*. Berkeley: University of California Press, 1993.

———. *Some Ottoman Documents on Jordan: Ottoman Criteria for the Choice of an Administrative Center in the Light of Documents on Hauran, 1909–1910*. Amman: University of Jordan, 1989.

Antonius, George. *The Arab Awakening: The Story of the Arab National Movement*. Rpt. Beirut: Librairie du Liban, 1969.

Antoun, Richard T. *Low-Key Politics: Local Level Leadership and Change in the Middle East*. Albany: State University of New York Press, 1979.

al-ʿAṭṭâr, ʿAdnân. *Thawrat al-ḥuriyya fî al-minṭiqa al-sâdisa bi-dimasq 1925–1926 wâdî baradâ wa al-muhâjirîn wa al-ṣâliḥiyya*. Damascus, 1991.

ʿAwaḍ, ʿAbd al-ʿAzîz. *al-Idâra al-ʿuthmâniyya fî wilâyat sûriyya, 1864–1914*. Cairo, 1969.

al-Azmeh, Aziz. *Islams and Modernities*. 2nd ed. London: Verso, 1996.

———. "Nationalism and the Arabs." *Arab Studies Quarterly* 17, nos. 1–2 (Winter and Spring 1995): 1–17.

Baer, Gabriel. *Fellah and Townsman in the Middle East: Studies in Social History*. London and Totowa, NJ: F. Cass, 1982.

Batatu, Hanna. *The Old Social Classes and the Revolutionary Movements of Iraq: A Study of Iraq's Old Landed and Commercial Classes and of Its Communists, Baʿthists, and Free Officers*. Princeton: Princeton University Press, 1978.

———. *Syria's Peasantry, the Descendants of Its Lesser Rural Notables, and Their Politics*. Princeton: Princeton University Press, 1999.

Beinen, Joel, and Zachary Lockman. *Nationalism, Communism, Islam, and the Egyptian Working Class, 1882–1954*. Princeton: Princeton University Press, 1987.

al-Biʿaynî, Ḥasan Amîn. *Durûz sûriyya wa lubnân fî ʿahd al-intidâb al-fransî, 1920–1943*. Beirut, 1993.

———. *Jabal al-ʿarab ṣafaḥât min târîkh al-muwaḥḥidîn al-durûz (1685–1927)*. Beirut, 1985.

———. *Sultân Bâshâ al-Aṭrash: Masîrat qâiʾd fî târîkh umma*. Beirut, 1985.

al-Bîṭâr, Shaykh ʿAbd al-Razzâq. *Ḥilyat al-bashar fî târîkh al-qarn al-thâlith ʿashar*. Damascus, 1961.

Blecher, Robert. "The Medicalization of Sovereignty: Medicine, Public Health, and Political Authority in Syria, 1861–1935." Ph.D. dissertation, Stanford University, 2002.

Bloch, Marc. *Feudal Society*, Translated from the French by L. A. Manyon. London: Routledge & K. Paul, 1961.

Bokova, Lenka. *La confrontation franco-syrienne à l'époque du mandat, 1925–1927*. Paris: L'Harmattan, 1990.

Bou-Nacklie, N. E. "Les Troupes Spéciales: Religious and Ethnic Recruitment, 1916–46." *IJMES* 25 (1993): 645–660.

———. "Tumult in Syria's Hama in 1925: The Failure of a Revolt." *Journal of Contemporary History* 33, no. 2 (1998): 273–290.

Bouron, Narcisse. *Les Druzes: Histoire du Liban et de la montagne haouranaise.* Paris: Berger-Levrault, 1930.

Brown, Nathan J. *Peasant Politics in Modern Egypt: The Struggle against the State.* New Haven: Yale University Press, 1990.

Burke, Edmund III. "A Comparative View of French Native Policy in Morocco and Syria, 1912–1925." *Middle Eastern Studies* 9 (May 1973): 175–186.

———. "The Sociology of Islam: The French Tradition." In Malcolm H. Kerr, ed., *Islamic Studies: A Tradition and Its Problems.* Malibu: Undena Publications, 1980.

———. "Understanding Arab Protest Movements." *Arab Studies Quarterly* 8, no. 4 (1987): 333–345.

Chatterjee, Partha. *Nationalist Thought and the Colonial World: A Derivative Discourse?* Minneapolis: University of Minnesota Press, 1986.

———. *The Nation and Its Fragments: Colonial and Postcolonial Histories.* Princeton: Princeton University Press, 1993.

Cleveland, William L. *Islam against the West: Shakib Arslan and the Campaign for Islamic Nationalism.* Austin: University of Texas Press, 1985.

———. *The Making of An Arab Nationalist: Ottomanism and Arabism in the Life and Thought of Satiʿ al-Husri.* Princeton: Princeton University Press, 1971.

Commins, David Dean. *Islamic Reform: Politics and Change in Late Ottoman Syria.* Oxford: Oxford University Press, 1990.

Cuno, Kenneth M. *The Pasha's Peasants: Land, Society, and Economy in Lower Egypt, 1749–1858.* Cambridge: Cambridge University Press, 1992.

Dalati, Aziz Amin. "The Ghouta of Damascus." B.B.A. thesis, AUB, 1938.

Dâwud, Aḥmad Yûsuf. *al-Mujâhid Saʿîd al-ʿÂṣ.* Damascus, 1990.

Deringil, Selim. *The Well-Protected Domains: Ideology and Legitimation of Power in the Ottoman Empire, 1876–1909.* London: I. B. Tauris, 1998.

Doumani, Beshara. *Rediscovering Palestine: Merchants and Peasants in Jabal Nablus, 1700–1900.* Berkeley: University of California Press, 1995.

Douwes, Dick. *The Ottomans in Syria: A History of Justice and Oppression.* London: I. B. Tauris, 2000.

Dowson, Sir Ernest. *An Inquiry into Land Tenure and Related Questions.* London, 1932.

Esherick, Joseph W. *The Origins of the Boxer Uprising.* Berkeley: University of California Press, 1987.

Fanon, Frantz. *The Wretched of the Earth.* Translated by Constance Farrington. New York: Grove Press, 1963.

Faris, Basim, ed. *A Postwar Bibliography of the Near Eastern Mandates.* 5 vols. Beirut, 1932.

Fâris, Jûrj. *Man huwa fî al-ʿâlam al-ʿarabî.* Damascus, 1952.

———. *Man huwa fî sûriyya, 1949.* Damascus, 1950.

Firro, Kais M. *The Druzes in the Jewish State: A Brief History.* Leiden: Brill, 1999.

———. *A History of the Druzes.* Leiden: Brill, 1992.

———. "Silk and Socio-Economic Changes in Lebanon, 1860–1919." In Elie Kedourie and Sylvia Haim, eds., *Essays on the Economic History of the Middle East.* London: Frank Cass, 1988.

Fleischer, Cornell Hugh. *Bureaucrat and Intellectual in the Ottoman Empire: The Historian Mustafa Âli (1541–1600).* Princeton: Princeton University Press, 1986.

Fortna, Benjamin. *Imperial Classroom: Islam, the State, and Education in the Late Ottoman Empire.* Oxford: Oxford University Press, 2002.

Gelvin, James. L. *Divided Loyalties: Nationalism and Mass Politics in Syria at the Close of Empire.* Berkeley: University of California Press, 1998.

———. "The Other Arab Nationalism: Syrian/Arab Populism in Its Historical and International Contexts." In James P. Jankowski and Israel Gershoni, eds., *Rethinking Nationalism in the Arab Middle East.* New York: Columbia University Press, 1997.

———. "The Social Origins of Popular Nationalism in Syria: Evidence for a New Framework." IJMES 26 (1994): 645–661.

Gerber, Haim. *Ottoman Rule in Jerusalem, 1890–1914.* Berlin: K. Schwarz, 1985.

———. *The Social Origins of the Modern Middle East.* Boulder, CO: L. Rienner, 1987.

Gilbar, Gad G., ed. *Ottoman Palestine, 1800–1914: Studies in Economic and Social History.* Leiden: Brill, 1990.

Gilsenan, Michael. "Against Patron-Client Relations." In Ernest Gellner and John Waterbury, eds., *Patrons and Clients in Mediterranean Societies.* London: Duckworth, 1977.

Goldberg, Ellis Jay, ed. *The Social History of Labor in the Middle East.* Boulder, CO: Westview Press, 1996.

Gramsci, Antonio. *Selections from the Prison Notebooks of Antonio Gramsci.* Edited and translated by Quintin Hoare and Geoffrey Nowell Smith. New York: International Publishers, 1971.

Guha, Ranajit. *Elementary Aspects of Peasant Insurgency in Colonial India.* Delhi: Oxford University Press, 1983.

———, ed. *Subaltern Studies* 1–4. Delhi, 1982–1990.

Gurr, Ted Robert. *Why Men Rebel.* Princeton: Princeton University Press, 1970.

al-Ḥakîm, Ḥasan. *'Abd al-Raḥman al-Shahbandar: ḥayâtuhu wa jihâduhu.* Beirut, 1985.

———. *Ṣafaḥât min ḥayât al-Shahbandar.* N.p., 1980.

Ḥannâ, 'Abdallâh. *al-'Ammiyya wa al-intifâḍât al-falâḥiyya (1850–1918) fî jabal ḥawrân.* Damascus, 1990.

———. *al-Ḥaraka al-'ummâliyya fî sûriyya wa lubnân: 1900–1945.* Damascus, 1973.

———. *al-Qaḍiyya al-zirâ'iyya wa al-ḥarakât al-fallâḥiyya fî sûriyya wa lubnân (1820–1920).* Vols. 1–2. Beirut, 1975 and 1978.

Himadeh, Sa'id. *The Monetary and Banking System of Syria.* Beirut: American Press, 1935.

———, ed. *Economic Organization of Syria.* Beirut: American Press, 1936.

Hobsbawm, E. J. *Nations and Nationalism since 1780: Programme, Myth, Reality.* Cambridge: Cambridge University Press, 1990.

———. "Peasants and Politics." *Journal of Peasant Studies* 1, no. 1 (October 1973): 3–22.

———. *Primitive Rebels: Studies in Archaic Forms of Social Movement in the 19th and 20th Centuries.* New York: Praeger, 1963.

Hourani, Albert. "Ottoman Reform and the Politics of Notables." In William R. Polk and Richard L. Chambers, eds., *Beginnings of Modernization in the Middle East: The Nineteenth Century.* Chicago: University of Chicago Press, 1968.

———. *Syria and Lebanon: A Political Essay.* London: Oxford University Press, 1946.

Joarder, Safiuddin. *Syria under the French Mandate: The Early Phase, 1920–27.* Dhaka: Asiatic Society of Bangladesh, 1977.

al-Jundî, Adham. *Târîkh al-thawrât al-sûriyya fî 'ahd al-intidâb al-fransî.* Damascus, 1960.

Kasmieh, Khairieh (al-Qâsimiyya, Khayriyya). *al-Ḥukûma al-'arabiyya fî dimashq bayn 1918–1920.* Cairo, 1971.

Kayalı, Hasan. *Arabs and Young Turks: Ottomanism, Arabism, and Islamism in the Ottoman Empire, 1908–1918.* Berkeley: University of California Press, 1997.

Kazemi, Farhad, and John Waterbury, eds. *Peasants and Politics in the Modern Middle East.* Miami: Florida International University Press, 1991.

Keydar, Çağlar, and Faruk Tabak, eds. *Landholding and Commercial Agriculture in the Middle East.* Albany: State University of New York Press, 1991.

Khalidi, Rashid. *Palestinian Identity: The Construction of Modern National Consciousness.* New York: Columbia University Press, 1997.

———. "Society and Ideology in Late Ottoman Syria: Class, Education, Profession and Confession." In John P. Spagnolo, ed., *Problems of the Middle East in Historical Perspective: Essays in Honour of Albert Hourani.* Oxford: Oxford University Press, 1992.

Khalidi, Rashid, Lisa Anderson, et al., eds. *The Origins of Arab Nationalism.* New York Columbia University Press, 1991.

Khoury, Philip S. "Factionalism among Syrian Nationalists during the French Mandate." IJMES 13 (1981): 441–469.

———. "The Paradoxical in Arab Nationalism: Interwar Syria Revisited." In James P. Jankowski and Israel Gershoni, eds., *Rethinking Nationalism in the Arab Middle East.* New York: Columbia University Press, 1997.

———. "A Reinterpretation of the Origins and Aims of the Great Syrian Revolt,

1925–1927." In George N. Atiyeh and Ibrahim M. Oweiss, eds., *Arab Civilization: Challenges and Responses: Studies in Honor of Constantine K. Zurayk.* Albany: State University of New York Press, 1988.

———. *Syria and the French Mandate: The Politics of Arab Nationalism, 1920–1945.* Princeton: Princeton University Press, 1987.

———. "Syrian Urban Politics in Transition: The Quarters of Damascus during the French Mandate." In Albert Hourani et al., eds., *The Modern Middle East: A Reader.* Berkeley: University of California Press, 1993.

———. "The Tribal Shaykh, French Tribal Policy, and the Nationalist Movement in Syria between the Two World Wars." *Middle Eastern Studies* 18 (January 1982): 180–193.

———. *Urban Notables and Arab Nationalism: The Politics of Damascus, 1860–1920.* Cambridge: Cambridge University Press, 1983.

Landis, Joshua. "Shishlakli and the Druzes: Integration and Intransigence." In Thomas Philipp and Birgit Schaebler, eds., *The Syrian Land: Processes of Integration and Fragmentation: Bilâd al-Shâm from the 18th to the 20th Century.* Stuttgart: F. Steiner, 1998.

Latron, André. *La vie rurale en Syrie et au Liban.* Beirut, 1936.

Lewis, Norman N. *Nomads and Settlers in Syria and Jordan, 1800–1980.* Cambridge: Cambridge University Press, 1987.

Longrigg, Stephen Helmsley. *Syria and Lebanon under French Mandate.* London: Oxford University Press, 1958.

MacCallum, Elizabeth Pauline. *The Nationalist Crusade in Syria.* New York: Foreign Policy Association, 1928.

Makdisi, Ussama. *The Culture of Sectarianism: Community, History, and Violence in Nineteenth-Century Ottoman Lebanon.* Berkeley: University of California Press, 2000.

Manna, Adel. "Continuity and Change." In Thomas Philipp, ed., *The Syrian Land in the 18th and 19th Century.* Stuttgart: F. Steiner, 1992.

Matthews, Weldon. "Pan-Islam or Arab Nationalism? The Meaning of the 1931 Jerusalem Islamic Conference Reconsidered." IJMES 35 (2003): 1–22.

Méouchy, Nadine. "Les formes de conscience politique et communautaire au Liban et en Syrie à l'époque du mandat français, 1920–1939." Ph.D. dissertation, Université de Paris, Sorbonne, 1989.

———, ed. *France, Syrie et Liban: Les ambiguïtés et les dynamiques de la relation mandataire.* Damascus: Arabes de Damas, 2002.

Méouchy, Nadine, and Peter Sluglett, eds. *The British and French Mandates in Comparative Perspectives.* Leiden: Brill, 2004.

Miller, Joyce Laverty. "The Syrian Revolt of 1925." IJMES 8 (1977): 545–563.

Mitchell, Timothy. *Colonising Egypt.* Berkeley: University of California Press, 1991.

Mizrahi, Jean-David. "Pouvoir mandataire et insécurité en Syrie et au Liban dans les années 1920: Le service des renseignements du haut-commissariat français au Levant." Ph.D. dissertation, Université de Paris, Sorbonne, 2001.

Moore, Barrington. *Social Origins of Dictatorship and Democracy: Lord and Peasant in the Making of the Modern World.* Boston: Beacon Press, 1966.

Mousa, Suleiman (Sulaymân Mûsâ), *T. E. Lawrence: An Arab View.* Translated by Albert Butros. London: Oxford University Press, 1966.

Mufarrij, Fuad K. "Syria and Lebanon under French Mandate." M.A. thesis, AUB, 1935.

Mundy, Martha. "Qada' 'Ajlun in the Late Nineteenth Century: Interpreting a Region from the Ottoman Land Registers." *Levant* 28 (1996): 77–95.

———. "Shareholders and the State: Representing the Village in the Late 19th Century Land Registers of the Southern Hawran." In Thomas Philipp, ed., *The Syrian Land in the 18th and 19th Century.* Stuttgart: F. Steiner, 1992.

———. "Village Land and Individual Title: Musha' and Ottoman Land Registration in the 'Ajlun District." In Eugene L. Rogan and Tariq Tell, eds., *Village, Steppe and State: The Social Origins of Modern Jordan.* London: British Academic Press, 1994.

Mundy, Martha, and Basim Musallam, eds. *The Transformation of Nomadic Society in the Arab East.* Cambridge: Cambridge University Press, 2000.

Mundy, Martha, and Richard S. Smith, eds. *Part Time Farming.* Vol. 2. Amman, Jordan, 1990.

Nashabi (Nashabe), Hisham A. "The Political Parties in Syria, 1918–1939." M.A. thesis, AUB, 1952.

Naṣr, Ḥasan al-Qaysî. *Qabsât min turâth al-sha'bî: ma'ârik wa qaṣâ'id.* Suwaydâ', Syria, 1997.

Peter, Frank. "Impérialisme et industrialisation à Damas 1908–1939." Ph.D. dissertation, Université de Provence/Freie Universität Berlin, 2002.

Philipp, Thomas. *Acre: The Rise and Fall of a Palestinian City, 1730–1831.* New York: Columbia University Press, 2001.

Philipp, Thomas, and Birgit Schaebler, eds. *The Syrian Land: Processes of Integration and Fragmentation: Bilâd al-Shâm from the 18th to the 20th Century.* Stuttgart: F. Steiner, 1998.

Provence, Michael. "Identifying Rebels: Insurgents in the Countryside of Damascus, 1925–26." In Thomas Philipp and Christoph Schumann, eds., *From the Syrian Lands to the States of Syria and Lebanon.* Beiruter Texte und Studien, vol. 96. Würzburg: Ergon Verlag, 2004.

———. "A Nationalist Rebellion without Nationalists? Popular Mobilizations in Mandatory Syria, 1925–1926." In Nadine Méouchy and Peter Sluglett, eds., *The British and French Mandates in Comparative Perspectives.* Leiden: Brill, 2004.

———. "Plowshares into Swords: Anti-Colonial Resistance and Popular Nationalism in French Mandate Syria, 1925–1926." Ph.D. dissertation, University of Chicago History Department, 2001.

Qarqûṭ, Dhûqân. *Taṭawwur al-ḥarakat al-waṭaniyya fî sûriyya, 1920–1939*. Beirut, 1975. Rpt. Damascus, 1989.

al-Qâsimî, Ẓâfir. *Wathâ'iq jadîda 'an al-thawra al-sûriyya al-kubrâ*. Damascus, 1965.

Rafeq, Abdul-Karim. "Land Tenure Problems and Their Social Impact in Syria around the Middle of the Nineteenth Century." In Tarif Khalidi, ed., *Land Tenure and Social Transformation in the Middle East*. Beirut: American University of Beirut, 1984.

Reilly, James A. "The Peasantry in Late Ottoman Palestine." *Journal of Palestine Studies* 10, no. 4 (1981): 82–97.

———. "A Peasant War in Syria: The Jabal Druze Revolt of 1925–1927." Unpublished paper, Georgetown University, 1983.

———. "Property, Status, and Class in Ottoman Damascus." *Journal of the American Oriental Society* 112, nos. 1–2 (1992): 9–21.

Ridâ, 'Alî. *Qiṣṣat al-kifâh al-waṭanî fî sûriyya 1918–1946*. Aleppo, 1979.

Roberts, Stephen H. *History of French Colonial Policy (1870–1925)*. Vols. 1–2. London: P. S. King & Son, 1929.

Roded, Ruth. "Tradition and Change during the Last Decades of Ottoman Rule: The Urban Elite of Damascus, Aleppo, Homs, and Hama, 1976–1918." Ph.D. dissertation, University of Denver, 1984.

Rogan, Eugene L. "Aşiret Mektebi: Abdülhamid II's School for Tribes (1892–1907)." IJMES 28 (1996): 83–107.

———. *Frontiers of the State in the Late Ottoman Empire: Transjordan, 1850–1921*. Cambridge: Cambridge University Press, 1999.

Rogan, Eugene L., and Tariq Tell, eds. *Village, Steppe and State: The Social Origins of Modern Jordan*. London: British Academic Press, 1994.

Russell, Malcolm B. *The First Modern Arab State: Syria under Faysal, 1918–1920*. Minneapolis: Bibliotheca Islamica, 1985.

Rustum, Asad. "Syria under Mehemet Ali." Ph.D. dissertation, University of Chicago, 1923.

al-Safarjalânî, Muḥî al-Dîn. *Târîkh al-thawra al-sûriyya*. Damascus, 1961.

Saliba, Najib Elias. "Wilayat Suriyya 1876–1909." Ph.D. dissertation, University of Michigan, 1971.

Salibi, Kamal. *A House of Many Mansions: The History of Lebanon Reconsidered*. Berkeley: University of California Press, 1988.

———. *The Modern History of Lebanon*. Delmar, NY: Caravan Books, 1977.

Salih, Shakeeb. "The British Druze Connection and the Druze Rising of 1896 in the Hawran." *Middle Eastern Studies* 13 (May 1977): 251–257.

Schäbler (Schaebler), Birgit. *Aufstände im Drusenbergland: Ethnizität und Integration einer Ländlichen Gesellschaft Syriens vom Osmanischen Reich bis zur Staatlichen Unabhängigkeit, 1850–1949*. Gotha, 1996.

———. "Coming to Terms with Failed Revolutions: Historiography in Syria, Germany, and France." *Middle Eastern Studies* 35, no. 1 (January 1999): 17–44.

———. "Practicing Mushâ': Common Lands and the Common Good in Southern Syria under the Ottomans and the French." In Roger Owen, ed., *New Perspectives on Property and Land in the Middle East.* Cambridge, MA: Center for Middle Eastern Studies, Harvard University, 2000.

———. "State(s) Power and the Druzes: Integration and the Struggle for Social Control (1838–1949)." In Thomas Philipp and Birgit Schaebler, eds., *The Syrian Land: Processes of Integration and Fragmentation: Bilâd al-Shâm from the 18th to the 20th Century.* Stuttgart: F. Steiner, 1998.

Schilcher, Linda Schatkowski. *Families in Politics: Damascene Factions and Estates of the 18th and 19th Centuries.* Wiesbaden: F. Steiner, 1985.

———. "The Famine of 1915–1918 in Greater Syria." In John P. Spagnolo, ed., *Problems of the Middle East in Historical Perspective: Essays in Honour of Albert Hourani.* Oxford: Oxford University Press, 1992.

———. "The Grain Economy of Late Ottoman Syria and the Issue of Large-Scale Commercialization." In Çağlar Keydar and Faruk Tabak, eds., *Landholding and Commercial Agriculture in the Middle East.* Albany: State University of New York Press, 1991.

———. "The Great Depression (1873–1896) and the Rise of Syrian Arab Nationalism." *New Perspectives on Turkey* 5–6 (Suraiya Faroqhi, guest editor) (Fall 1991): 167–189.

———. "The Hauran Conflicts of the 1860's: A Chapter in the Rural History of Modern Syria." IJMES 13 (1981): 159–179.

———. "Railways in the Political Economy of Southern Syria 1890–1925." In Thomas Philipp and Birgit Schaebler, eds., *The Syrian Land: Processes of Integration and Fragmentation: Bilâd al-Shâm from the 18th to the 20th Century.* Stuttgart: F. Steiner, 1998.

Schölch, Alexander. "The Emergence of Modern Palestine (1856–1882)." In Hisham Nashabe, ed., *Studia Palaestina: Studies in Honor of Constantine K. Zurayk.* Beirut: Institute for Palestine Studies, 1988.

———. "European Penetration and Economic Development of Palestine, 1856–1882." In Roger Owen, ed., *Studies in the Economic and Social History of Palestine in the 19th and 20th Centuries.* London: Palmgrave McMillan, 1982.

———. *Palestine in Transformation, 1856–1882: Studies in Social, Economic, and Political Development.* Translated by William C. Young and Michael C. Gerrity. Washington, D.C.: Institute for Palestine Studies, 1993.

———. "Was There a Feudal System in Ottoman Lebanon?" In David Kushner, ed., *Palestine in the Late Ottoman Period: Political, Social, and Economic Transformation.* Jerusalem: Yad Izhak Ben-Zvi, and Leiden: distributed by E. J. Brill, 1986.

Scott, James C. *The Moral Economy of the Peasant: Rebellion and Subsistence in South East Asia.* New Haven: Yale University Press, 1976.

———. *Weapons of the Weak: Everyday Forms of Peasant Resistance.* New Haven: Yale University Press, 1985.

Scott, James C., and Nina Bhatt, eds. *Agrarian Studies: Synthetic Work at the Cutting Edge.* New Haven: Yale University Press, 2001.

Seale, Patrick. *Asad of Syria: The Struggle for the Middle East.* Berkeley: University of California Press, 1989.

———. *The Struggle for Syria: A Study of Post-War Arab Politics, 1945–1958.* 2nd ed. (1st ed. 1965.) New Haven: Yale University Press, 1986.

Seikaly, Samir M. "Land Tenure in 17th Century Palestine: The Evidence from the *Fatâwâ al-Khairiyya.*" In Tarif Khalidi, ed., *Land Tenure and Social Transformation in the Middle East.* Beirut: American University of Beirut, 1984.

———. "Pacification of the Hawran (1910): The View from Within." Unpublished paper presented at the Proceedings of the XII Congress of CIEPO, n.d.

Shambrook, Peter A. *French Imperialism in Syria, 1927–1936.* Reading, UK: Ithaca Press, 1998.

Shanin, Teodor. *Defining Peasants.* Oxford: Blackwell, 1990.

———, ed. *Peasants and Peasant Societies.* 2nd ed. Oxford: Blackwell, 1987.

al-Shaṭṭî, Muḥammad Jamîl, *'Ayân dimasq fî al-qarn al-thâlith 'ashar wa nisf al-qarn al-râbi' 'ashar min 1201–1350h.* Reprinted from various editions. Damascus, 1994.

Sluglett, Marion Farouk, and Peter Sluglett. "The Application of the 1858 Land Code in Greater Syria: Some Preliminary Observations." In Tarif Khalidi, ed., *Land Tenure and Social Transformation in the Middle East.* Beirut: American University of Beirut, 1984.

Sluglett, Peter. "The Mandates: Some Reflections on the Nature of the British Presence in Iraq (1914–1932) and the French Presence in Syria (1920–1946)." In Nadine Méouchy and Peter Sluglett, eds., *The British and French Mandates in Comparative Perspectives.* Leiden: Brill, 2004.

Spivak, Gayatri Chakravorty. "Can the Subaltern Speak?" In Cary Nelson and Larry Grossberg, eds., *Marxism and the Interpretation of Culture.* Chicago: University of Illinois Press, 1988.

Swedenburg, Ted. *Memories of Revolt: The 1936–39 Rebellion and the Palestinian National Past.* Minneapolis: University of Minnesota Press, 1995.

Tanenbaum, Jan Karl. *General Maurice Sarrail, 1856–1929: The French Army and Left-Wing Politics.* Chapel Hill: University of North Carolina Press, 1974.

Tauber, Eliezer. *The Arab Movements in World War I.* London: Frank Cass, 1993.

Tell, Tariq. "Guns, Gold and Grain: War and Food Supply in the Making of Modern Jordan." In Steven Heydemann, ed., *War, Institutions, and Social Change in the Middle East.* Berkeley: University of California Press, 2000.

Thompson, Elizabeth. *Colonial Citizens: Republican Rights, Paternal Privilege, and Gender in French Syria and Lebanon.* New York: Columbia University Press, 2000.

Tibawi, A. L. *A Modern History of Syria Including Lebanon and Palestine.* New York: St. Martin's Press, 1969.

Tomeh, Ramez George. "Landownership and Political Power in Damascus: 1858–1958." M.A. thesis, AUB, 1977.

ʿUbayd, Salâma. *al-Thawra al-sûriyya al-kubrâ: 1925–1927 ʿalâ ḍauʾ wathâʾiq lam tunshar.* Beirut, 1971.

Van Dam, Nikolaos. *The Struggle for Power in Syria: Sectarianism, Regionalism, and Tribalism in Politics, 1961–1978.* New York: St. Martin's Press, 1979.

Van Young, Eric. *The Other Rebellion: Popular Violence, Ideology, and the Mexican Struggle for Independence, 1810–1821.* Stanford, CA: Stanford University Press, 2001.

Vincent, Andrew. "The Peasantry of the Ḥawrân in the Nineteenth Century." M.A. thesis, AUB, 1982.

Wahlin, Lars. "Occurrence of Mushaʿ in Transjordan." *Geografiska Annaler* 70B (1988): 375–379.

Warriner, Doreen. *Economics of Peasant Farming.* London: Oxford University Press, 1939.

———. *Land and Poverty in the Middle East.* London: Royal Institute of International Affairs, 1948.

———. *Land Reform and Development in the Middle East.* 2nd ed. London: Oxford University Press, 1962.

Weber, Eugene. *Peasants into Frenchmen: The Modernization of Rural France, 1870–1914.* Stanford: University of California Press, 1976.

Weber, Stefan. "Images of Imagined Worlds: Self-Image and Worldview in Late Ottoman Wall Paintings of Damascus." In Jens Hanssen, Thomas Philipp, and Stefan Weber, eds., *The Empire in the City: Arab Provincial Capitals in the Late Ottoman Empire.* Beiruter Texte und Studien, vol. 88. Würzburg: Ergon Verlag, 2002.

Weulersse, Jacques. *Paysans de Syrie et du Proche-Orient.* Paris: Gallimard, 1946.

Wolf, Eric R. *Europe and the People without History.* Berkeley: University of California Press, 1982.

———. *Peasant Wars of the Twentieth Century.* New York: Harper and Row, 1969.

Wright, Philip Quincy. "The Bombardment of Damascus." *American Journal of International Law* 20, no. 2 (1926).

al-Zâqût, ʿAṭâ Allâh. *Aḍwâʾ ʿalâ al-thawra al-sûriyya al-kubrâ.* Damascus, 2000.

Zeine, Zeine N. *The Struggle for Arab Independence: Western Diplomacy and the Rise and Fall of Faiṣal's Kingdom in Syria.* 2nd ed. Delmar, NY: Caravan Books, 1977.

INDEX

www.ingramcontent.com/pod-product-compliance
Ingram Content Group UK Ltd.
Pitfield, Milton Keynes, MK11 3LW, UK
UKHW032029240225
455518UK00001B/75